PRAISE FOR *MORE*

"An insightful and heartfelt view of what mothering looks like for an ambitious outdoor athlete. Written in the form of a journal for her kids, *More* is an entertaining read for anyone, and a must-read for anyone considering parenthood."

—Tommy Caldwell, professional climber, environmental activist, and *New York Times* bestselling author of *The Push*

"A professional rock climber shares the challenges of maintaining her career after becoming a mother. In this epistolary memoir, Burhardt relays the emotional challenges of becoming a mother while attempting to retain a sense of her own identity. Raw, passionate, and stinging."

—*Kirkus Reviews*

"Majka gives a beautifully honest account of the questions and inner dialogue so many people face with motherhood. For anyone questioning the balance of adventure and parenthood and marriage, *More* offers a sincere look into how to unwrap the past, present, and future."

—Beth Rodden, mother and top American rock climber

"How do you, as a diehard climber and mountain guide, navigate the maelstrom of being a new parent and sustaining a marriage when both partners are also wedded to a life of adventure? As Majka Burhardt reveals in her searingly honest epistolary memoir, you don't. You simply make it up as you go and hope to survive, much like you would on a serious alpine climb. *More* portrays this whole messy reality—with humor, beauty, and an unsparing eye for the visceral details."

—Matt Samet, author of *Death Grip* and former editor of *Climbing*

"Majka's writings not only made me laugh out loud, but I was impressed by her willingness to share her most vulnerable inner thoughts and fears as a mother during this critical time of political, social, and environmental turmoil. This series of letters offers an insightful perspective about how our intense love for our children can enable us to do what's best in the face of all the challenges of life and the frequent messiness of motherhood."

—Lynn Hill, climbing legend, mom,
and El Capitan free-climbing pioneer

MORE

MORE

Life on the Edge of
Adventure and Motherhood

MAJKA
BURHARDT

PEGASUS BOOKS
NEW YORK LONDON

MORE

Pegasus Books, Ltd.
148 West 37th Street, 13th Floor
New York, NY 10018

First Pegasus Books cloth edition March 2023

Interior design by Maria Fernandez

This is a personal memoir and all events, places, and people are represented to the best of the author's recollection. Some names have been changed to protect privacy.

Library of Congress Cataloging-in-Publication Data is available.

ISBN: 978-1-63936-349-0

10 9 8 7 6 5 4 3 2 1

Printed in the United States of America
Distributed by Simon & Schuster
www.pegasusbooks.com

For Irenna and Kaz

Dear reader (Dear you),

What follows is my story, intertwined with those of others. But make no mistake—it's not complete. How could it be?

A memoir is never not monocular. Add to this the fact that the one you hold in your hands today was not written as a look back in time. Instead, it is a compilation of in-the-moment moments—the unfiltered reality of my heart as it grew and twisted and healed its way through early motherhood.

Some things will be different from what others remember. Some things will be different from what I or others want to admit. It has all created the journey that got me—got us—here.

My sister says we all live on the same diamond, just on separate facets. This is my facet.

—Majka Burhardt
September 1, 2022

April 1, 2021
Letter | Four-and-a-Half Years Old

Dear Irenna and Kaz,

Becoming a mom has been the loneliest thing I have ever done. I am supposed to tell you it's beautiful, soulful, and satisfying. And it is—but those emotions are all easy to process when they crash over you. It's the grief, the fear, and the uncertainty that will knock you to your knees and leave you alone, again and again, having to get back up.

In the past five years, what I have wanted more than anything is to find my own mother, to help me rise. And not my mother now, your Grandma Pooch, because she is a phone call or plane ride away in Montana. I wanted my mother when she was becoming a mother. The impossibility of having this has not stopped me from desperately desiring it. *How do I do this?* I want to ask. *Why do I feel this way?*

But I cannot find a portal to my mother when she was a young mother. What I can do is give you me.

One day, you might find yourself buckling under the enormity of love and growth so strong they make you feel like you're constantly ripping out a part of yourself to be yourself. One day, you might need the memories and stories you never knew. These are those stories. This is our story.

If that day comes, my babies, know this: You are not alone. You were never alone.

November 18, 2015
Video Journal | Six Weeks and Five Days Pregnant

I am attached to the world by four metal teeth, each penetrating a frozen smear of water no more deeply than a grain of rice.

Actually, *we* are attached.

I have one ice tool in each hand and a crampon on each foot. I'm anchored to the world by filed tips of steel the same size as you, all of us together on the barely frozen November ice.

I've never thought about the relative attachment strength of a grain of rice to ice until I learned that this was your size at six weeks in my belly.

I'll make you a deal: you stay in my belly and grow bigger, and I will handle the climbing. So far, two hundred feet up a six-hundred-foot scar of ice and rock, swinging weapons disguised as climbing tools at a frozen gash still seems reasonable. This is my sport. When I'm ice climbing, I feel whole.

Today, your dad and I are climbing and I'm testing how it feels to swing tools at ice with a stowaway. Your dad has had nothing change in his body in the past six weeks.

Do you want to know a secret? This isn't your first ice climb. A month ago I carried you up this same climb—the Black Dike on Cannon Cliff—without knowing it. On that day it felt great to be out in front, levitating on frozen water tendrils.

Today, my pants are tighter and I'm letting your dad go first. It sucks. For me, at least. It's likely your dad's dream has come true. We've spent eight years tabulating whose turn it is to be in the lead while climbing, all the while pretending we're not keeping score. I wonder if he will be up for making a deal that, in the future, I can get back on demand anything I've given up during pregnancy?

Likely not, I think.

You should know that for most of my life I have pushed myself to do whatever is bigger and harder, as if achieving at the edge of difficulty makes the feat more worthy.

I already feel myself slowing down to accommodate you and can't tell if I should be proud of myself or terrified.

December 1, 2015
From the Notepad | Eight Weeks and Four Days Pregnant

You are two.

December 4, 2015
Audio Journal | Nine Weeks Pregnant

It's 10:59 in the morning, it's forty degrees out and sunny, and I'm driving to Portland, Maine, to see my physical therapist and trainer to talk about growing you and staying strong at the same time. Don't worry—I have my two hands on the wheel. Just like there are two of you. You each are growing hands, hopefully two apiece, in my belly. I'd like to tell you I am writing you a letter, but it's good to fess up now that I've always been a talker.

A man crosses the street in front of me with a one-year-old on his shoulder. A dad and his kid, no doubt.

Before, I might have thought the scene sweet at best, delaying my drive at worst. But today? Envy. Total body-shaking envy. Because all I can think is that I won't be able to do that with my children—you—because there will be two of you. What will I do instead? Walk across the street with one of you on my back and one on my front? One on my shoulders and one in my arms?

I want you to know I had a plan for this. And I want you to always be wary of what comes next whenever anyone tells you they have a plan.

I had a plan that your dad and I would try to have kids. That was all I knew I could commit to, and all I asked your dad to commit to as well. If the try worked, the plan would land on us having one kid—and no more—so I could finally wrap my head around motherhood. That we could seamlessy give up our comfortable, childless lives solely based on the fact that we'd only be parenting one child—a kid who would be easy. A traveler. An independent kid. A kid we'd take everywhere. *We could handle it,* I told myself.

In my plan, Peter and I could both still be driven. I could have my career and I could be a professional athlete, and, and, and . . .

My life has largely been about and, and, and. I grew up seeing that you could do everything because that's what my parents did. Granted, they might have been able to do everything because they were divorced and each had the means to hire a full-time nanny who transferred between parental homes with my sister and me in an alternating two-day and five-day shared split set on an endless loop for my childhood.

For right now, I want you to know: I want everything. I want to be a professional climber, I want to direct a revolutionary international conservation organization, I want to be able to write, I want to be a good partner, and I want to be a mom. Your mom. A mom of twins.

———

You should know I'm not driving anymore. I can't drive when I cry this hard. Instead I am on the side of the road with the car akimbo, straddling pavement and frozen dirt.

Twins. My body is shaking from sobbing.

Buying tickets to Kenya! reads a text message on my phone. It's my climbing partner Kate. I cry harder.

So fun! I write back while snot drips on the phone.

Next time you'll have to come, she writes back.

I'm laughing *and* crying now. How is anything I have ever planned going to be possible with two of you? How can I plan now when I have never known so little about anything in my life?

I also cried and laughed when I found out you were not just one, but two.

"Here we go," I said to your dad when I heard the news.

"Here we go," I say to the empty car interior, speaking to all of us now—you two as cherry-sized orbs, and your dad and me together.

....

December 4, 2015 (Later)
Audio Journal | Nine Weeks Pregnant

I'm still driving to Portland.

We're going two hundred percent. That's my new plan. I discovered two hundred percent last year in Mozambique on our second expedition to launch Legado—that big, revolutionary international conservation organization I mentioned I am still working to make happen. It was two A.M. in the small town of Gurue, Mozambique, and I had to get a team of eighteen people speaking five languages, seven hundred feet of climbing rope, two hundred pieces of climbing protection, two gallons of ethyl-alcohol preserve, three microscopes, ten tents, sixty-two cans of tuna, and one snake hook to the base of a 2,000-foot granite wall twenty-two miles distant that caps off the 7,940-foot Mount Namuli—where we'd live for the next month. "We give it two hundred percent," I told everyone. And I kept asking for that and giving it for a month.

That's the world I have been in since, accelerating Legado at every possible moment. You wouldn't think it would have led me to you. But then again, you don't know about my toe rot.

—⁓—

Five months ago, I landed in France to climb after three back-to-back Africa trips for Legado. Thirty-eight years into my life and I was just ready to contemplate motherhood, but thus far the combination of anti-malaria pills and not actually seeing your dad was serving as birth control. France was going to be our first concentrated time together in six months. But within the first hour of sinking my hands and feet into perfect granite cracks high above the Vallée Blanche glacier near Chamonix, I didn't want babies; I wanted more climbing.

I told your dad I wasn't ready, and I knew that at my age it might mean I'd never have kids.

Two weeks later, I got a hole between the pinkie and second toe of my right foot. A hole all the way to the bone filled with crackling, oozy, smelly gunk, created by the simple act of my toes rubbing against each other when stuffed in my climbing shoes and in the mountain boots I wore while hiking to and from the climbs. Nothing sexy, nothing rad. Just a hole. Climbing was out until it got better. Then the rain started. And when, while trapped in the deluge in a twelve-by-twelve apartment in Chamonix, my best friend in New Hampshire called to tell me she had had her second baby, I crumpled to the floor and sobbed. *What if I've done my math wrong?* I thought.

Is it really worth sacrificing having children to go climbing when one measly hole in your toe can shut down your whole life plan? Does being a mom relate to foot rot? Should they even be in the same equation?

That night, I told your dad I wanted to make a baby. For real.

Two hundred percent. Turns out I was heading here the whole time.

―――

Once we started trying to make you for real, it didn't work right away. I cried when I got my period and interpreted my tears like data points on a graph tracking my ever-increasing desire to pursue motherhood. But in hindsight, maybe the tears were just hormones.

We tried again. I took it easy. I decided that if this was going to be my one shot at having a kid, we'd go to the doctor, make sure my uterus was shaped correctly and my tubes were patent. I was ready to get a barrage of tests. Not because I thought we needed them, but because I wanted to be sure. Because, at (by then) age thirty-nine, I wanted to give myself the best shot.

I decided to take it easier, but not count on you appearing in my uterus. So when I got tired on the uphill approaches to climbs, I slowed down. But then when the ice came in on Cannon Mountain in a flash-freezing event, I did one of the earliest-season ascents ever on the Black Dike with my friend Alexa. I led each pitch, and with every tool and crampon placement, I felt my winter body coming alive.

Tap, swing, kick, tap, tap, kick, kick.

That is my music.

I went back to taking it easy the next day, resting instead of climbing, ordering new picks and crampons and putting away my rock-climbing gear to prepare for the frozen season.

I was ready for whatever was to be.

And then on the day I was supposed to call to make an appointment with my OB-GYN, at an exact point in my cycle, I decided for the heck of it to do a pregnancy test. Peter napped on the couch while I peed on the stick. A faint line showed up, which seemed both confusing and significant enough to wake him up.

"I think I may be pregnant," I said.

"How can you be 'maybe' pregnant?" he asked.

I peed on another stick. The same faint line appeared. I Googled it. The internet was in agreement—false positives don't happen, and a faint line is a line. I was pregnant.

I didn't sleep that night. *We're doing this,* I kept telling myself. By the middle of the night, the *we* part of my statement was gone—*I* was doing this. I lay awake in heavy moonlight while Peter slept with seemingly no care in the world. All I could think was if I was the one tipped us over the edge to have children in the first place, then it seemed I would also be the one who carried the dream forward into the future.

Every day for that first week of knowing I was pregnant, I spent half the day wondering if we should just put you back. Not actually wanting to go through the steps of having an abortion, but fundamentally feeling like growing a baby (because I didn't then know I was growing two) wasn't what I wanted to be doing anymore. And then the first week dissolved into the second. And the third, and the fourth. And through all those early weeks, the same thoughts kept crossing my mind: *I am happy. I am excited. I am on board. I am doing this—but what if we just made a horrible mistake?*

A mistake in getting pregnant. A mistake in creating permanence in the form of another being in the middle of marriage—something that, even without kids in the mix, is fraught and imperfect and many times the opposite of permanent.

I don't know anyone who is a parent who is happy in their marriage. I look at the moms and dads I know and the relationships they have . . . and they're awful. I know I'm not supposed to say that. And I am definitely not supposed to write that. I want to find another family we can emulate, but I don't know any. *None of you have what I want to have.*

I am being naïve and an ass. I know. I don't have a clue what I'm talking about, standing on this side of the great, raging river of parenthood and marriage.

I told Peter we needed to find a new model. He said he wasn't ready for a minivan. I told him I meant marriage.

December 4, 2015 (Later Still)
Audio Journal | Nine Weeks Pregnant

I'm back on the side of the road ugly-crying. Your dad just texted me that his departure date changed for his trip to climb with his friend Bernd in Patagonia, the alpine-climbing wonderland at the tip of South America. *Leaving earlier than I thought next week—thanks again for the support, sweetie!*

I need to turn off my messages, or get a new husband and friends.

The husband I do have is an internationally certified mountain guide who spends half of his working time training the US military special-forces teams in high angle rescue and mountain mobility and the other half guiding civilians on everything from their first day out to their dream ascents here at home and around the world. And then in his spare time? You guessed it. He climbs. Though you will be part of his spare time soon and part of both of our all-the-times. For now, you're already my all-the-time. But not your dad's . . . yet.

Did you know I was supposed to be climbing in Patagonia this winter? Golden granite, blue ice, and the most perfectly jagged alpine skyline you'll ever know. Even after I saw that faint blue line on the pregnancy test, I thought I'd be able to pull off alpine climbing while pregnant. The only hiccup was that I was tired and nauseous all the time, and I suddenly couldn't quite imagine doing a three-day ascent of a mountain, much less a one-day push, much less a seven-hour approach hike to even get to the climbing.

Three weeks ago, Peter decided to go to Patagonia alone and I told him I would support him. To be fair, we both decided he would go, but only his decision was active. So I used frequent-flier miles from all of those Africa trips and booked myself a trip to Mexico instead.

I then spent three days hating him for deciding to actually take me up on my offer to still go to Patagonia, resenting the shit out of him for believing I meant it when I said I would be okay with him going there without me.

I didn't mean what I said. I don't know what I meant.

—⁓—

There are people who don't tell anyone they are pregnant until halfway through their pregnancy. I told my climbing-equipment sponsors when I was five weeks along. Of course, back then, I thought I was only telling them about one of you.

I always wake up too early at the Banff Centre Mountain Film Festival. This year was no different, except this time my four A.M. wake-up had to do with nausea instead of jet lag. By 4:15 on my first morning, I had already quested out of my complimentary hotel room in the dark to the Banff Centre gym.

Rowing, squats, chops, Spiderman push-ups. Check, check, check, check. Pull-ups were next and I was already being smart and more conservative, so first I slung my skinny black rubber band around the bar to give me an assist.

I stepped into the band and jumped. But I missed the bar and the tension band shot me backward, depositing me flat on my back on the black floor matting. I erupted into tears first from the surprise, second from the pain, and third from the general emotional shitshow that is being pregnant.

Two things worth noting: not many people go to the gym at 4:15, and Canadians don't believe in providing Kleenex at the gym.

I left the gym shortly thereafter to look for breakfast. My friend and sometimes climbing partner Sarah Hueniken was opening the door to enter the gym as I was rushing out. "I'm pregnant," I said, instead of hello.

Later that day I told my first gear sponsor, testing the waters with an athlete manager who was also a dad.

He was having coffee. I was drinking water, seated in the Maclab Bistro and trying to shift my weight off my bruised backside.

"You're only five weeks though?" he asked.

"I know it's early," I said, "but I'd rather you know why I'm not going to Patagonia this winter . . ." I could not bring myself to also say it might be why I wouldn't be sending him many pictures of me climbing ice for the company's catalog and marketing materials. Back then, I still thought an ice season might be possible.

You had still not made your public debut as my belly dwellers. But I almost announced you one night a few days later in Banff while sitting on a panel celebrating forty years of the festival with five other climbers, among them Tommy Caldwell and Sonnie Trotter. That night the moderator, Ed Douglas, asked them, both dads, what it was like to be a parent and a climber. Tommy and Sonnie gushed about how great it was to be able to climb professionally and travel everywhere with their families.

Ed said something about how incredible it was that they were ushering in a new era in which climber babies could be born and live a vagabond life full of adventure with their families. All I could think was what a bunch of bullshit it was. Neither Tommy nor Sonnie has a wife whose own career is also built around climbing. *How does it work then?* I wanted to demand. Sarah was on the panel too, but neither of us counted as parents in this conversation—yet.

My growing belly strained against my black tights and red dress while I debated announcing why I was so uncomfortable in my clothes and discomfited by this discussion to the twelve-hundred-person audience. But instead I kept you private and promised myself that, when it was time, I'd speak up.

That was three weeks ago. Three days ago, I lay on the ultrasound table while Peter stood next to me and a technician named Mabel scanned my belly. Less than a minute in, she paused the wand and looked away from her computer and directly at me.

"Have you been doing anything special?" she asked.

I knew.

"Am I having twins?" I asked.

"That's what I see," Mabel said.

I'd like to tell you that the first words out of my mouth were not these, but I have already committed to being honest. "Are you joking?" I asked.

"I don't joke about these kinds of things," Mabel pronounced.

I grabbed your dad's hand and started laughing. I didn't notice the tears until he reached over to wipe them off my cheek. "Babe—" he started to say.

"Only the positive," I interrupted him. "Only the good things."

I haven't slept in the three days since. I research double strollers and tandem nursing instead. "We've got this," I tell your dad whenever I see him. But soon, when he's in Patagonia, I will only have myself to tell.

December 5, 2015
Audio Journal | Nine Weeks and One Day Pregnant

Mount Avalon is a 3,442-foot peak that sits forty-five minutes from my house in the White Mountains, with a well-trodden 3.5-mile round-trip hike up its eastern flank. Only 3.5 miles.

That is what I told your dad. Again and again while sobbing into his lap, still wearing my hiking pants with the top button undone.

"Maybe you need less hiking and more napping," he said, tentatively stroking my hair.

And that is why I am now in bed at 2:10 in the afternoon wearing pajamas and an eye mask and with our dog Ptarmigan underneath the covers beside me while I record a voice memo to you.

I started today's hike listing all the other hikes I would do this winter. Travel was easy on nontechnical ground, and my hiking partner, Anne, and I made good progress through the snow.

"Kearsarge, Crawford, Baldface—new and old summits," I told Anne.

"One at a time there, tiger" was her noncommittal reply.

Eighteen months ago, Anne and I spent twelve days in Turkey climbing limestone by day and sharing various tiny sleeping trailers by night. Ten weeks ago, she was my partner when I launched myself onto mottled gray granite peeking out from the changing New Hampshire leaves. The rock was crisp and dry, I was strong and able, and each time I twisted an appendage into the fissure splitting the granite, it stayed put. Or at least until at three-quarter height on the eighty-foot Screaming Yellow Zonkers, where I came careering off, bouncing onto the rope, safe but unsuccessful.

Do you know I wrote down the gear for that crack as a note to myself in my phone before I left the cliff that day? Each piece I needed to place the next time, in the exact order. I only do that for my favorite unsuccessful climbs—climbs I mean to return to.

And now Anne and I are hiking partners.

Remember the hole in my toe? It mended. A week of rest, and this summer I had the best alpine granite-climbing season I've had for years in Chamonix. The grand finale was thirteen pitches of swapping leads with your dad on, the Trélaporte's California Dream, one of the better chunks of French orange granite. (And yes, I have a granite obsession—good for you to know that now.) For every foot I climbed along the fifteen-hundred-foot route, all I could think about was wanting more. I stood on the summit and eyed the neighboring Aiguilles greedily. "Charmoz next, then the République, then the Grépon," I said, singling out the spires in the Mont Blanc massif like a drunk pool player calling pockets.

On dinky Mount Avalon today the snow composition changed higher up, and for the last mile gaining the summit I winced with effort each time I shucked a foot out of the heavy snow. Anne pretended to have the same problem. When we'd hiked Chocorua together two weeks ago, she brought me extra snacks I told her I didn't need but then proceeded to devour.

This time she gave me a hug as I got back in the car at the trailhead and didn't say anything about my tears.

I have to stop talking now because your dad just yelled up the stairs that it doesn't sound like I am napping.

December 6, 2015
Audio Journal | Nine Weeks and Two Days Pregnant

Last night, I spent my sleeping time awake, trying to figure out how we are going to go places together. When your dad woke up, I had my question ready.

"What do you think are the chances I can fly by myself with two babies? If I can hold them both, do you think I can get them both on the plane for free?"

Your dad is a good guy. He knew to scoop me close before he told me it was likely one free kid per adult.

We're looking for a new, bigger house. Legado—the organization I founded with $11,000 and a harebrained idea about combining science, conservation, and climbing—is about to crack open. My spring and fall are already stacked with events around North America to present my new film, *Namuli*, about its origins. I might have a salary for the first time in my adult life. But not maternity leave. How am I going to work more and grow my career while also finding time to be with you—unless we all do it together?

By 6:20 this morning, my career-plus-motherhood concept of having an infant who can travel and accompany me at climbing and film events had vanished. Or at least my vision of doing it independently had, since this *infant* had become *infants*.

"I could swap kids for trips, trading them out each time," I reasoned. "We could get a nanny."

All through breakfast I researched childcare options, until by nine A.M. I'd compiled a spreadsheet of options to help me analyze what we could afford and how to budget for it. When I learned that two kids in full-time daycare cost almost twice as much as an au pair, I told Peter our guest room would need to be permanently occupied for years to come. "We have the jobs that can make this work," I told him—and me—"if we keep doing the jobs."

I then created an Excel cell for the frequent-flier miles saved up during our climbing trips to Patagonia, Namibia, Europe, and beyond, to use instead on an au pair to fly with me and the babies so I could save my career.

And for the rest of the day, I tried not to feel like a version of myself had died in the decision.

December 7, 2015
From the Notepad | Nine Weeks and Three Days Pregnant

An alarm on my phone just went off. Apparently in the middle of the night I decided it would be a good idea to buy stock in Sunsweet prune juice.

December 8, 2015
Audio Journal | Nine Weeks and Four Days Pregnant

Good morning! It's 4:13 A.M. I am somewhere between my home in Intervale, New Hampshire, and Portland, Maine, because that's the closest airport to our home. Today I'm going to catch a six A.M. flight that boards at 5:42 A.M. to go to Mexico for a beach week with my friend Kristie. But don't let that fool you. Kristie and I have been climbing partners for ten years—from first ascents in Ethiopia to supporting each other through some of our hardest rock climbs at home. But on this trip we are going to be surfers—if I can make it to the flight to Mexico. Correction: if *we* make our flight to Mexico.

That just sounded like I am talking to someone other than my babies. My babies!

First of all, it's total bullshit that the first trimester of pregnancy is even possible. It makes no sense from an evolutionary standpoint why I'm battling extreme nausea if what I'm supposed to be doing is keeping the two of you in me, making you healthy, advancing the human population, and obeying the biological drive to propagate the species.

In case we all suffer from amnesia because you guys will be so dang cute and so dang worth it and I will be so dang sleep-deprived that I can't remember what actually happened during this time, let's just be clear about how I feel right now.

It's 4:15 A.M. I woke up at 2:55 A.M. Before that I woke up at 2:05 A.M., 1:05 A.M., midnight, eleven P.M., and ten P.M.—and I went to bed at nine P.M. Before I went to bed, I had three cookies and then a fourth cookie topped with peanut butter. Even with all those cookies, I still went to bed nauseous. I woke up and had a cup of coffee. I had potato pancakes—which I made at three A.M. And a fried egg. I ate them from 3:20 to 3:35; it's now 4:16 A.M., forty-five minutes later, and I feel nauseous again. How is any of that practical? How is it practical that I haven't taken a shit in days? I feel completely full and congested in my digestive tract, and yet the only way to keep myself from not feeling horrible is to keep eating. None of this makes sense.

I went to the doctor yesterday. I heard one of your heartbeats, probably Baby A. They are calling you Baby A and Baby B. I am calling you Baby A and Baby 1 because—let's just be honest—B is not a good way to start your life in terms of being your own person.

Next week we'll have another ultrasound to check if you're sharing a placenta. And while I am planning for you to be great sharers, I'd like to keep you separate right now while you're in Mamma's belly so you can be safe and healthy and thriving.

I gave us a mantra last night.

I make healthy, robust babies who go full-term easily. I am a strong, healthy, pregnant warrior goddess.

Now my job is to repeat it again, and again, and again. Until I believe it.

December 9, 2015
Audio Journal | Nine Weeks and Five Days Pregnant

Yo vomité. In case you ever need it, that is how to say, "I puked," in Spanish. "I puked for three days" is: *Yo vomité durante tres días.*

The first time was smack in the middle of Sayulita, Mexico's, town square in front of five children. My knees buckled and I barfed directly on a flower bed while squeezing my legs together to try to stop a trickle of pee from becoming a full-on public display of urination. "*Yo soy okay*," I said to the kids in the square first, and then to you, so many times to you two over the next days.

Kristie is surfing. WhatsApp tells me Peter is heading to Aguja Mermoz as his next peak in Patagonia to climb. I am curled in a ball on damp sheets under a fan working against the Mexican heat, trying my hardest to keep down the Pedialyte and wish for this stomach virus to end so I can go back to my regular all-day "morning" sickness while just being pregnant with twins.

December 20, 2015
From the Notepad | Eleven Weeks and Two Days Pregnant

"The first thing I want you to know is that I'm okay," your dad said.

New York City streets are no place to have a phone call with someone in the mountains of Patagonia. I can't tell whose phone is more full of wind.

"What happened?" I asked.

"Ben and Jess were two hundred feet up the chimney on Exocet, and Jess dislodged an ice chunk that clocked Ben in the back. But he's okay."

"Did Ben get hit by ice before or after you and Bernd climbed the first part of the chimney?" I asked. I knew Peter had gotten that far on the Exocet route on Aguja Standhardt from a text sent last night, when he and his climbing partner Bernd eventually made it back down to town— El Chaltén—from their basecamp fourteen miles up the Torre Valley.

"Before. We made sure he was okay before we went up. And then the Polish team got hit today—we just heard."

I'm midway in my cab ride from Chelsea to Midtown for a meeting about the upcoming film on Legado. The Polish team is a husband-and-wife pair who climbed behind Peter and me on Fitz Roy—also in Patagonia—almost a year ago. I saw them only once before I took over the lead a thousand feet into our climb.

"He was knocked unconscious by ice fall from above," Peter said. "But she got him down."

Exocet is the climb I most want to do next in Patagonia. Or had been wanting to do, before everything changed.

I check my phone. I have three minutes before my meeting.

"I have news too," I said. "I can't get the genetic test—it doesn't work for twins. If we want to make sure both babies are okay, I have to get two amnios."

"Double the risk," Peter said.

"Double is our new single?" I offered.

"I don't even know what that means," Peter said.

"I don't either, and I have to go," I said, then added, "Are you done with Exocet?"

"For now, yes."

December 25, 2015
Audio Journal | Twelve Weeks Pregnant

It's 5:32 A.M. You wake me up early, little stinkers.

Today, we are back from Mexico and New York and are now in Montana seeing your Grandma Pooch. There is new snow falling along Swingley Road as I head back toward Little Mission Creek Ranch.

I don't feel very good. I am hungry and nauseous, I feel sad, and I'm tired because I don't sleep well. I don't feel like me. And I'm really afraid I'm not going to feel like me for a long time.

I feel like me when I get to be powerful. I feel powerful when I climb and get to be my complete, independent self. But I am not independent anymore because now I am three people: I am us. Three people, six hands, thirty fingers, thirty toes. And all those fingers and toes add up to no power—it adds up to me feeling muted. Is this prepartum depression? Is that even a thing?

I wanted to be a powerful pregnant athlete goddess. Instead, I stopped doing push-ups, decided ice climbing felt too uncomfortable with this belly—not to mention that its doubly swollen state made it an exaggerated target for dislodged chunks of ice—and am trying really hard not to be mad at your dad because he has more freedom than me. It's all so typical. I feel typical. I hate feeling typical.

I don't want to be the pregnant mom-to-be resenting her husband. I don't want to resent your dad. We are supposed to support each other as athletes and as climbers, but how does this still work when those parts of me are on a giant pause? How are we equals now when in my spare time I'm researching changing tables and strollers and nursing pillows and in his he's eating fucking baked goods in El Chaltén waiting for the weather to change so he can do yet another climb?

I know I am becoming a mom because keeping you two healthy is already my main priority—which is why I am here and not in Patagonia. Your dad also wants healthy nuggets, but he *is* in Patagonia. I never expected him not to climb when I was pregnant. But I think the more true statement is that I never really expected anything about this time because I didn't know we'd even get here. If he could be pregnant, would I go to Patagonia? Probably.

Will I go next year as my comeback?

I've almost made an entire climbing career out of comebacks. Two back surgeries, shoulder surgery, a torn finger ligament, a broken foot—but I have no idea how to come back into the game with two infants.

My friend Kevin, who climbs like it's as easy as breathing and is a dad, heard I was having you two and sent me a text to congratulate me. He said that in the future, when I'm a badass with twins in tow, I'm going to get even more points. I know that shouldn't matter. But to me it matters so damn much.

I need a mind shift. I need to own this. I am going to have you in June, and I am going to do it my way. Strongly and powerfully and honestly and humanly, and I am going to kick ass.

I am strong, healthy, happy . . .

Maybe that's it—I need to say I'm happy.

I am a strong, healthy, happy, pregnant warrior goddess, goddammit!

That sounded convincing.

I don't feel the happy though. I've got to find the happy.

All right. It's Montana. It's Christmas.

Next Christmas, I am going to have six-month-old twins.

Riddle me that.

December 27, 2015

From the Notepad | Twelve Weeks and Two Days Pregnant

Your aunt (my sister) cross-country skis like a caffeinated jackrabbit. Up down, up down, I can see her hamstrings and quads syncopate through her tights. I follow her track across the barest skim of snow as we thread our way up Mission Creek Trail. She arrived yesterday and offered up a ski within ten minutes of unfolding herself from the sixteen-hour car ride.

"How is it feeling?" she asks.

I kick and glide and realize I am imitating her bouncing even though it's not my personality or my ski style. I force myself to stop. "Okay," I say. "Tight on my belly."

"I skied all through my pregnancy with Jeannie," she says, "up until I fell on top of her."

"Oh yeah, when did that happen again?" I ask, pretending to remember this detail.

"Thirty-two weeks—then I was on bed rest."

I nod to her back, remembering that part.

"But there's no way you're going to be able to ski that long," she adds.

I do the math. When I'm thirty-two weeks along it will be May, with no snow left in New Hampshire to even ski on. I want to point this out, but instead I slow down and let the space between us grow.

Four weeks ago, she was the fourth person we called to share the news.

"Ready to be an aunt to twins?" I said when she picked up.

"You're going to be huge!" she said in return.

Will you be like this together? I made most of my choices in childhood based off ones my sister had made two years before me. She ran; I threw discus and shot put. She sang; I wrote. Always another lane. But now I follow her across the Montana trails.

Later, I am upstairs working, and she is on a post-ski run. Your grandma is at the barn in town training for a horse show in January in Idaho.

My mother raised strong girls, read a note card taped at eye level on our pantry cabinet throughout my childhood. When my mom moved to Montana, the note card didn't come with her—it didn't need to anymore.

January 3, 2016
From the Notepad | Thirteen Weeks and Two Days Pregnant

"This," my friend Cameron, an acupuncturist, said, pointing to my belly and circling the air. "This you can do."

"And this," Cameron, the athlete and mom, said, pointing to my head and making the same motion. "You can probably do this too, but it will be harder."

Everyone has opinions now. My mom has always had them.

"One day," she has told me countless times, "I hope you have a daughter who announces at nineteen that she's going to be a full-time climber and then at twenty tells you she's marrying a thirty-one-year-old mountain guide."

I hope one of you is a girl. I am terrified you are both boys, because raising strong girls is what I was shown how to do. And while I think I can pivot to raising two boys, I really want a shot at one of each. I hope we find our way together. I am terrified of what that way might be.

I imagine you are going to teach me just how much is really possible in my life. But there is something more. Something I don't even know.

Something that I can already tell is coming.

....

January 23, 2016
From the Notepad | Sixteen Weeks and One Day Pregnant

In two days they are going to put a seven-and-a-half-centimeter-long needle into my womb—which is to say, your home—twice. It's the *twice* part that had me calling your grandma.

"Remember how you said you'd come if I needed you?" I said.

"Absolutely."

"I need you."

Today, I picked her up at the Portsmouth, New Hampshire, bus station two hours from our home up north. But first we spent the day texting about her ever-changing arrival time. My mom has special travel powers in the form of her stepdaughter's/my stepsister's (your step-aunt's?) airline job, which means she gets to come see us for a twentieth of the price—but double the connections and triple the time of a normal flight.

"Do you think you will start buying tickets when the babies come?" I ask her once she's settled into the passenger seat of my car.

"I have a friend who bought an RV and parked it in her daughter's driveway for the first three months of her granddaughter's life," she says in response.

I merge onto the highway and consider the length of our driveway.

"But that wouldn't work for me," she continues. "Not with my riding schedule."

"There are horses in New Hampshire," I say. "Maybe we can find you one to ride."

"Maybe. How are you feeling, honey?" she asks.

"Remember the heartburn?" I ask.

"I don't remember any of it," she says. "I just did it."

....

February 1, 2016
From the Notepad | Seventeen Weeks and Three Days Pregnant

My friend and climbing partner Caroline is ice climbing in Norway. Instagram and your dad tell me this.

If Caroline and her husband, Adam, have one kid who is three years old, when can trips like hers be a reasonable goal for me, with two kids?

....

February 8, 2016
Letter | Eighteen Weeks and Three Days Pregnant

Dear Toots and McGoots,

Those aren't your names—don't worry. I promise we will have better ones picked out by the time you make your debut in June, because even though you are due July ninth no one is going to let us get past June 30th.

Last week, I found out that you're a boy and a girl, and it seemed like the right time to write you your first letter. Yes, it's one letter for both of you. You might as well get used to sharing from the start.

I have not been eagerly waiting to be a mother. I'm thirty-nine, and I've been focused on doing everything else instead.

Last year had me ringing in the New Year on top of Patagonia's Fitz Roy, leading a thirty-eight-person symposium about how to disrupt traditional conservation work, spending two months working three back-to-back stints in Ethiopia and Mozambique, climbing the most difficult ice of my life at home in New Hampshire, writing a proposal for my third book, taking five weeks to climb perfect alpine granite in Chamonix with your dad, and finishing a film that has been four years in the making.

I've been busy. I like being busy.

Theoretically, it's been possible for me to become a mom for decades. That's a long time to choose to pursue things that are not what most people dub "the greatest role you can have in life."

For me, I've been on the fence about becoming a parent. Not because of you. Because of me.

For most of my career, people have told me that if I were to have children then I would have to change my life, stop traveling, tone down my climbing, and basically give up my ability to create and expand. Each time someone told me any of that, I wanted to punch them, but I haven't (and neither should you—ever). Instead, I have chosen to stand taller and stronger against such limiting beliefs. Or I did in theory. And now it's time for reality. In fact, the only way your dad and I could get to the place of trying to have a baby was to tell ourselves it was possible for us to become parents and not lose ourselves in the process. Then again, that's likely what every parent tells themself before they step off the high dive.

But you are not *a baby*, and I am the first one laughing about the irony of it all.

You are entering a bold and beautiful world. I have spent my time in it hurtling my beliefs, passions, and curiosity up against each other, and in fact have made this my career. It has not always worked. Sometimes

I ache for a more normal trajectory. But when it does work, it catches my breath and grounds my soul in a way that makes me know I belong in the universe.

You two are not "the normal way."

When I reflect on the most important, striking, heart-in-stomach things I have ever done, they have always been the result of doing what people would call "too much." I general-contracted my dream house at age twenty-two; I put up first ascents on sandstone towers in Ethiopia as my first climbs back from shoulder surgery; and I kept driving in a nor'easter that shut down the Eastern Seaboard, making it to North Conway on a bet to myself that it would matter and ended up falling in love with your dad.

And as you grow inside me, I know you will be the pinnacle of what I have done and will do. I know you're like your mamma because already—in utero—I can tell that your Team Twin motto is "More." You make me pee eight times a night, eat double the amount of pork I had thought previously possible, and cry with something I can only know as the biggest love I have ever felt. In all of that, we fit right in together.

I'm not saying I have this figured out. You can't get to be my age and see your sister, cousins, strangers, and friends go through parenthood and think anyone ever has it figured out. While we may never figure it out entirely, somehow we're going into this bold and beautiful world together.

I can't wait to see what more looks like, with you.

March 12, 2016
Audio Journal | Twenty-Three Weeks and One Day Pregnant

Okay, you little buggers, we have just flown to Lincoln, Nebraska, to Minneapolis, to Seattle, to Oakland, back to Minneapolis, to Chicago, and finally to Portland, Maine. You two were super troupers while

Mom gave five presentations showing the film and talking about how Legado came to be in six days, amid a lot of up-down-up, down-up-down on planes and countless other modes of transportation. That is pretty exciting. Today we are coming home and don't have to get on a plane for eighteen days—which feels like a success.

Today you are twenty-three weeks old in Mamma's belly, which means we are shooting for you to stay there another fifteen weeks. That feels like a really long time to me. And then I also feel like it's going to go quickly.

I have a big belly. Really big.

"Don't worry, you're getting close," the flight attendant told me today while I tried to cram past her in the galley.

I snorted and told her I am not due until the end of June—three and a half months away.

The surprise on her face made me realize how different I look, and that what makes me different is you. You *two*. In the early months you were in there, but there was no physical manifestation to the outside world of your double presence. Now I watch people's eyes widen at the orb of my belly and the announcement of what's to come.

I get to see you again next week. A "twin viewing," your dad and I call the ultrasounds. He comes to as many as he can, and then we report the news back to all your grandparents. You have six of them. You should know now there are a lot of dynamics at play on my side of the family. Your dad and I are going to work really hard to keep our family not so complicated.

Sometimes I worry about your dad and me. I worry about our fundamental ability to do this, and to do it well by supporting each other. We're teeing up roles without even knowing it. I'm either working or getting ready for you, and he's either working or climbing. I already see how my need to plan and prepare lets him do less of both.

I had a boyfriend before your dad who loved birds. One day we were lying in bed and he was telling me about blue jays. "The mamma birds, it's their job to sit on the nest," he told me. "It's biological, just like humans."

I left that boyfriend shortly thereafter. Now I'm the mamma bird.

April 4, 2016
From the Notepad | Twenty-Six Weeks and Three Days Pregnant

Today two strangers touched my belly. It would have been three had I not put a box in front of it at the post office to ward off my third interlocutor.

It is as if contributing to the human race makes you public property.

I am no different. My hands used to almost itch to hold someone else's belly. I hope I asked. I think I did it then to try it on. I wonder if I will do it again to remember.

A note of clarification though: it's women who want to touch me.

"That belly getting hard to haul around yet?" Rick, the owner of International Mountain Equipment, one of the US's oldest and crustiest climbing gear shops, based near us in North Conway, New Hampshire, asked today. I stopped by to sell old ski-touring boots in my current empty-the-house pre-twins mania.

"Not yet," I told him.

Rick shook his head. "Do you ever need to rest it?" he asked. Then he patted the counter. "You can prop it right here if so."

April 16, 2016
Audio Journal | Twenty-Eight Weeks and One Day Pregnant

Hey guys,

You're sitting outside in the sun, or the closest you can get to it with my shirt rolled up and my tummy exposed to collect all the spring New Hampshire warmth we can.

Today you two are twenty-eight weeks old in my belly. Which is a really big deal. Because this means that if you were born today (which you're not going to be, because you're going to be born in June), you would have a really good chance of survival.

Like I said, it's a big deal. We did a really good job getting here.

This past week, you, my little girl, moved from being at the top of Mamma's belly, on top of your brother, to being all the way down so you are eye-to-eye with him. Which hurt like hell, but that is not the point of this story.

Sometimes I can look down and see you two kick without feeling it. It looks like there are alien limbs coming out of my belly. It's pretty wild to have four feet kicking me, and four knees and hands poking out all over the place. You, little boy, are big, big, big. You are tracking a full two weeks ahead in growth. And you, my dear little girl, are tracking just exactly at your number of weeks. So altogether we have a lot of baby in Mamma's belly.

Today is a good day. Some days it's a harder day, but today is a good day.

I love you, little nuggets. I've loved you from the start, and want you to always know that. Nowadays it's just not as hard as it was back then to have you growing inside me. Nowadays I can let the love lead. And I love your dad. Which is a good thing because I think we're going to need that, and more.

April 21, 2016
Audio Journal | Twenty-Eight Weeks and Six Days Pregnant

Maybe one day you will each have kids. Maybe one day it will help to listen to these audio files and hear what your mom thought when she was pregnant with you. Or maybe it will scare you shitless. Or maybe it will do both.

Perhaps it is supposed to do both.

I love you.

Today, we're going to have a good drive to Twin Mountain, grab your Grandma Sarah (your Gramgram, as we've decided to call her), and go give a *Namuli* show at Williams College in Massachusetts. There's a word in New Hampshire for the more poorly behaved Massachusens—Massholes!—which we'll talk about when you're a little older.

April 21, 2016 (Later)
Audio Journal | Twenty-Eight Weeks and Six Days Pregnant

"What's your next trip?"

"Do you have another movie coming soon?"

"Did you know when you were in college that this is what you'd do?"

Tonight, I stood in front of an audience of Williams College students fielding questions after I'd screened *Namuli* for them. Nobody asked about what was growing in my body or what might happen when you're out on the other side.

It wasn't the theater lighting. By Q&A time, it was plenty bright. Maybe they just didn't see the now fifty pounds of belly protruding over my knees. When I was in college, had I ever encountered anyone who was pregnant? I couldn't recall a single person, but I knew better than to assume I'd somehow spent four years of my life without seeing life about to arrive somewhere around me.

We choose what we see. We choose what matters.

"I'm also pregnant with twins," I told the crowd. "This is my number one next trip," I told us all.

After a beat I added, "That is, until I take them with me on a film tour in October when they're three months old."

—⁓—

I'm back in the hotel room brushing my teeth by eight thirty. My stomach pushes my nightgown up and out and exposes my crotch—something I had not noticed until I was sharing a room with your Gramgram. I grab my phone and send myself an email reminder to purchase a nursing-and-sleeping setup. And then I send another one about buying bigger underwear.

May 4, 2016
Letter | Thirty Weeks and Five Days Pregnant

In hindsight, choosing a birthing class seventy-five minutes away should have been a red flag.

Or maybe I should have just not talked.

Carla, the doula instructor, started us off with introductions. Name, how far along we were, and where we lived.

"I'm Mariana; I'm thirty-six weeks along," began the first woman.

Before she could continue, I spoke up: "That's it?"

Penny was next. "I'm thirty-five weeks—"

"But you're tiny," I interjected.

It was then that Peter grabbed my hand. I squeezed his back and tried to free my paw. He squeezed harder.

———

Later, on the drive home, we were stalled in construction traffic. Peter gave a heavy sigh.

"Babe," he said. "That was not okay."

"What do you mean?" I asked.

"I know I'm not a pregnant woman, but I cannot imagine anyone wants to be told their very significant pregnancy is less than yours."

We started moving again, our Toyota Matrix rumbling over the torn-up asphalt. I braced my hands on my thighs and gasped.

"Okay over there?" he asked.

"Okay," I said. At the next bump I put one hand on the roof and the other on one thigh as I peed onto the seat. Just a little.

"But seriously, they were tiny," I said.

"Maybe try something other than 'tiny' next time."

Ahead of us loomed eight more miles of alternating dirt and pavement.

"Or we can just not have a next time," I said.

"Also a good idea," Peter said.

———

I'd wanted that birthing class because it was through a birth center run by doulas. Once we were on a smooth road, I took out my phone and signed us up for a class with nurses at the hospital ten minutes from our house instead.

May 16, 2016
Letter | Thirty-Two Weeks and Three Days Pregnant

Dear McGoots and Toots,

I know, I promised new names. We will get there; we still have five weeks to come up with them. Five weeks until you launch yourselves into the outside world. Five weeks until I hold you in my arms instead of in my belly.

We are on a three-person journey every millisecond of every day—but it is the nights I want to talk to you about. It is the nights when I lie awake in the dark at eleven, one, three, and four, and I wonder just what we're all getting ourselves into. Those are the moments when I need to feel you kick and squirm, and yet those are the moments when you're most silent. And so from now on, I'm going to knock.

——

Seven years ago, I met a Himba woman in northwestern Namibia. It was early evening in Marienfluss Valley—that hour-long slice of time when the whitened grasslands turn temporarily gold. Your dad, Kate, and I had just climbed a rock route in the shade of a 113-degree day on a granite cliff that was the backdrop to a Himba family's mud-and-grass home. We had no common language with the Himba. It was 2009, and we were twenty days into a thirty-five-day expedition whose budget for a translator had evaporated with the global financial crisis. The Himba family had been watching our team climb, and we'd been living on their land. We had developed a system of pointing and gesturing to get by. One woman and I were particularly hitting it off that night. She reached for a bright-green rope I had as confirmation that we'd actually been the ones climbing the rock face. I nodded, and she shook her head.

This woman had a baby on her back—nine or ten months old, I guessed. Old enough to make faces back at me when I made them at him. His mother and I switched from communicating about rock climbing to communicating about babies. She turned to give me better access to the little boy, and when she moved sideways in the light I saw her belly pushing against the orange-and-yellow blanket that covered her bare body below. I looked up at her, and then together our eyes traveled back to her stomach. Within a moment she'd grabbed my hands and pulled them close. She flicked the woolen blanket out of the way with her elbows and settled my palms on the taut skin of her belly. We kept them there while her baby inside kicked. The woman and I both smiled. And then she reached for my belly.

The Himba woman did not reach for me with an open palm, but rather she took her right hand and made it into a fist, hovering this above my navel. When she touched me, her knuckles brushed my skin as if knocking on a door. She rapped. Twice. She pointed at the rock face above with her other hand. She shook her head, rapped again. "No, no, no," she said.

I'm sorry to say that I never got the woman's name. In the year after meeting her I wrote an essay, for a book, about her knocking on my belly in the context of being fine with not having children and my clarity and comfort with the fact that my life and the travel, climbing, exploration, risk-taking, and boundary-pushing that come with it did not necessarily predispose me to motherhood. And this was all right—I could have an empty belly.

Life is ironic. You two might just be the largest ironies, and joys, of my life and your dad's. I'd like to tell you that I am excited, ready, and happy every moment as I prepare for your arrival. But I don't want to lie to you. I don't want you to expect total certainty from me as mom, or from yourselves if you should ever be expecting parents.

The doubts and fear, for me, are the worst at night. During those sleepless stretches in the dark I wonder and worry. And as I said, it's those moments when you stinkers are silent that I most want and need your flips and flops to reassure me that you are okay in my belly and that we will be okay when you're out of it.

So last week I started a new plan: When you're silent, and I'm scared, I do what the Himba woman did. I knock. And now, you answer.

May 30, 2016
Letter | Thirty-Four Weeks and Three Days Pregnant

On Saturday, I call Kate. I know I have been avoiding her. I have two voicemails and over a dozen missed texts—too many moments when her name pops up on my phone and I don't pick up or respond.

The climbing community is full of where-you-are-going conversations. The assumption is always the journey outward—rarely the journey inward. It is about destinations, trips, journeys, and always going.

Kate's one of my best friends. We've climbed together all over the world on dozens of trips, but last year, while climbing in Chamonix together, we were off step. I was fresh off three back-to-back Legado trips to Africa, and she was fresh off sending the Leaning Tower, a test piece of technical and physical difficulty in Yosemite Valley. Being high above my protection on small holds felt unfathomable to me. It was effortless to her. I saw myself as wildly behind.

That was the trip when I was ready to forgo a whole life with you in exchange for a life of solely climbing. Kate was in part the motivation—or rather the inspiration of the sinking feeling I had when I suddenly felt like a second-class climber in comparison. I saw Kate slipping away from me and our lives diverging. I thought it was about Legado and my choosing to work and climb in the mountains with the people who call them home, and her choosing to elegantly and simply climb them.

Who knew that toe rot would be the hero of our story?

———

I make myself call Kate. I stand outside on the long, broken strip of asphalt that is our driveway and use a Chuckit! to throw a tennis ball for Ptarmigan. The Chuckit! I bought two months ago when I stopped being able to bend down and pick up the ball for him. Over and over I throw the ball while Kate and I catch up. She shares how she is fresh off a big road trip to the Black Canyon of the Gunnison, with its fearesome dark-rock big walls, in Colorado; canyoneering in the Utah desert with girlfriends; working on a whole new level of strength as a boulderer; and about to go try the notorious 1,000-foot 5.12 rock climb Romantic Warrior in the Sierra Nevada and add another huge climbing achievement to an ever-growing list.

I don't want to only talk about being pregnant and babies, so I ask her for specifics about each adventure. But talking about climbing seems off to me as well. We've never only talked about climbing. In fact, we rarely give each other a climber-speak, spray-down, blow-by-blow recounting of our climbing escapades. That is done more in passing. Before I was pregnant it went like this:

> *Her: I finally did Leaning Tower.*
> *Me: Amazing. I did this hard ice route called Within Reason.*
> *Her: Was it scary?*
> *Me: Sorta.*

And then we'd always go on to talk about where we were traveling next, or what it felt like to be on a recent trip, or about how to love and live with partners who climbed as much as we did. But on the phone today, I am torn.

"You still haven't told me how you're doing," she says.

I feel like I'd be a complainer if I really tell her what my day-to-day life is like. That I wake up and make high-pitched groaning noises as I stand up to go to the bathroom. That I take the stairs one at a time—both up and down—matching each foot, hand locked down on the railing the whole way. That I have a hydration bag next to the couch so I can, while lying down, drink some of the gallon of water I need every day. That I might have to lie down eighty percent of the time for the last four weeks of this pregnancy.

This isn't about Kate. And I know it. She's the most empathetic and sweet person around. We've traveled the world together, and she's seen me struggle plenty. Maybe too much. Maybe that is the problem. I want to be strong and invincible for a moment—for her and to her.

"Hold on," I say as Ptarmigan drops the ball into the ditch. I mute myself before I bend to retrieve it, to cover the inevitable groan.

"I'm thinking my first trip with the twins will be to the Red this fall," I say when I unmute, talking about the small sandstone crags of the Red River Gorge, in Kentucky. "They will be four months old then, and I have always wanted to go climbing there."

"I could meet you there," Kate says. "Wait, I'm going to Iran then."

"Maybe Greece after the Red?" I say.

"What about Peter?" Kate asks.

"What about him?"

"How's he feeling about trips?"

"He wants to go to Patagonia, of course," I say. "But I probably need to wait at least a year after giving birth for that. Maybe we can all go at the same time then."

I miss Kate. I miss that life of mine. "Or Chamonix next summer?" I offer.

I keep brainstorming trips because I want that life back. And while I know deep down I will get back some form of that life, I also don't want to think of it as "having it back." Because what I am doing is going forward into something new. I don't want to compare my life to what it was, but to be in what it is. And I know that. And it's up to me to create it. It always has been.

Ptarmigan is lying in the shade, and I've plopped down in a chair next to him. The air is heavy with pending New England rain. "We're still looking for a new house," I tell Kate. "Of course, you know me and my Treadwall"—a rotating, perpetual-motion climbing wall used to train endurance—"I need to make sure there's space for that so I can get my body back."

I cringe and pause at my own awkwardness, but Kate doesn't notice. Soon we're saying goodbye.

I heave myself up and call Ptarmigan to go inside. I need to stop saying things like "when I get my body back." It's not coming back. It never does—it goes forward. I need to go forward with it.

June 4, 2016
Audio Journal | Thirty-Five Weeks and One Day Pregnant

Hey babies,

We got to thirty-five weeks, which means you can be born at our local hospital in New Hampshire and not the one in Maine that has a NICU.

We are three weeks away at the most from having you. And I have been lying down for more and more of every day. I'm not really leaving the house at all. Maybe once a day just to run an errand. Sometimes just to go to the doctor. Sometimes driving myself—sometimes not. Lately I have had a few scares and have gone to the hospital, and your dad and I decided it might be better for me to stop driving.

I always thought that pregnancy would be this incredible experience with my body; I never thought it would feel so much like it was shutting me down. And even as you jut out into the world from my belly, I feel so small. Like I have been enclosed in a cocoon instead of feeling large, open, vast, and ready to meet anything.

Your dad and I made a plaster cast of my belly last weekend, and I walked outside with it on while it dried. It was hanging on my skin and I felt, for the first time, like the cast was all of my pregnancy and I could feel myself—my original self—behind all of that pregnancy. When I popped the cast off, I thought for a moment that maybe I could just lift off the pregnancy. It was just a moment. Just a thought.

June 10, 2016
From the Notepad | Thirty-Six Weeks Pregnant

"Do you want to take a joy ride?" I ask Peter the day the minivan arrives from the used-car dealer.

"Do you?" he says.

Peter helps me climb into the passenger seat, and we set off for a half-mile "road trip" in ninety-four-degree weather with the windows down.

Four houses down the street I give a mini-grunt as I lean over and play with Peter's hair at the base of his neck. This is the move I used to telegraph that I wanted to kiss him in five-degree weather in his beater Subaru when we met eight years before. This time his hair is damp, and I would scooch over to kiss him if I could still scooch.

"Did you ever think you'd have a minivan and be chauffeuring your very pregnant wife full of twins around in it?" I ask.

"I never thought any of this," he says.

—⁓—

June 14, 2016
Audio Journal | Thirty-Six Weeks and Four Days Pregnant

All right, you two, you've gone catawampus in Mamma's belly. I worry about you squishing each other. Well, to be fair, I mainly worry about you, little boy, squishing your sister. You're big—above the ninety-fifth percentile—while you, little girl, are on the smaller side. We've been nervous about that all along, but the doctors tell us to think of you as individuals and not to compare you to each other. It's hard not to, of course, because you're also the same, stacked side by side, or as they say in Quebec, "side by each."

This has been by far—far, far, far, far—the hardest physical thing I have ever undertaken. Now I am lying down all the time. I don't, as a rule, do that much. Every day I spend the majority of my time lying on my side with my belly seizing in contractions when I shift.

For the past thirty-six weeks my whole goal has been to keep you in. I am finally at the point where I can start to think of moving you out. I am so ready to get you on the other side. To have you grow breathing air. And to let me grow being a mamma while I shrink at the same time.

I'm nervous. About giving birth to you. But I am not scared. I know I can't plan it, can't control it, can't make it be anything but what it will be. I might have tried to do that if there were just one of you, but you've already taught me how to give in to the two hundred percent of you.

June 15, 2016
Audio Journal | Thirty-Six Weeks and Five Days Pregnant

I am ready to have you guys. Your dad told me today that he'd like to wait until next week.

I said it was no longer okay for him to suggest that I continue to remain pregnant for his convenience. He didn't intend to be mean or insensitive, but just him saying it shows what different trajectories each of us is on right now.

His life is about to change, to get bigger and smaller at the same time—bigger because you guys are in it, smaller because his freedom will shrink dramatically.

For me, it's the opposite. My life has been getting narrower and narrower the further into pregnancy we get. And it's going to open up when I am on the other side of this.

Last night, the two of you shook your booties to a beat of your own making, pulsating your backsides and heels against the edges of your spherical home, in and out of time to twin syncopated hiccups.

"I can't believe they're coming out," your dad said. "It's not like anything else in life."

"Birth?" I asked him.

"All of it. Compared to everything else, this is happening no matter what."

I waited for him to go on. I had nowhere else to go.

"Take Fitz Roy," he started.

"Are you about to compare having children to climbing Fitz Roy?" I interrupted.

"Wait for it," he said. "Listen—we were planning to climb it the whole time, but at any moment, we could have turned around, right?"

The two of you stopped moving, as if you were also doing as asked and listening to his story.

"If the snow was unsafe on the hike in, we could have bailed," he continued. "If the temperatures were too warm for the ice to be safe, we could have bailed. We could have even skirted the summit and traversed and rapped down."

I took his hands and put them on top of each of your rumps. "Pay attention down there," I said. "You are not an *if* or *maybe* or *might*. You are *ours*."

We stood together, layered—you then me then him—and then I belched.

"It was a malt day," I say, shrugging my shoulders.

"Malts." Peter shakes my stomach. "Never forget that you two were grown with malts."

I am glad you are about to come thundering into my life. No matter what, I am giving birth to you. You're going to be these creatures I can hold, whose fingers I can touch—you're going to be my babies.

I don't think there's ever been anything that has happened in my life that has felt so inevitable. And even still, *inevitable* feels too passive to describe this. Maybe *profound*, *true*, and *unassailable* are more accurate.

In so many spheres of life you can change your mind. You can *not* get married, you can *not* go to college, you can *not* go to Mozambique, visit your grandmother, or hold your niece—but you can't, at this point, thirty-six weeks and five days pregnant with twins, alter your course.

And I don't want to change course.

In the middle of last night, I thought I was going to have you. A lot is going on with my body; it's changing, I can feel it. It's getting ready. And I got scared. If I move, you move, rejiggering yourselves so that my uterus contracts. Which meant each time I woke up because my hands were numb from being barnacled into claws while I slept or because I had to pee, we'd all get braced for action. "We've got this," I whispered to you while rubbing both of you head-to-toe through the skin of my stomach.

Do you know my words willed you to be two? When I started trying to get pregnant, I told myself I'd make healthy, robust babies with ease. And I never thought *babies*, being plural, meant anything. It was just more grammatically correct. Before I got double amnios and they drove a 7.5-centimeter-long needle into my belly—twice—I started saying,

"I make robust, healthy, full-chromosome babies with ease." Mantras are one of my things, and I wanted you to grow the whole way. And now we're here.

For the past thirty-six weeks I have wondered if we would really get here. There are all of these off-ramps—things that could go wrong, things that could not go entirely right. I could have you early, I could lose you. But not anymore. You're mine. You're ours.

June 29, 2016
Audio Journal | One Day Old

One day, I will tell you the story about how I went through forty-one hours of labor to bring you into the world. About how for a quarter of it I was in a fever dream, about my water breaking over a green exercise ball that would later fillet my legs open while my body desperately tried to release you. That is a story for another time. You are the story for now.

Irenna Burhardt Doucette. You are strong, with long, lean legs that make you look like a giant. You are five pounds and fourteen ounces of power. You have eyelashes and fingernails. You nursed the minute you touched Mamma's chest. You carry the name of my grandma, Irena, but have an extra *n* to make your name all your own. She was one of Poland's early female lawyers—a force to be reckoned with who created my dad and loved my mom.

Kaz Raymond Doucette. You have dark, curly hair and love to get it wet under the water. I want to inhale your round cheeks. You didn't have an official name until today. Now you get to carry the legacy of my dad, Krystzof Kazimierz, and your dad's grandpa Ray forward—but on your own terms, as Kaz.

You're used to each other. This should not be surprising to me after you spent thirty-eight weeks and four days together in my belly. But it is. You each nook into the other's cranny in your shared hospital bassinet.

You both fit under my armpits, tucked tightly inside the folds of the robe I threw into the hospital bag at the last moment. It encircles us all each time we nurse. Which is all the time.

You were born yesterday. Today is your dad's and my third wedding anniversary. I told your dad it's perfect this way. You will have your special day, and we will have ours. This year, we're spending our special day making it all about you.

Maybe I'm a fool to think it won't always be all about you.

July 4, 2016
Audio Journal | Six Days Old

You are growing. I am healing my body, which let you into the world, and ripping open my soul now that you're here. Everyone is here and doing what they are supposed to do.

July 6, 2016
From the Notepad | Eight Days Old

Last night's iPhone note entry:

10:30 P.M.:
   Both wet, change
   Both nurse eight min
   I poop

K poop
Both nurse ten min
I wet
Both nurse five min

12:48 A.M.:
Both wet, change
Both nurse four min
K tries to fall asleep, ice water behind ear to keep him awake
and nursing
K poop
Both nurse ten min
I poop
K poop
Both nurse four more min
I poop

3:10 A.M.:
Both three poops and two wet
Twenty-five-ish min of nursing

4:20 A.M.:

Now I am wide awake and you're not. Each time you feed it's supposed to be for thirty minutes. Is it thirty minutes cumulatively? I ask your dad. But he's finally back to sleep after our night shift has ended, and we're back in our bed.

Maybe I should wake him up. As the resident diaper changer, he's the one to double-check the poop numbers too. Did Irenna poop before or after nursing?

How long do I have to keep track of this?

I'm switching to paper.

July 9, 2016
Audio Journal | Eleven Days Old

Your grandma is leaving today. But first she's out on a three-hour, forty-five-mile bicycle ride on roads busy with summer-vacation traffic.

This morning, she was holding you, Irenna, and stroking your jaw-line, if you can even be said to have a jawline at one week old. "I hope you're smart like me," she said to you. "And athletic."

Then she drank her coffee. "And compassionate," she added eventually.

Three months ago, your grandma was cycling in Arizona and had what she mandates we call a "ministroke"—though she also mandates we don't talk about it, so we rarely get to call it anything. For this visit, her bike arrived in New Hampshire before she did. I can't stop her from riding any more than she can make me take a nap.

"If I have a stroke and get eaten by a bear, so be it," she told me today, over her shoulder, while biking down our driveway in ninety-two-degree heat.

You will get to know that your grandma is an amazing, daunting, and formidable woman. She loves fiercely, she loves completely, and like most other things she does in life, she loves competitively. I hope to god that you guys get to know her so, so well. And I am scared to death that you won't. And that is my fault because I waited until I was thirty-nine and she was seventy to have you.

One day when you have kids, I will come help you. I will try to remember how hard it is, and how wonderful it is at the same time, to have my mother around. To have her hold my babies and love them. To have her nudge you with hands that were always loving and always a little rougher than I wanted them to be.

Maybe I'll remember how nice it is to see her come in and just depend on her to be here. Also how wild it is, when you're almost forty years old, to share your house with your mother, who helped create many of the systems you use but also does things differently.

To watch her learn how to recycle, to watch her break the rules and use the scrubby on the pans we asked her to wash with the sponge. To watch her demand domestic independence and lack of supervision because, after all, what does it really matter if we don't eat organic eggs sometimes?

She'll be back from her ride soon. Let's go pick out some good outfits to wear when we say goodbye. As if you *wear* outfits—we're in survival dressing mode every time your dad or I work your eight limbs into any item of clothing. I already gave away everything with buttons, no matter how cute it was. Nothing is cuter than zippers in this new life of ours. Your dad streamlines further by keeping you naked except for a swaddle and a diaper. And since he runs point on the poo diaper changing and is the swaddle king of the Northeast, he gets to make that decision most of the time.

Your dad and I have spent eight years refining our climbing systems together, so that we can automatically hand off the climbing gear as we swap leads at belay anchors. It seems right then that in these past eleven days—a maelstrom both of love and getting our asses kicked—we're already developed just as proficient with a system with you.

Every day and night we're a team conveyor belt as he delivers you to eat with me and cleans you up to eat again. Last night, between the two of you, he changed eleven poo diapers—the current all-time record.

Irenna, you have a special look you give him right when he starts to put on a fresh diaper and you fill it up before he can even finish doing up the Velcro tabs. It cracks me up every time, though I try not to laugh too hard as it still feels like it's going to blow out my C-section stitches and pour pee and afterbirth out of my vagina—*and* I don't want to hurt your dad's feelings.

But today we will do outfits with buttons come hell or high water because I need more pictures of you with your grandma. One day you're going to need them too. She hasn't even left, and I feel she's already too far away. This is why people want to stop time. And how they learn to keep going.

I love you two. You're eleven days old today. Kazaroo, you've been on my chest in a carrier the whole time. We got you settled while Mom was recording you this letter. Irenna-bear, you're in the cradle that Grandma made for you. We had an okay night. I put jeans on for the first time in three months. It's a big day. I love you, little buga-boos. I love you for cracking my body and my heart wide open and not stopping.

July 20, 2016
From the Notepad | Twenty-Two Days Old

I now know that if you're repeatedly vomiting, your body can still nurse two newborns. I don't think I was lucid through most of the nursing sessions between retching for god-knows-what-reason last night, but I pulled it off and you got fed.

I was already exhausted. What do I call this new state?

July 30, 2016
Audio Journal | One Month and Two Days Old

It took eight months of my life as a full-time climber to have a friend wrenched from the world for the first time; it's taken four weeks as a mom.

Gary Falk fell twenty-four hundred feet to his death off the same pedestal of rock he'd stood on hundreds of times on the side of the Grand Teton. The same pedestal of rock your dad has stood on dozens of times, me a handful. I can close my eyes here in New Hampshire and conjure the gray-gold, three-by-three granite platform in Wyoming.

But my brain never stays with that image long, replacing it with scenes of Gary and Kate's four-year-old and nine-month-old children. I wonder, in the moment their dad died, were they napping? Crying? Barreling gleefully down a slide at the park?

Gary's day was just another one at the office for a mountain guide. Or it was supposed to have been. In this moment, I hate mountain guiding. I hate being one myself. I hate being married to one even more.

———

I'm getting ready to go climbing for the first time in eight months. Not today, but soon. Where does this fit, where does Gary fit, where does the death of a friend who does the same thing as you ever fit?

Each time I learn of a loss in the mountains, I run a mental weave pattern: How well did I know them? Have I traveled the same steps they took before their death? Where is the fault line in the accident narrative that I can find to separate me from it being my story? I have been running this mental calculus for twenty years, but now that you're part of the math I feel doubly exposed, with all my nerve endings out there, frayed and waiting to be *zung, zinged,* and *zapped* by the world.

I didn't know Gary well, but your dad did. I've been running theoretical drills of losing my partner to climbing since I was nineteen. Now that partner is your dad.

This week in the Bugaboos in the Purcell mountains of British Columbia, a climber dislodged a boulder the size of a EuroVan just by touching it as he walked by it, and it crushed him. Something that had been there for thousands of years took the length of a heartbeat to finally move and forever stop a life. *What are the chances of that happening again?* my mind automatically asks to insulate me from the accident.

Your grandparents and my nonclimbing friends are not so secretly hoping I'll stop climbing now that I have you. I won't talk with them about it; pushing past their trepidation with my determination has always been my way. But what if this—having you, being your mom—does change me? If I felt exposed climbing in Chamonix last summer after not climbing for months because of international work, what will it feel like now after a longer hiatus and a new role as a mom? Not to mention the seventy pounds of weight I gained and the fifty pounds I have lost and whatever it feels like to balance this new body of mine on tiny rock edges?

Before our drive today, I sat down and nursed you in front of a webcast of the Democratic National Convention I'd been saving to see for two days.

I was crying by the time Hillary Clinton took her first three steps toward the stage.

I want to raise you both in a world where she is president, not a world that would elect Donald Trump. I don't want that other world. And next to any of this, climbing seems superfluous.

"We have to campaign," I told your dad the other day.

He winced.

"I will campaign," I said.

Your dad asked me if I ever paused and realized how much work this is. But I don't pause. I just pick you up, love you, feel crushed by the enormity of my responsibility to you in the world, and try to be grateful I got to put on my underwear today.

August 3, 2016
Audio Journal | Five Weeks and Two Days Old

Did you know that the day I gave birth to you I sat in a recliner naked from the waist up, torn apart from waist down, and typed out an email, one-handed, that said, "Of course I'd be happy to meet as soon as possible about a grant to fund the next five years of conservation work on Mount Namuli."

Now we're working on that grant together. Or at least we do it every day from 6:43 A.M. to 7:14 A.M.

I am pretty sure I am quickly approaching some version of carpal tunnel syndrome from the combination of holding your heads to nurse and contouring my arms around those same heads to type while you sleep on my chest. I don't care. Perhaps I'm deranged from the lack of sleep and the constant contact high of your milky smell and the allure of the largest funding amount I've ever fielded or could dream of as even possible.

I could tell you about plenty of times when all of the pieces I am trying to put together are not working. For now, I'll take the intoxication of the moment.

August 7, 2016
Audio Journal | Five Weeks and Six Days Old

We're driving home from Aunt Cate and your now–Uncle Mike's wedding. You were in the wedding party as yourselves, but also as an extension of me. I walked down the aisle carrying one of you on each arm.

I am feeling . . . what? So tired. So sad. So happy. So human. I feel like a mom. It's not a part I'm playing anymore. It's who I am.

After we walked down the aisle, I handed each of you to willing friends and stood in the ceremony as myself. But the rest of the night was all about you. In and out of the house to the reception with one or both of you in my arms. Leaking milk onto the electric blue of my dress when I held neither of you. Choosing Kaz as my only dance partner as I walked laps around the outside of the tent to get him to finally sleep against my skin, feeling that I was where I needed to be while simultaneously wishing I could dance with others on the walnut floor.

Given all of that, a mom must be what everyone else sees me as too. But not necessarily as *me*.

My mom asked me when you were born if I was just so proud of moving through the world with you guys. It hadn't really crossed my mind to be proud of being able to move as a unit with you. Likely because I don't do it that much yet. What we do as a unit a lot is nurse, which for this week at the wedding has meant a lot of time with me topless on the couch and your dad and his family and friends pitching in to change you and swirl you around in a giant system of love and carries and cuddles and kisses. I want to live in this system forever. Or I do during the days. The nights I could do without, and all this week I tried to give your dad sleep and extra time with his family. Which means I had neither for myself. Which again means I am a mom.

Mom of twins. It turns out it's not the last thing in my bio, as it is on my updated Instagram profile. Right now, it feels like the first thing.

———

You are almost six weeks old, and I am not ready. It is going too quickly. I am not ready for you to be bigger, and I don't think I ever will be. Our life, our time together, seems so fragile. And it's fragile. And it's strong. And it's just life.

Above all, I feel so vulnerable. So stinking vulnerable.

You're vulnerable and strong too. I saw that this week when we had to go to Dartmouth Health Children's with Irenna.

They put you in a headlock, little girl, and they inserted that probe into your eye and put it down your nose to clear your tear duct. You screamed at first, but then you stopped screaming and you just sat there with your eyes opening and closing, your nose wrinkled. I stood next to you rocking, not because I held a baby in my arms but because I didn't know what else to do.

Watching you tore me apart. And it also bound me together. I didn't want to witness your pain—I never want you to feel pain. But I also don't want to miss it. I want to be present in all of it.

At the same time, I could hear Kaz in the adjoining room crying for me. He was with a young woman named Jane whom I'd hired to be my extra hands for the five-hour round-trip drive to the hospital as well as the two hours we ended up spending there. None of us had what we needed just then, but we did the moment we were all back together.

I want to love you to pieces and not miss it, and not go too quickly to the next thing, because you guys are my next thing. You're my thing. I'm a mom.

August 20, 2016
Audio Journal | Seven Weeks and Five Days Old

I'm cutting my fingernails in the driveway; I usually cut yours on the couch.

"Rope, rack, helmets?" I ask your dad as he walks out of the gear room and opens the car.

"Breast milk, babies, their aunt to take care of them?" he asks in response.

"Let's go visit my other life," I say, settling into the front seat as we set off down our long driveway, Peter at the wheel.

—⁓—

Six years ago, I wrote an article for *Climbing Magazine* about the eternal comeback after my second back surgery. When I wrote it, the thought never crossed my mind that one day I'd be coming back from having twins.

But coming *back* doesn't take you anywhere but *back*ward. As I said, I'm moving forward.

I know it's possible; we've all done it. All athletes recover. All athletes create new iterations of themselves, wondering what each version will be like.

Sometimes I think this is the real beauty of climbing: you get a chance to start again and climb your way back up—through the grades, through risks that seem minor and reasonable until you're back to the edge of yourself and moving forward into what's possible.

August 20, 2016 (Later)
Audio Journal | Seven Weeks and Five Days Old

I was apart from you for exactly three hours and eighteen minutes while I went climbing. It took me twelve steps inside the door before we were one again. You latched onto me and I held onto you, covering your cheeks, foreheads, noses, and ears with my chalky fingerprints.

Your dad is going into the garage of our new house to assemble the Treadwall so I can start training again. It's rock season now, and ice season is coming. Or that's how I used to think about it. Now it's simpler and not dependent on the weather—baby season. Twin season.

Our new home is in Jackson, nine minutes from our yellow house in Intervale. It's a house that came on the market the day you were born and that we bought before you'd been outside my belly for twenty-four hours. I told you I like to do it all at once, right?

August 25, 2016
Audio Journal | Eight Weeks and Two Days Old

"There's still no news from the search for Kyle and Scott," Peter says from the kitchen.

We've just gotten settled on the blue couch in the living room. My feet are propped on a step stool, my lime-green My Brest Friend tandem nursing pillow strapped around me like an inner tube, extra pillows under each arm to support my arms and in turn your heads.

I look down at each of you. "When did they go missing again?" I ask Peter.

"Five days ago, maybe more?" His knife clunks on the cutting board. Carrots.

I never met Scott Adamson. I last saw Kyle Dempster three years ago when he came to our valley's ice-climbing festival to share tales of his time on the Himalayan giants K7 and the Ogre I. They're both lost on the side of the Ogre II in Pakistan now, and I know none of us wants to admit what we already know—that they are lost forever.

August 27, 2016
Audio Journal | Eight Weeks and Four Days Old

No one told me not to bring a stroller to boob group.

No one told me, either, that you were supposed to cover your boobs at boob group.

But it's impossible to nurse the two of you covered, and it's also the last thing I want to learn how to do.

It's also impossible to extract a double stroller from the back of a small room once fifteen nursing mothers, their infants, and other miscellaneous toddlers have filled it up.

We are like a small semitruck everywhere we go. Or a double-wide. Or a . . .

And shoes. Before I am done, we have to talk about the shoes. I had a box of fourteen pairs of hand-me-down shoes for infants, which I have already given away. Who in the world puts shoes on babies?

The women at boob group. Each and every one of them.

August 28, 2016
Letter | Eight Weeks and Five Days Old

Life is no longer singular for me. Not in focus, not in priorities. You did this to me.

Yesterday I found out that Legado got another major new grant—and it's the one program in Africa to get the grant this year. You might not think this is relevant to your lives yet, but it's actually very much so.

I somehow was able to give birth to you and apply for this grant all in the past two months, on top of the news of other possible funding. I suppose this means I have finally assembled a team of the right people to work with me and that I have had at least *some* maternity leave (albeit unpaid). Both are signs of progress.

Your mamma started an organization that now has a grant from a consortium including the Global Environment Facility and the United Nations Development Programme. These huge organizations and changemakers—names that I studied in school and thought would no longer be part of my life when I took up climbing full-time—are now behind and beside me as we create this together.

Six years ago I saw a photo of a granite rock face in Mozambique. It wasn't a good photo or even a good-looking rock face, but it was something—it was new. I'd never heard of or thought of rock climbing in Mozambique before that photo.

Two months later I was putting together an expedition. But not to that rock face. To one much bigger: Mozambique's 7,936-foot Mount Namuli. And not just to climb—to launch a program to conserve that mountain and its biodiversity. With its people. I had the support of my climbing sponsors, but to do the big work I needed more support. Which went a little bit like this:

"Hi, my name is Majka Burhardt, and I'm launching a new program on Mount Namuli combining climbing and scientific research to protect a globally important area for biodiversity."

I'd then spend three minutes talking about Namuli, its forests, and the importance of biodiversity, awaiting the inevitable response: "This sounds ambitious. Where have you done this before?"

I tried out lots of answers.

I did a similar climbing program in Namibia but did not have the science team or community focus. That experience inspired this work . . .

I specialize in creating teams that tackle new problems . . .

No, I have never flipping done this, but I believe it's a good idea and want you to give me money to do it.

Eventually I went to Namuli with a small team and backed by funding solely from my climbing sponsors. The larger project took three years and ten times as many nos, but then we started getting yeses. Today we're partnered with a Mozambican conservation organization and operating a full-time program working with Namuli community members to try to create a plan to protect their mountain.

I say "to try" because this is a story for you, Irenna and Kaz, not for our funders.

We tend to compartmentalize our lives, believing that our personal interests and the working parts of our lives rarely if ever intersect. I was taught that the people running the United Nations Development Programme couldn't or wouldn't understand climbing. But here it all is—climbing, conservation, livelihoods, development—sandwiched together in Legado. And Legado is sandwiched between the two of you.

I'm turning forty in thirty-seven days. That seems like real adulthood. And I am a mother. And I have this flourishing organization connecting more dots than I ever thought could be connected. And I'm crying, the good and big and happy and scared-at-the-bigness-of-life tears.

—⁂—

August 31, 2016
Audio Journal | Nine Weeks and One Day Old

Why do I feel like I have spent my life multitasking in preparation for having you? How insane I was for thinking it was for a career. How insane I was for thinking we're not going to end up right here. Right now, Irenna, you're tucked against my chest, sleeping in a carrier. I'm changing Kaz, and I'm dictating this letter.

Next week, an au pair, Anna, will come to live with us. She's from Germany and is a trained confectioner. Which could be my downfall next to my salvation.

The closer Anna gets to us, the more torn I feel about having an au pair in the first place. That's not true. Your dad and I both work full-time, so we need help to pull this—you—off. I made the plan for this long ago, but now, ten days from Anna moving in, I wonder if I should just chuck it all and hang out with you all the time.

Except.

I have work I *want* to do.

I feel I am going to miss the best parts of you. I don't want to miss a thing, but trying to work and care for you without any help makes me feel crazy—and maybe that constant tension between the things we want to do and the things we need to do is the crux of motherhood.

Yesterday I spent four hours dealing with financial paperwork after our grant came through. Amid the spreadsheets and the calls, I kept shoving pacifiers in your mouth, Kaz, and trying to pick you up, Irenna-bear, and set you down so you wouldn't cry. But that doesn't feel like the way I want to mother.

I want to be present.

I want to enjoy you. I want to do things by myself and create powerful things in the world.

I don't know how this is all going to work out, but we're trying to do it.

September 8, 2016
From the Notepad | Ten Weeks and Two Days Old

We're back in our positions. Tonight, Peter is making tacos and cole-slaw. The cabbage scratches as he pushes it across the grater. I raise my knee, which lets me hold Kaz's head stable just long enough to slot the nozzle from the CamelBak I've hung above my couch nursing station into my mouth.

"I saw," I say when I finish drinking.

"Saw what?"

"That woman. I don't know her." The water tastes funny, and I look down at the nozzle and realize the inside of it is laced with green algae.

"*Didn't* know her," I correct myself. "Julia."

Swish, scratch, swish. Peter grates the carrots next.

"This is not normal evening conversation," I say. I blow on Irenna's face to keep her from falling asleep on the job. "Or maybe what I should say is that I don't want it to be."

"Do you want me not to tell you?" Peter asks.

"You didn't this time—I saw it anyway."

I want it not to have happened. She broke a hold off the side of a granite mountain on a traverse that mirrored one Peter and I had done four years earlier. Already I've justified that it's not the same. But I transpose the two events in my head. "All I can think of is which hold, which mountain, which ridge?" I say

"But you know it wasn't the Palisade Traverse," Peter clarifies to me.

"Why should it matter?" I say, to both of us.

I think of the sun rising on the side of North Palisade—a fourteen-thousand-foot peak deep in the eastern Sierra Nevada—coaxing me out of my sleeping bag for the third day of movement despite my body's best wishes. I think of how much I relied on Peter back then.

"My water hose has gone to shit," I say.

"Again?" he says.

Later that night, after the twins go to bed, I find a tube cleaner in the basement, rotor green sludge out of the clear tube, refill the water bag, and hang the system back on the wall for the next day's hydration.

September 10, 2016
Audio Journal | Ten Weeks and Four Days Old

Today, my mom called and announced that she's finally decided to find a new therapist.

"I'm tired of feeling so damn angry," she said.

My mom doesn't believe in FaceTime, which is good. I can make approving noises and she doesn't have to know that I'm crying.

I love her. And I don't want to wait until I am seventy-one to stop being angry.

"You know that saying you and Peter have?" my mom asked.

"Wanna trade?" is the top thing Peter and I ask each other these days, but I am pretty sure this is not what my mom meant.

"Your sister stitched it on the quilt square she added to the stole we all made for your wedding," she said. "I think of it all the time: 'From Judgment to Love.'"

I cried more. Maybe Mom at seventy-one and me at thirty-nine are more alike than I ever want to admit.

From judgment to love.

From judgment to love.

As I go about my day, I repeat it like a mental string of rosary beads.

It doesn't work. Being the daughter of two lapsed Catholics is not in my favor. All I feel is judgment and anger. They are becoming my default.

I feel them when he leaves the toilet seat up and I collapse on the skinny rim of the bowl because I still can't control my abdominals to squat that low; when he tells me how tired he is while scrolling through his phone or computer and while I nurse two humans; when he says he doesn't feel he can be with both kids alone after he comes home from work and it's what I've been doing all day; when he cooks my eggs too runny and when I have to depend on him to cook them in the first place.

Breathe, Majka. Control your own reactions. Start there. From judgment to love.

I don't want to feel like shit and be angry at Peter. I have to give him my best. I am scared that he won't show up and give me the same.

And if he doesn't . . .

If he never steps up . . .

Or if he does and I don't see it . . .

Or it's not enough . . .

Or if I can never stop being angry . . .

Then what?

And I am desperately scared that Peter won't step up, and it will be like it was with my first husband, Eddie. I chose against that first marriage. I don't want to choose against this one.

September 10, 2016 (Later)
Audio Journal | Ten Weeks and Four Days Old

Okay, I can do this.

I have a new plan. Gentleness, affection, listening, and understanding. It's for your dad and me, but really it's for you.

Start small. I know how to do this. I'm going to do my best to be generous and kind, give him affection, give him breaks, give him what he needs, ask what he needs—and I am going to hope it comes back to me.

For a week.

And if it doesn't come back to me by next Tuesday, then I will let myself talk about it. To me, this is life right now, and I want him to understand it. What we need to do is take it by the horns and make it good.

Your dad is fighting it. I need him to be the great dad I know he can be. I love that one—the one who wakes up and offers ideas for breakfast in alternating British, German, and Australian accents and says, "I love you," to each of you while snorting piggy kisses into your cheeks. How do I help him get back to that dad? How does he help me be that mom?

September 11, 2016
From the Notepad | Ten Weeks and Five Days Old

Two grown men singing "Welcome to the Jungle" as they bicycle baby feet in time to the music.

This is what it takes for me to take a shower.

It's on again when I get out, Axl Rose howling about bringing *it to your shan-n-n-n-n-n-n-n knees*. I hear your dad sing in time to the music. "Bearski, knee, knee," he croons to Irenna, using his new nickname for her.

"Go like this and see if Kaz likes it too," he tells Uncle Richard.

Uncle Richard is not your dad's brother. He's one of his best friends. Who happens to spend a lot of time at our house, using it as his New Hampshire home base and guiding headquarters, four hours from his real home in Maine. He spends so much time here that I told him when I got pregnant that if he wanted to keep up his New Hampshire guesthouse he had to be on board with all things twin. This man who never wanted babies of his own now jumps in wholeheartedly.

From the shower, I can hear Uncle Richard and your dad guffawing and singing, and I imagine them flapping each of your limbs in time to the music. No one is crying. I debate shaving my legs.

Maybe I need to see your dad with greater curiosity and amusement, like I see Uncle Richard.

When I was in my early twenties trying to climb harder and harder routes, a stronger climber told me to "fall upward." If you stopped trying and hung on the rope or fell, it was a failure. If you fell because you were trying, at least you were heading in the right direction.

Maybe that is what your dad and I are doing. Falling upward, with you. Being your parents is the ultimate *onsight* for us, a climber term for a no-falls, first-try ascent of a climb you have no prior knowledge of. But in climbing, you can fail on an onsight and walk away—and then find another climb to try onsight. In parenting, you onsight—and either succeed or fail—but then have to keep going on the same "climb." How can I expect Peter to crush it if he's never done it before? We had no idea what we were getting ourselves into, times two.

Uncle Richard now knows how to swaddle you. Your dad taught him. So we will have forever changed Uncle Richard, even if just this little bit. I am ten weeks into the steepest learning curve of my life. Correction: We are. Your dad and I are. There is no going back to the people we were—to each other, to anyone. There is only falling upward for us too.

September 12, 2016
Audio Journal | Ten Weeks and Six Days Old

I am sitting in the parking lot at Story Land, the headliner New England children's amusement park that happens to be five minutes from our house in Jackson. One day we'll go visit it inside. I've had my car idling in the shade for twenty minutes to keep you, Kaz, sleeping, while you, Irenna-bear, nurse with me in the front seat. We almost made it home. But Irenna, you woke up with a blood-curdling cry, so now I'm ruining the climate because I need one moment without both of you crying, and the second I click that bloody key over to turn off the car, I know you, Kaz, will wake up.

Our au pair, Anna, started yesterday. She lives with us and has a bedroom upstairs. She works forty-five hours a week tending to you, tending to anything in the household that relates to you. I think I thought I'd have childcare for those hours of the day, allowing me to work—but I am realizing I don't have childcare. I have *help*. Childcare assumes I could hand you over to Anna. But watching both of you at once is too big a job to ask of her. I only just now feel comfortable doing it—and then not all the time.

So instead, we do it together. I have one of you napping in a chest carrier while she has the other. And I know I am lucky as hell to have Anna, but shouldn't it feel easy if I have help?

I could *not* work. I could give up my career and be your mom, and your dad could support us. Except . . . your dad could die any day at work, and then where would we be? Me, single parenting you two, covered in grief while I fight my way back to a career to support us? It's better this way. And I love my work, and it's never crossed my mind not to do it. Which is maybe what I should have said first.

And no, I don't think your dad is going to die every time he goes climbing. Or that I will die. How would we climb if we thought that way? How unbalanced is it that I'm justifying how we rationalize climbing right now—as if that were the goal instead of being your parents?

I thought by now I'd be working. But what I am doing instead is spending any precious mental energy creating domestic systems and getting Anna comfortable with you and your needs so that I can—eventually, theoretically—work.

Help costs too much money for this not to work.

And the two of you nurse so much I'm starting to see how much easier this would be if I wasn't breastfeeding.

Except.

I don't want to make a choice between nursing you and working—which is for me, and you, and us. Maybe I could pump, squirreled away in my home office, but it's a loft with no sound insulation from the rest of the house, and my body is forever permeable to your cries. It's easier to come to you when you need to eat than to hear you needing me but then feed a suctioning machine instead.

This is why people leave home to go to work. This is why I want to stay home and work.

I want a break. I feel horrible for saying that.

I don't know if you should be napping when I have you, or if I should give you to Anna when you are napping so that she can more easily manage you. But then I wouldn't get you when you are napping.

And no one is likely getting anything great from your dad and me these days because not one of our family four-pack is sleeping at night anymore.

And now you are waking up, Kaz. Oh boy, you're okay, Kaz. Keep sleeping, bug. Someone needs to sleep.

September 13, 2016
Audio Journal | Eleven Weeks Old

We're back nursing in the passenger seat of the car, stalled out in our journey, again, a mere five minutes from home. That's mostly when I record your letters. It's being with you doubled up and attached to me while I speak to you both for now, and for posterity's sake. And for the company of my own voice as well.

Irenna, you have only wanted me since I came home from Boston, where I went three days ago to pick up Anna at the train station and spend three hours teaching others to climb at a nearby climbing gym, to momentarily tag back into my life as a pro athlete. The nine-hour trip was triple the longest time I'd been away from you before. Last night, you were not satisfied after nursing every hour since two P.M.— you needed more at bedtime. We sat in the dark on the couch in your room as your brother slept. You gently tugged at my right nipple, and your hand came up like a starfish on my breast. I traced your fingers with my left hand. The softest fingers, the softest surfaces I have ever touched. So delicate, so perfect, so mine.

"I will not give this up," I told you. "I cannot."

Your only response was to nurse and squeeze me more.

"I have no idea how we're going to do this, Irenna-bear," I said.

But then again, I never do.

———

Earlier today, I learned that we are at yet another elevated stage for a grant that would transform our ability to work on Namuli. I also got an invoice for $11,000 that we don't have the money to cover, signed a contract for a book with Patagonia, and realized I had no idea how to make it to a speaking event in October on top of my commitment to show the film in Banff, which I hoped to squeeze in "en route" to a day of meetings in DC, which was "en route" to go be a climber again in Kentucky.

And amid all of it, I realized this would all be easier if I were not breastfeeding.

It's day three of us having Anna as our au pair, and I know to even have her, and a fledgling organization that can pay me so I can pay for her, is a luxury. But it feels more a Band-Aid than a solution.

I dash upstairs to be at my computer when there's any window of time—always with one of you asleep in a carrier on my chest. If I stand up with my laptop perched on boxes, I can type and bounce you to keep you sleeping. This almost works until whichever of you is with

Anna cries, and any mental focus or capability I have is replaced with electrified breasts from my milk letting down.

My idea was to plug back in. Sure, my work would be "modified." But I'd do it. Writing emails and conducting meetings to lead an organization that's supporting mountain communities to conserve their home, which also happens to be one of the most biodiverse places on Earth—all while jiggling one of you enough to get a nap while being sure someone else is jiggling the other of you so that you nap at the same time and then nurse at the same time, just so we can do it all over again. This is not modified work . . . It's insane. Which is why I gave up on it again today and went for a nap drive.

So here I am. Tandem nursing in the Story Land parking lot, where fantasy lives.

September 16, 2016
From the Notepad | Eleven Weeks and Three Days Old

Will you be in Banff for the festival? I text Sarah Hueniken. I'm asking early to stake out time in what I know is her busy life. She is balancing her full-time guiding, building an ever-advancing career as a pro climber, and taking on a new role as a more permanent fixture for her partner's two kids.

Yes! Climb? she responds.

For five minutes, I let myself scheme a plan to have my eighty-one-year-old stepfather and seventy-one-year-old mother manage my three-month-old twins for eight hours while I climb in Banff. Then I note to myself that this would be the day after they have traveled all day just to support me at the festival and will likely already be exhausted.

By "climb" do you mean hike for an hour with a twin strapped to your chest? I write back eventually.

Exactly, Sarah says.

September 19, 2016
Audio Journal | Eleven Weeks and Six Days Old

I'm sitting in the driver's seat of my van, with the computer wedged against the steering wheel, sweat dripping between my engorged breasts, and the windows and doors shut so I can't hear you two screaming while Anna and your dad try to console you inside the house. Before having you I would have never guessed how far your cries can travel. Plus Ptarmigan is barking because you are crying, which makes you cry even more. Despite all this chaos, the van should be the perfect office for me. Except my iPhone is dying and my transformative funder is telling me they want to fund our *work* but not fund *us* to do it.

I take notes on my computer and try to pay attention. I don't even feel like I belong in this conversation anyway. I never wanted to create a behemoth conservation organization. I don't want to say yes to terms that will turn Legado into something I didn't envision. We're trying to create a new way for these places in the world and their people to use their own power to create their future. And it has come down to me fighting for that goal—all while crammed in my van and hiding from my kids.

October 4, 2016
Letter | Three Months Old

Dear Kaz and Irenna,

Today I turn forty. That's old, or young, depending on whom you ask. But I don't care what anyone else thinks about the relative age of forty. I only care about turning forty in respect to you two. Today you are three months and one week fresh in this world. And while you can bet on the fact that I'm going to do everything in my power to be around when you turn forty, today I can't seem to get past the fact that I might not make it there. (Yes, I'm being morbid, and I Googled it—the average life expectancy for Americans is 78.74 years.)

Here is the thing—I remember when my mom and dad each turned forty. But you won't. And while I remember the celebrations of my parents' birthdays and the "Forty and Sporty" T-shirt I picked out for my dad, I don't know what they were like when they were forty, what their wishes and dreams were, what they were afraid of, what they were proud of, and what they wanted. Your grandparents are alive today, and I could pick up the phone and ask them those questions, but what I really want is to ask them those questions forty years ago. Because this birthday seems big and scary to me, and I've been trying all day to figure out why—while knowing all along it's because it's my first birthday as a mother.

So today, I will tell you what I hope, what I'm scared of, and what I know. Use this when you want to know me better; see proof that no one, ever, really has it figured out; or remind me that when I started out on this journey of parenthood, I neither knew how to adjust a car seat nor that I needed to wash the rolls of fat under your chins to keep stale-milk neck cheese in check.

Here is what I hope: That you will be strong and vulnerable. That I will learn how to be a parent who is content with any iteration of our time together. That I will find a way to work in the world and make a difference while staying true to my evolving desire to spend time with you. That we will explore the world together powered by our feet and arms and lungs. That one day you will both nap at the same time. That you will forgive me for the mistakes I will surely make. That I will forgive myself.

Here is what I'm scared of: That you won't like climbing. That you will like climbing. That I'll die before I know you as adults, that any of your six grandparents will die, and that the poodle will die. That when any of the aforementioned losses happen, I won't be able to take the pain away from you. That you will want a cat.

Here is what I know: Being a mother has already been the most powerful force I've ever felt in my life. It makes me gasp. It makes me weep. It makes me love you so fiercely I am afraid I will burst. And it makes me happy. Everyone says it goes too fast. I understood this when you were less than a day old and I already wanted to go back and hoard the moment I first held you in the world again and again and again. I want the first time I saw you together, naked on your dad's chest rising and falling with his big breaths, again, and again, and again. Each hour and day that go by makes me want more of you. And let's be clear—I don't want more children because you're it for your dad and me. But more of each of you. More time, more kisses, more smiles, and even more poop if it would give me everything else. And I also know that time will not suddenly expand and gift me more of itself—thus, the only way to get more of you is to be vigilant with our time in the world.

And that is me at forty: exhausted, inspired, and awed by the two of you. I'd tell you more, but it's time to stop now and go to bed. Let's all get some sleep. We're going to need it—we have our lives together in front of us.

November 1, 2016
Audio Journal | Four Months Old

We're in Minnesota, where I grew up but you never will. Anna, you, and I flew here yesterday, during which time we went through six changes of clothes—the bonus being that only three were poop-up-the-back blowouts. We've been making the rounds with cousins and aunts and uncles and sisters by blood, sisters by marriage, and sisters by friendship.

We live 1,474 miles—and my whole adulthood—from this place. Sometimes I wish we could collapse and invert all that and I could live here and have all my life and family piled together. Instead, Kaz, today you got to suck on my Uncle Mark's hand, which is the closest you will ever get to my Grandpa Omar, his dad, twenty years gone already.

We're staying with your aunt, and at night she pulled out the photo albums of your cousins when they were babies, twelve and ten years before you ever entered the world. There was Jeannie with my Babcia Irena—your namesake, little girl. The one who will never get to hold you. There was Sawyer cuddled the same way your grandparents cuddle you now—except in the photo they are younger, brighter versions of their present selves.

I text your dad before going to bed. *Here's a list of the photos we need: more of them alone, more together, Kaz rolling over, Irenna's sly smile, their perfect bellies and expanding worlds.*

....

November 3, 2016
Audio Journal | Four Months Old

This morning I sat on a god-knows-why-it's-sticky public-bathroom floor in the Minneapolis–Saint Paul Airport with my syncopated nipples spraying milk from their ducts. This, apparently, is your mom getting back "out there." This is being on a film tour, together—the thing of greatness I planned when you were in my belly.

Greatness last night was me at a fundraising dinner, milk leaking through my blouse while I tried to solicit support and new donors, only to be inundated by ideas about how to grow cedar trees more sustainably—never mind that there are no cedar trees where Legado works.

Greatness this morning was my hands-free pumping setup so I could simultaneously pump and email the Africa lead for our primary funder about when to meet the director of the Global Environmental Fund next week in DC.

Greatness, or desperation, was deciding to pump extra while watching my next Tuesday—five days away—get stacked with meetings, panic slowly growing in my belly as I realized I hadn't brought enough frozen milk to buffer all of these susequent days away from you on this two-country, four-state tour. The only one who can solve that is me, so I turned the pump on high and hoped your grandma was still rocking you and keeping you asleep in the stroller outside the airport bathroom, on leg two en route to Canada, so I could increase my milk supply enough to make this whole deranged plan work.

Greatness was triggering the explosive-liquids wand during the third level of the Minneapolis security screening with the milk I had just pumped—then being asked if I'd rather relinquish the milk or undergo further testing, to which I said, while thinking of the meeting with the director of the Global Environmental Fund and all of the people on Namuli who could benefit from their support, "No, I will not relinquish those five ounces, which represent one-eighth of the food my children need today, and which allow me to try to make a difference both in the larger world and in their world as a mom."

Oh, and it's your dad's birthday today. He's in New York State climbing with his best friend. Just him. Just them. No babies.

Greatness would be me feeling genuinely supportive of this in just a fraction of the spirit of my original offer. It was not as if he was going to come on the film tour with me anyway. That was never on the table. That was never something I even asked.

November 5, 2016
From the Notepad | Four Months Old

Banff night one:

Cocktail parties are made for new moms. I nursed you, changed into my party clothes, and was at the festival-opening party for exactly forty-eight minutes.

I hugged and said hellos to almost as many people and deemed it a success. Then I came back to you and your grandparents.

"Does it feel good to be here, honey?" my mom asked when I got back.

"It feels right," I said.

———

Night one, later:

It's four A.M., and the two pack-and-plays I had to wheedle from the hotel (*Our policy is one per family, ma'am*) are empty. The three of us are strewn diagonally in bed, with pillows for bumpers securing our perimeter.

"Wake me up if you need me," my mom said last night before she crawled into bed in her own room next door. But who would do that to a seventy-one-year-old woman who just spent the entire three hours of the flight walking the plane's two-foot-wide aisles, alternating carrying and bouncing each four-month-old twin while I held the other?

November 6, 2016
From the Notepad | Night two

I fell asleep at my own film premiere.

First I got to introduce it.

When I got back to the rental townhouse, the two of you were in the living room, screaming in my friend Misti's and her sister's arms. Misti and I met in Ethiopia when I helped create the country's first-ever trail race and she ran in it, but tonight she offered to be a babysitter and even brought a plus-one.

"They were so awake, it seemed like we might as well just leave the bedroom and come upstairs," Misti said with a shrug.

"Thank you so much," I said. "Really."

November 6, 2016
From the Notepad | Day three

We made it out to meet people today. The three of us rolled into the coffee shop at 2:45 for our 2:30 meeting with Jane.

Jane, a friend of mine and Patagonia's longtime photo editor, had texted me the day I arrived. *I wanna see those babies!*

"Isn't it amazing?" she asked today as Irenna spit up chunky breast milk on her forearm.

"So amazing," I said as I wiped the milk off with a crusty cloth.

"Remember to love this," Jane said. "Okay?"

I nodded. All around me were people I knew, people I had climbed with, shot photos and films with, traveled with, and more.

"We're going climbing in the Red together next," I said. Louder than I needed to.

November 9, 2016
Letter | Four-and-a-Half Months Old

I went to bed with Hillary in the lead, and all of us on a smattering of camping mattresses on the floor of my college friend Eric's basement on the outskirts of DC. When you woke at two A.M., I wedged the three of us into a chair while you nursed in tandem.

Peter read the news. "Trump," he said.

Can you taste agony through breast milk? I can't stop the tears. I hold you both tighter and sob, rocking you and me and all of us together. "No, no, no," I say over and over. "This can't be right."

Irenna fell into the crack between the camping mattresses, and no one slept very much that night.

November 9, 2016 (Later)
Letter | Four-and-a-Half Months Old

At six A.M., I am out of the shower and putting on business clothes. I pack my pump to head into a somber DC. Meetings stacked on each other, punctuated by pumping breaks. I take up the only bathroom in the Corner Bakery at seven thirty A.M. I stand next to the sink and brace the pump on its rim, trying not to touch anything I don't have to, feeling guilty about the fifteen minutes it takes for my breasts to empty, during which time no one else can get in here. Later I pump while sitting fully clothed on the toilet in the Global Environmental Fund's women's restroom stall, willing my milk to fill the bottles faster so I can make it to the Nature Conservancy's African watershed roundtable on time.

Five meetings and four locations later, I'm back nursing you on Eric's couch while talking to my program assistant on speakerphone while yelling to the cabdriver through the open door of the home that he's found the right house and I'll be out shortly. We get to the DC airport just in time for an evening flight to Kentucky. Peter is almost there already, having completed the Herculean task of driving from New Hampshire to Kentucky with a pit stop in DC with a cooler full of frozen breast milk, because despite my best efforts I didn't end up at this point in the trip with enough milk to get through twelve hours away from you on my last day of meeting, while you were under Anna's care.

When I set this schedule, this part was supposed to be the reward—the hyperefficient way to get in my first climbing trip after a film tour and a stopover in DC to secure more funding for Legado. But it made me almost lose you.

Over ten days I have cleared us through five airport-security check-points in two countries. Anna and I have a flow now. She provides the extra hands, and I put what needs to be held into those hands in whatever order I need. On and off the plane, I handle the changing. I decide if the shit-up-the-back outfit should just be tossed or if it should live in a Ziploc for a four-hour flight and ensuing car trip before I try to salvage it through a fetid and equally long reclamation effort of soaking, scrubbing, and washing/re-washing. Then I deliver one of you fresh to Anna to trade for the other.

Tonight, Kaz gets first dibs on the Reagan National Airport bathroom change with me. I excuse myself and step around the women in line to get to the changing area. Then I flip and flop him down and around, and we're up. I'm back with Irenna on the same Koala Kare fold-down four minutes later.

"Weren't you just here?" a woman in line asks.

"It's magic, isn't it?" I say.

She laughs. She makes clucking noises at Irenna, and Irenna coos back.

"Want me to hold her so you can go?" she asks.

I deposit Irenna into her outstretched hands and grab my purse before saying thanks. "I'll be superfast," I say.

Inside the stall I sit down and unleash a torrent of pee with one long exhale. On the inhale I Kegel the pee, then shoot up off the toilet as I undo the latch of the door.

But Irenna is still there, safe and sound in the woman's arms. I do up my pants while my heart races. *Dumb Majka, so dumb,* I think. *This is how it would happen.*

"I have a granddaughter just like this," the woman says.

Okay, maybe not with this woman, but dumb. Very dumb.

When Irenna and I get back to Anna, I offer for Anna to go to the bathroom next.

"Anna?" I say when she starts walking away.

"Yes?"

"Don't ever give one of the babies to someone else and go into the bathroom stall, okay? Come find me instead."

"Of course," she says, raising an eyebrow slightly—Germanically—at the thought.

While she's gone I text your dad: *Travel rules to remember: on closed vessels such as planes, it's okay to have strangers hold babies—in sight.*

Your dad responds with a question mark.

Just something to keep in mind, I write back as they announce boarding for our flight.

For the next two hours en route to Kentucky, I play "nurse a twin, any twin," the whole plane ride. Once we land, I drive Anna and me and you in the pitch-black night to a cabin to be a climber again.

November 10, 2016
Audio Journal | Four-and-a-Half Months Old

I am making bad choices on this multistate and multicountry trip. Thinking I could pull off being a traveling climber with four-and-a-half-month-old twins was only one of them.

After we arrived in Calgary, Canada, it only took five minutes of your uncontrolled crying before I let my eighty-one-year-old stepfather, your PapaD, take the wheel and get us to Banff even though I promised myself I wouldn't let him drive. I sat in the back sandwiched between you two, and when I could no longer convince you my knuckles were my breasts, I unbuckled my seat belt and hung the real thing over you one at a time, my face smashed into the seat back as I leaned over your car seats. I willed PapaD to keep us safe as the snow piled up on the mountain roads, alternately consoling and terrifying myself with the knowledge that if we crashed I'd be the first one to go, ejecting straight through the windshield, topless, into the Canadian winter.

Back at home we had our system. I'd nurse you at the same time, every time. Especially at night. During the day, your dad or Anna would help swap you into my arms and change you. At night, it was all your dad and me.

But there is no such thing as a system when traveling with you—without your dad, swapping Anna for your aunt, your aunt for my mom, my mom for anyone who will hold either of you, any time. And the nights?

The first night away from home I set you, Kaz, down first on the couch in my sister's basement. You rolled over and nearly suffocated on the throw pillow during the ninety seconds it took me to get Irenna out of her pack-and-play to join you. You nursed together for all of a minute before Irenna pooped. Kaz, you will keep nursing when you poop. Irenna? Never.

The diapers were across the room. So I tried to stand up and shuffle over to them, all while trying to keep Irenna from wailing and to keep Kaz nursing. I started to pee from the effort.

I was the one who cried first that night. Irenna next, and then when I forced Kaz off my nipple, all three of us. We cried until Irenna was changed and we were back to nursing, perched on the floor, surrounded by diapers in a godawful position for my body—but ever so worth it for the quiet.

Now we're back with your dad in a dank, dusky cabin in Kentucky. All night I nursed you on the brown leather couch, the seat sticking to the undersides of my thighs. It made the sound of peeling tape each time I tried to move. I am so grateful to have your dad back in the system, until I realize there is no system anymore. You two are no longer sleeping at the same time, and I have done that to us. And each time one of you cries, I am too damn tired so I can no longer walk out to the living room and make your dad and your other twin half get up too so we can all four be in this downward spiral together.

Which is why by three in the morning all four of us are now lying on this tiny full-sized mattress with its sheets that don't fit. Your dad sleeps. I just turn back and forth between the two of you, unraveling the final threads of the system that took me—took *us*—four long months to make.

November 12, 2016
From the Notepad | Four-and-a-Half Months Old

Irenna-bear, you like to wake up when I am exactly thirty feet above you. Kaz, you're agnostic to where I am on a climb. You just generally want me, and you make sure everyone knows it.

It's day two of our climbing trip and I've climbed two pitches total—about one-eighth of what I'd usually climb otherwise. One of you squealed at all times for both.

I have always wanted to climb in the Red River Gorge. But maybe I should not have planned an excursion to the climbing mecca of the Southeastern US as my first trip back. Or maybe I should have done my research better . . . on the lack of cell service we'd have . . . or considered how, as parents of four-and-a-half-month-old twins, we'd not be okay with said lack of service and therefore not want to leave Anna with said twins at the cabin while we climbed, forcing us to go en masse—parents, twins, and our climbing friends—to the crag . . . or about how there is a sleep regression at four months, which might feel like double hell if you're going through it with twins . . . or how some kids start teething at four months old.

Where are you supposed to do this research?

"It's so great to see a mom out climbing," yet another person said to me this afternoon. I hate those people. *No, this is not me out climbing,* I want to say. *This is my body vibrating with every squeal Kaz makes when I am twenty, forty, eighty feet above him, willing my fingers to hold an edge, willing my abs to stick together, and willing my heart and head to even want this in the first place.*

It sounded good and possible in concept. Nurse, cuddle, toss each of you into our friends' willing arms, and go up. Everyone tries to help. Bernd can even get you to sleep in the morning, reciting French pastries—*pain au chocolat, pain aux raisins, tarte aux fraises.* Hjördis can wear either of you like the boss-mamma she is, and she jiggles you to keep your minds off me. But I am the one everyone needs.

My friend Sasha arrived last night with her husband. I had you in the stroller on the road this morning while she was off to climb, and then again when she was back, and then again when she was going out for groceries. Sasha is a problem-solver. "What if . . . ," she asked each time. "What if I get you teething rings? What if I get you groceries? What if we find you a new cabin with better cell service?"

What if, I think, *I just let it go?*

November 13, 2016
Audio Journal | Four-and-a-Half Months Old

Last night, I walked up to a high point on the road where I had cell service and called my new twin-mom friend, Rebecca. She's married to a mountain guide but happily abstains from climbing herself, and she's ahead of us in parenting by six years. When I'd told her I was planning this trip a few months ago, she'd told me I was insane. "Don't go camping," she exclaimed. Technically we were not camping; we were in a cabin. Even so, I start off by apologizing.

"I ignored your advice," I said. "I'm sorry. And I failed. Total failure."

"Don't be too hard on yourself," she said. "Your only failure was thinking you were cool."

"I didn't think I was . . . ," I started to say, but Rebecca was not done.

"You're not cool," she said. "You're the opposite of cool, so stop trying to do cool shit and just be."

So now we're back at the airport and you're asleep in the rental car. Anna is going to the bathroom before we start our traveling circus show, and I am whispering our reality into posterity.

Only three days in, we're bailing on the eight-day climbing trip I spent six months planning.

Your dad is focused on the math, working on an equation that nets him more climbing. I am focused on getting you—us—home. Today we will take our sixth and seventh flights in twelve days. Your dad's consolation is a day of climbing without us, then packing up the cabin and starting the seventeen-hour drive back to New Hampshire tomorrow.

"I don't think this is working," I said to him yesterday.

"Why don't we try again tomorrow? You can get some sleep, and I'll take the kids with Anna," he offered.

I looked around the cabin that would have been a luxury to me for most of my life as a spendthrift climber—a decadent waypoint between days spent trying hard. Now all I see are the crusty sheets that covered our beds when we arrived—sheets we then changed ourselves—the freezer that can't seem to keep my milk frozen, and the peeling laminate living-room floor I paced on nightly and hourly, trying to get one of us to sleep.

"I haven't napped since I gave birth. Do you know that?" I asked.

"How about—" your dad started to say.

"I want to go home," I said. "Wait—that's not true. I don't want to go home. I want to climb. But that's not what this is. This isn't what I want. Not when it's this hard and not what they need."

I didn't ask if he was disappointed. He didn't ask me either. This used to be what we did best together.

We tried so damn hard. Each on our own. I know he went to the mat for us—driving the whole way from New Hampshire to Kentucky, loaded with groceries and gear and sleeping and changing paraphernalia, which he then got ready for us. Then he waited up until one A.M. to greet me and Anna and the babies when we arrived. And *then* each day he cooked as well as prepared the climbing gear. All without a single complaint.

Trying hard used to work for us. Or at least it gave us a shot. In Namibia we got stymied by 113-degree heat on our objective in the north and drove four days back south to attempt a line on the Brandburg, the country's highest mountain instead. Then the route we spotted up the face turned out to be caked with mud and bird shit, so we spent a week cleaning it and getting it ready. We ran out of water on the wall, and Peter was the one who found a racoon-sized depression in the rock filled with sludge, which he cleaned out so that it would refill with water we could drink—and gladly did. I was the one who took on headfulls of dried bird excrement to get a key section of the climb ready; as a thank-you, when it was time to link it all together, Peter let me lead this crux, glory pitch, a strenuous, 190-foot leaning fissure perfectly sized for my hands and feet. He tried, I tried, we tried together. We saw each other trying, then.

Now he's climbing and I don't want to hear about it. I'm starting yet another plane rodeo, and he doesn't even know the wheels of your stroller have to come off to fit through security or that I can now make that happen with just one hand.

I see Anna coming back from the bathroom inside the airport, which means it's time to catch the plane. How about you stay asleep just a little longer, until we have to wake you up and go through security? And since we're making deals, if you could then go back to sleep once we're on the plane, that would also be good. I'd keep trying for other deals, but we already know how this is going to go.

I have eight outfits and two cases of wipes ready, but not much else to give you today.

<hr />

December 7, 2016
From the Notepad | Five Months Old

"I can't straighten my leg," your dad says on the phone.

"What do you mean?" I ask.

"Something snapped," he said.

It's dumping snow outside my mom's window here in Montana. Your dad is in Alabama. I'm here to guide ice in Hyalite Canyon near Bozeman and host a strategic planning session for Legado with our team. He's there to instruct US special forces. I can't get him onto a plane and home any more than he can help me pump enough milk to get through thirteen hours away from you while I'm up on the ice tomorrow.

We hang up the phone. You play peekaboo with Grandma Pooch in front of the fire and I miss it while I call doctors and insurance companies and hospitals to cajole a Monday-morning appointment for your dad and the surgery, likely, to come.

December 11, 2016
From the Notepad | Five-and-a-Half Months Old

Every morning we go with Grandma to visit the horses. Today was Rose.

Irenna, you went first. Grandma Pooch shucked off her mittens to get a better grip on you in your slippery snowsuit as she held you close to Rose's nose. When you sucked in your breath, Grandma squeezed you closer. "You're going to love horses," she said to you.

Kaz, you didn't want to see the horse, but that didn't stop Grandma. Or me, really.

That was this morning before eight. Now I've just nursed you down for your naps, and I'm running back to my team for strategic planning. We're not even a full day into our session, but they already know how to keep going without me.

December 12, 2016
Letter | Five-and-a-Half Months Old

Tonight you cry at 10:15 P.M., jolting me from my deepest and first sleep of the night. Peter is on crutches now, his right leg incapable of straightening until a knee surgery repairs the bucket-handle meniscus tear that's held his leg hostage for a week now. He clomps, and I walk, to your room, neither of us awake enough to want to talk to the other.

Since you were born your dad has been the twin picker-upper while I sit on the couch to be the nurser. But now he sits and I deliver you to him one at a time—at least, that was the plan. I arc wide around him to get you, Irenna, and the moment you smell me, you try to nurse. When I hand you to your dad, you start to cry. I set off for you next, Kaz, but I forget to give your dad's outstretched, frozen leg space. I stride directly into Peter's injured limb with a *thud*. He growls/screams like an animal in pain.

Your screams come next. Both of you at once. I swipe you, Kaz, sit down, and try to nurse, but everyone is crying around me. Even me.

"I can't do this," I yell. It feels good. I do it again, roaring. The loudest I have ever yelled. We all are shocked into silence.

December 16, 2016
Letter | Five-and-a-Half Months Old

The first email comes from one of my sponsors: "Your pass is registered . . ."

Hours later, from another sponsor: "A pass in your name . . ."

A third: "Let us know if you need a pass . . ."

It's time for the Outdoor Retailer Show. At least, it's the build-up for the moment when the entire industry, pro athletes and all, converges in Salt Lake City for a giant trade show. Or, I suppose, what I used to think of as the entire industry.

I went with you in my belly last year, right after I'd shared to the world that there were two of you in there. By then I was already walking around belly-first.

"You're pregnant?" Ron, an almost-pro climber turned athlete manager for a climbing brand, said when he ran into me on the convention-
center floor.

"Not just pregnant," I said. "Twins."

His first response: "You are so fucked."

———

It wasn't just Ron.

"Wow, good luck with that!"

"Poor Peter."

"Probably the last time we'll be seeing you here for a while."

Like I said, that was last year. This year, I compose one email that
I copy, paste, and send to each of my sponsors: "Have so much fun at
the show. All is good here in New Hampshire—climbing and slinging
twins galore."

December 19, 2016
Letter | Five-and-a-Half Months Old

The night we all screamed will be the last night for months that Peter
helps with any nighttime feedings or needs. Today, a week later, we
finally talk about my screaming.

"I'm sorry," I say.

"I understand," Peter says. "You were at your limit."

He leaves it at that, and I am caught between wanting to leave
it too and wanting to have someone—my someone—sit me down
and tell me they have got me. But now Peter is attached to an ice
machine postsurgery, and I'm already onto the next iteration of my
motherhood self.

December 20, 2016
From the Notepad | Five-and-a-Half Months Old

Notes from the Night Weaning Journal

6:15 P.M.: Nurse, diaper, book, nurse again—until done, sing, dark.

7:00 P.M.: Both twins in cribs.

7:05 P.M.: Five-minute wait while they cry—check in. "Night night, you can do this, I love you, Mom and Dad love you."

7:15 P.M.: Check-in. "Night night, you can do this, I love you, Mom and Dad love you."

7:30 P.M.: Check-in. "Night night, you can do this, I love you, Mom and Dad love you."

9:30 P.M.: Change diaper, nurse Kaz for eight minutes, put him down, start check-ins. Note: if he is awake at nine thirty, *no milk*—just check-ins. Wait until asleep to feed. After you do fifteen-minute check-ins, *never* go back to five or ten.

8:00 A.M.: If they cry the whole time for an hour, do fifteen-minute check-ins, then after one hour even if they haven't slept, get them up. *Keep awake* until the next nap. If they sleep, they can sleep two hours, but then the next nap starts later. Add two hours, adjust, make sure to start after twelve, put the twin who slept least down first for a nap. Move Irenna to closet.

December 28, 2016
Letter | Six Months Old

Dear Kaz and Irenna,

I have seven minutes before you need to wake up from your nap. Then I need to nurse you, and then I need to go on a hike with my earphones in to make it a meeting.

So, with what little time I have, some thoughts: Today, you are six months old. Here is what I never knew:

That I would love nursing you so completely. That the time I spend with you—together, holding hands, exploring each other's ears and eyes, or one-on-one, with total trust, total nuzzling and inward focus on just us—would complete every sense I have. I didn't want to count on nursing, or to want it in case we couldn't. And each time I do it I feel grateful for this connection we get to have.

I had a goal to nurse you this long, and here I am. Here *we* are, more like it. This is a time I will not stop. When you are mine and I am yours.

I am not sure right now about the pieces of my life and what order they are supposed to orbit in. The obvious way would be to do things in separate pieces. Love you from eight A.M. to ten A.M. Work from ten A.M. to two P.M. Climb from two P.M. to four P.M. But nothing about you, or me, or us, works separately. We work together.

January 5, 2017
Letter | Six Months Old

"Did you know Kate and Gilbert and Brittany are in Patagonia?" Peter announces from his pole position, icing his knee on the recliner with his computer and snacks at the ready beside him.

I'm cooking dinner and both of you are kitchen bugs, strapped into vibrating seats on top of the counter with little stuffed owls—what we call *hoot hoots*—hanging above you. God knows why they are there because you rarely bat at or even acknowledge them.

"Yeah, I did," I say, "in Torres del Paine." Where I have still never been. Gilbert is another one of my climbing partners, and I wince thinking of the three-pack with Brittany added in. Brittany has always been more fun and climbed harder than me—things unlikely to change now that I'm a mom.

"Do you know what they're trying to climb?" Peter asks.

I head to the sink and turn on the faucet to do the dishes. "I can't really hear you," I say.

January 10, 2017
Letter | Six-and-a-Half Months Old

I just sat in the van at the end of the driveway. I looked left, looked right. I depressed the brake harder. And screamed at the top of my lungs. Silence rang after. I did it again. I looked left again, right again, and turned out of the driveway. Nothing had changed. *Maybe it's not for me. What should have changed?*

January 16, 2017
Letter | Six-and-a-Half Months Old

It's taken Kelly and me twenty years of knowing each other to climb together. We first met on the Kahiltna Glacier in Alaska, but today we went climbing fifteen minutes from my house here in New Hampshire.

When in season, Repentance is not a hard route—or it shouldn't be for me. That's an asshole comment. But it's the one I kept making to myself as I seconded the mixed rock-and-ice climb's first pitch—that is, climbed it while belayed from above by Kelly, who'd just led it. The crux was freshly or barely bonded—depending on how you thought of it—comprising a series of vertical rivulets that had yet to become a cohesive block of ice. It's like the ice was suspended midformation—not solid yet, but present enough to temporarily puncture with tools, kick with crampons, and use to move up into the frozen world.

Over email and text messages pre-climb, Kelly and I had belittled ourselves to each other about our general lack of fitness to climb anything worthwhile. He's post–back fusion surgery, and I'm six months postpartum and still nursing. When we met to carpool in the Glen gas-station parking lot, eight minutes from my house, he announced that he'd forgotten his water bottle. I told him the benefit of climbing with me was that we'd always have milk in a pinch. "Disgusting!" he screeched.

I pumped en route to the climb, handing him the keys to the minivan as I hooked myself up.

"Have you ever had a pumping climbing partner?" I asked him.

Kelly said he had sisters, friends with kids. But then he paused. "No."

During our mutual berating, we joked about finding someone else to be our ropegun—to lead all the pitches and get the rope up for us—or about taking it easy instead, on moderate terrain. But we both knew it was bullshit. As I followed Kelly's lead, I looked up at the second pitch the moment the ice came into view; at the belay anchor, instead of handing him the ice screws and rock protection, I left them racked on my harness. I might not have one hundred percent wanted to lead the pitch above. But I one hundred percent did not want to belay while Kelly took the sharp end again.

—⁓—

Ice makes you remember your fear. Today was my fourth day out on ice since I was two months pregnant. The other three days didn't really count because they were out guiding novice and intermediate climbers, coaching them on low-angle, easier ice. This one did.

I wanted to be welded to the ice. I slammed my tools so deep with each swing that I burned extra energy trying to get them out. *Idiot*, I told myself, wrestling to loosen yet another placement. I reset my body, stemming my left leg out and above my hip in the exact position my physical therapist and I discussed *not* doing while my abs tried to re-engage to support my twice-sugeried back and post-twin-pregnancy body. I looked down at Kelly and said that normal mothers of six-month-old twins did not do this.

But maybe they should.

—∿∿—

Eight years ago, while I was warming up on a climb called Where Night Meets Light on Trollville cliff in Jackson, a swing of my right arm unleashed a chunk of ice that swept me off my feet. I hadn't thought of that fall in years. Today, it's all I thought of. *What happens if I loosen my tool and that lens of ice erupts? Will it take me out? If it does, will this screw hold my fall the way the last one did?*

I examined each fracture. I placed one screw for Irenna. Another one, a mere two feet above, for Kaz.

Right now, Peter is at home on crutches. His local ice-guiding work is piling up for me to do while he's recovering, and the weight of our household, our children, and our lives is all stacking up to something I don't want to acknowledge. "Don't worry, we're fine. We'll be fine," I've been telling Peter. On Repentance, placing another screw, evaluating my options, I realized I had to stay whole at any cost.

I peered up and around the final granite chockstone blocking me from the top of the climb and the trees above. I leaned my body horizontally to clear the chockstone and placed my crampon points precisely in mico rock blemishes, inspecting the foot placements in the dying light of day. My left hand pulled on my left tool high above my head, and I took my right tool off the wall to balance it on my left shoulder while I eyed the next move. *This would be,* I thought, *a bad place to drop my tool.*

And then I dropped my tool.

"Tool!" I screamed to Kelly, watching the metal spark as the tool ricocheted across the chimney and dropped to the ground 350 feet below. I looked up. I was fifteen feet from easy ground. *This was not a hard climb.*

"Are you okay?" Kelly yelled up.

"Yeah!" I yelled back. "I've got it."

Climbers are proponents of invention driven by necessity. We are constantly devising new gear and techniques to safeguard our lives and achieve our objectives: camming devices to fit parallel-sided cracks; downturned, sticky-rubber rock shoes for overhangs; monopoint crampons for tehnical ice. On Repentance, driven by my own necessity, I cammed my knee, levered down on my one tool with both hands, and forgot to protect my core against the rock as I hauled and scratched my way to the top, trading eventual bruises for success. I was not scared. I was only determined.

I would not characterize myself as competitive. But then what should I call this drive to do it, to finish it, to do it myself? To prove that I could do exactly this at exactly this time?

I belayed Kelly up as my breasts zinged and ached with a four-hour backlog of milk—I'd last pumped in the car before the climb, and now the adrenaline was amping things up. Kelly followed the pitch by headlamp, and by the time he joined me I had the ropes rigged and ready to rappel. I shot myself into the blackness. One hundred feet down I paused and put knots in the bottom ends of the ropes. With every ten feet I rappelled the cords fought me, twisting and knotting when I just wanted to zip home. I was ten minutes from the car and twenty minutes from my home. Or I should have been. But Repentance didn't let me off so easily.

February 3, 2017
Letter | Seven Months Old

Dear Kaz and Irenna,

Do you know I try to switch whose name is first each time I write to you? I will inevitably forget this.

Just over a month ago, your grandmother left our house after her most recent visit. I've never felt as far from her as I did when she was here in our house alongside us. I have not wanted to write these words and set them in ink—in pixels—but they are burning in my heart.

Your grandmother did not have an easy childhood, an easy life, an easy marriage to my father, or an easy time being stepmother to PapaD's six children. I am not sure those are the stories, however, that I am supposed to tell you now.

Here is how I want to be with you and your children: I want to love you, and them, completely. I want to trust that my love for them is felt and understood. I want to trust that their love for me is not in jeopardy or does not jeopardize their love for their other grandparents, aunts, uncles, siblings, or others. I want to be confident that our relationship—during whatever sliver of time it occupies—is right. I almost wrote that it would be enough. But really, with those we love the most, it's never enough, though it can so often be too much.

While my mom was here over Christmas, I had to remind myself to be nice to her. To not look at her and judge her choices to spray surface cleaner near the butter, to trim a metal nail with our best knife, to put the plastic recyclables in the trash—to not see all of these as failures but rather as parts of her personality. For she is immovable; she does not like to be course-corrected or adapted. My mother was trying to help, but her help created more work. I tried to tell her to relax instead, but that only made her purse her lips and tense her back and keep wiping down the counters undeterred. I know enough from my childhood that the expectation was for me to offer effusive praise for any gesture or action. She is the supreme mother, in her view, and she wants that role to be continually venerated. And it's exhausting.

I want to carry forth a different legacy for you. I want to listen to your way of living and let *you* show *me* how to do it. I want to take in those microadjustments with grace and understanding that this is your life, not mine. I want to love you unconditionally. I want to love you without anger and judgment and insecurity about how much you love me. I want to bring you peace and ease.

"You're being like your mother," your dad told me last week. And it stopped me in my tracks. I was toeing the line of traits I didn't want to emulate. But then came a swift and visceral reaction. I love my mother. I admire my mother. I want to be like her. Perhaps what I am learning now is that I want to be like parts of her. The best parts. And I'd like to have the wisdom and courage to look at the other parts—those we both share, those I'm on the precipice of sharing—and know enough to fight them off.

February 7, 2017
Letter | Seven Months Old

I have found one room in our house that is soundproof from your cries. I use it today to video-chat with a scientist named Bernie about a Mulago Foundation fellowship for me in my capacity as the founder of Legado. Bernie is on their vetting team, and is my first step to becoming a Mulago fellow. As we talk, I try to forget that behind me on my Skype screen is the climbing wall and I'm sitting on a bouldering mat—and, as it turns out, the room is not as soundproof as I thought. I focus on talking about Legado's prestige, its funding, and its connections—and on pretending I am not a new mom.

After fifty minutes, Bernie cuts me off mid-explanation. "Let's cut to the chase. You are not a fit right now. To be a fit you'd need to be operating on three sites, have the metrics to back up change, and have a destination where there are eighty mountains globally that could benefit from this."

I act like I agree. But in my heart I feel bottomed out. Because if I'm being honest, I am not sure I want this for Legado. Or that I want this for me.

Am I going to have to spend everything I have to find a point of success with Legado? Will I have to leverage all of my social capital, all of my resources, and then more to make this happen? Is this the one thing I want to do that with? Or is this just the thing I rolled into?

Where am I inspired? Where does it make sense in my life? When does it make me sing?

I'm trying to find my connection to this (again). And to make a connection for other people. And what I'd like is for it to be easier. For it to be set up with funders who want to work on Mount Namuli, who believe in the work we are doing, and for my role to be drawing the lines of connection between everyone. Instead I feel like I have to draw the map, build the roads, trace the lines, and then go and get it funded each step of the way.

And right now I am not totally convinced. Or convinced at all. Is that because I don't totally believe in Legado? Or because I'm burned-out? Or scared? Or all of it? What's going to shift my perspective? Having money would shift me. Having the support that money entails would shift me. But it takes work to get money. And to get money, at the start, I have to believe. I have to be passionate. I have to *believe*.

What am I doing? Why am I doing this? Maybe that is the question I actually need to answer: *Why* am I doing this?

———

In 2011 I stood at the base of Mount Namuli for the very first time after having seen it only in my mind. A team of five of us hiked the final six of fifteen hours in darkness and woke in the morning sleeping on the ground in front of the house of the Lomwe Queen of Namuli, with the mountain's granite walls looming above. We had to start there, with her and her community, then with the granite wall to climb, then with the hunt for a chameleon that lives on Namuli to see if our idea of combining community, conservation, science, and climbing would actually work. After three years of raising money, creating a partnership with a Mozambican conservation organization, planning a film, pausing a trip with tickets in hand because of spiking violence in central Mozambique, and waiting, we came back and put the pieces together.

We put up a new climbing route, discovered new species for science, and started the first collaborative surveys with the Namuli communities to understand their priorities and how they used their forest. On our last day on the mountain, Raimundo, who lives in the house closest to where we camped and helped us find nearly every snake and chameleon, told me that where we climbed was where he gathered the best grass for his home. Raimundo and I decided that next time we'd climb up there together.

Twelve months later, last year, I saw Raimundo in a hotel conference room in Beira, 475 miles from Namuli. He, other Namuli community members, our growing conservation team, and I were there to spend three days talking about how we might do this work together. Raimundo made me promise to learn Portuguese—the dominant language in Mozambique due to its colonial past—in my extra time. I had babies with that time instead.

My brain is on fire with memories, and in this moment I get the jolt I need. Our actions matter.

I can no longer exist in a vacuum of adventure. I need to see each adventure land with impact. I need to feel it take my breath away and scare me—not from the risk, but from the reality. Because the reality of it is the very fact that our actions do matter—our adventures have impact—and I'm trying to understand the weight of my own. The first time I climbed the massifs in Ethiopia, I knew I couldn't ignore the connection beyond the mountains. I had to see each adventure for what it was, what it is—that it is more than just a mountain.

Mountains are our legacy, for those of us who believe in them—those of us who find our church, our souls, and our peace in them. It's easy to protect the mountains of the West, those big, bad, jagged expanses that are just straight wilderness—though in reality that status is largely because white settlers took that land from the Native Americans and declared it so. Conservation has been created based on a similar concept of wilderness: a place devoid of human dwelling. It's much harder to protect (and to define what *protecting* is) amalgamated ecosystems—these mountains where people, rainforests, and farmland blend together in a complex dance.

The word we should really be using instead of *protection* is *connection*. Holding space for the people who live in this place to make connections between their lives and their home, and listening to what they need to support themselves and what matters to their legacy. That's flipping why you called it Legado—Portuguese for *legacy*—Burhardt.

⁓

The sheer vertical expanse of Namuli brought me there. The surrounding green and the people kept me there. And along the way I think I've learned that I'm kept there by the knowledge that we can't just look to the easy places. As climbers, as outdoorspeople, we are drawn to the difficult, the challenge, the edge. This is the edge of activism for conservation. This is where it will ultimately count the most. This is taking the thicker way through life.

I will find the money and the fellowships to do this the way we know it needs to be done.

March 2, 2017
Audio Journal | Eight Months Old

I'm feeling weird. Your grandma, my mom . . . I'm feeling really separate from her. I don't think I know who she was as a mom. I am pretty clear on who Gramgram—your dad's mom—was and is as a mom, but not very clear on who my mom was as a mom.

As it turns out, recording these audio journals for posterity when you are forty years old and have eight-month-old twins while finally unpacking boxes from moving and going through all of your old pictures and seeing photos of your 1998 wedding to your first husband is a little tweaky in the head.

As it turns out, being a mom is a little tweaky in the head.

I keep coming back to this sticking point: I love you guys so much. It's the best thing in the world and it's terrifying and I want to just love you and kiss you and be with you. I just have this nagging disbelief that my mom ever felt that way toward me.

March 3, 2017
Audio Journal | Eight Months Old

I miss my mother. And she's alive.

I feel exposed at both ends—middle-aged, I suppose, frayed at the top and bottom. Eight-month-old twins on one end and parents in their seventies on the other. Someone is going to leave me—it is inevitable.

I look at photographs of my childhood and at scrapbooks of art in my two-year-old's crayon scrawl, and I sob. *Who was I then? Who were my parents?*

I should put the old pictures away, but I can't. There's a photo of me at twenty-one on a mountaineering expedition on Denali, standing at fourteen thousand feet with a breast-cancer prayer flag clutched in my hands. Four names scrawled with Sharpie on the flag—my sister, mom, and both of my grandmas. These were the women I stood for. Two are gone. Two feel far away.

I know your Gramgram right now as a woman, a mom, and a grandma. I see her every week when she and Grandpa arrive from their home, an hour away in Whitefield, with pies and tools and love and listening. I know her deeply and intimately and easily, and feel both lucky and terrified by the trespass this somehow represents against my own mother. Because I feel I know my mom less every day across all of these platforms.

"Did you love me?" I want to ask her. "Did it hurt to leave me every day? When you came home, did I love-maul you? Could I not stand to be away from you? Did that break your heart or make it bigger? Did you and Dad fray apart before I lay in your arms, or as I did?" Each story I've told myself about my childhood—each memory—is now refracted through the prism of my own motherhood. I want to access it all, to learn the *real* story. I want proof, records, letters, videos. I want to see . . . what? Love? Poignancy? The rawness? I feel taken apart by the rawness. Maybe I want to know that it was there in the people who made me too.

I want to ask my mother, "What did it feel like to have babysitters see our firsts? Did you drop everything when you came home at night from your ever-busier career, and for both days on the weekends? Did we play? Did you tuck me in a crib and walk away?" I'm a decently adjusted forty-year-old woman who is proud of the work my mother did in the world, and intellectually I understand what she had to do—yet I still want to know if she loved me.

Because if she did love me as much as she said, then how did she grow to become so hurt and unsure and sometimes so mean?

"Mom," I said today, "the kids love seeing you."

"That's not true. I am just a body to them. They already have a grandma."

"Oh mom," I sighed, "that is so not true. You're my momma, their grandma through me—it's that special."

"Save it, Majka; I don't believe you. Don't patronize me."

I don't want to be like her. I don't want to carry those pieces forward, yet I feel the anger and frustration in me boiling and boiling. Maybe that is a piece of it as well—that I am becoming her. And that I am becoming my sister with a wary voice, snapping quickly, not rising to the level of kindness I want to operate at, but staying below the line. Here are the two women I least want to be like in their anger and to whom I am likely the most similar.

If I love you two more than my mom loved me, will it make me different from her then and now?

I feel exceptionally separate from Peter too; I feel I can have real conversations about where I'm at with everyone except him right now. We don't seem to have open channels for each other—or hold them open. We are misfiring—who wants to talk about what when, who wants to type, who wants to scroll Facebook. This can't be my marriage. I am so acutely aware that this is how it unravels. How it's the time we use to lay down stitches together that will keep us together, because otherwise we will reach a point where nothing can sew us back up. Losing my first marriage has to count for the wisdom I can use to save this one.

March 3, 2017 (Later)
Letter | Eight Months Old

Dear Kaz and Irenna,

One day, maybe when you're thirteen, or thirty, you might wonder if I loved you. You might have a child and feel your heart exploding with love and ache with the richness of that love, and wonder if I ever felt that way about you. Or maybe you'll be better adjusted than I am and never wonder. We can hope for that. But just in case . . .

Today, you are eight months and three days and seven hours old. I cannot imagine being away from you. I take hours apart from you—days, but never a night. Never a trip, never a time zone or a plane or a country, ocean, or continent. And yet the other part of my heart—the part I spent years growing before you—lies six time zones, 7,849 miles of Atlanic Ocean, and the entire width of Africa away.

The way I see it, everything in my life has prepared me to pull off Legado or leave it all behind. I have done what I love wholeheartedly.

Charted my life by my passions, multiplied by my interest, and expounded to the power of what I don't know but can still learn. And now I have you two beings grounding me at home. And my work is shifting to the concept versus the doing. For now.

We're one month away from a go/no-go on Namuli. Or really, I should say another one. I am learning how to navigate fundraising. How to synthesize my complicated relationship with Mozambique and Namuli and the mountains, and make a pitch that sells.

Why am I doing this? That's a damn good question—one I keep asking. Maybe I need to change it to: "Why am I doing this *today*?"

Sometimes the answer is "because it's what I started and I don't know how to stop." And other times—when I find that kernel of awe, when I am blindsided by the power of the people on Namuli asking our team where I am—I know I cannot leave. And yes, there is pride. There is deep, deep ego and pride at work. And each donation we receive, each speech I give, each young woman who asks me how I put my passions together to create a career, I dig myself deeper and push myself further into this.

March 14, 2017
Letter | Eight-and-a-Half Months Old

Dear Kaz and Irenna,

If you're still wondering about the love . . . when I come home from a day away guiding or speaking and you devour me with your hands and eyes and mouths, I feel that I am in the place I am meant to be. When I nurse you before your nap and you settle into my arms and we talk about your dreams to come, I feel the most content I've ever felt. I used to think superlatives were lazy and absurd. Now I constantly feel the happiest, the most loved. I miss you the most when I am gone.

When you were little—right now—I did everything I could to be with you. And I know that there might be a cost. There is a cost. I don't feel present in my work in the same way I did before. And it's not because I don't believe in it or care about it. It's because you are always in the background. Literally. And figuratively. You are downstairs squawking and screeching. You, Irenna, might be making your first set of linked crawling moves. You, Kaz, might be standing for the first time unsupported. I write down your naps, I nurse you before and after each one, and then we power-play before I go back to work. Irenna, you're a stinker because you've decided you like to nurse for thirty minutes after each nap—a way, I think, to keep Mamma even closer, longer.

I could do this differently. I could rent an office, go to the library, sequester myself. I think I would be in awe of what I could get done. But then I'd be attached to a pump and missing your squeals. And so I am home, working around the margins of your naps and waking times, when you're out exploring the world in the stroller with your dad or Anna. And the truth is, the only way this is even possible is because of the domestic team we've assembled. The privilege is not lost on me. There's Anna, who spends extra time making homemade lasagna to then puree it for you. Who every morning comes downstairs and asks, "Where are my bugs!" just like your dad and I do. We even have Holly, who comes every two weeks to reset the house by cleaning it from top to bottom so I can breathe.

Before I had you, my vision was that I would go everywhere with you easily. Now, eight-and-a-half months into it, I am unsure what this means. I am now so keenly aware of the exhausting logistics of all of us going anywhere. This fall we traveled far and wide, and I worked as we went. We brought Anna, to make it possible. And I am still tired when I recall what we did. In another life I can see going to climb sandstone cracks under the warm spring sun in Zion and Indian Creek right now. In that life, I am your mom and nothing else. But to be your mom and to drive Legado forward, to write a book, to make money, to tend to my career so it is here when I need it—to do all of this and take you to Zion . . . I don't know how.

Will I get better at being fractured and discombobulated? At grabbing exactly twenty-three minutes of work and diving into an annual organization budget—and out of it—in that narrow window?

I know the solution. I leave the house. I am able to focus. I am able to get things done. And then I come home and devour you. But I don't want to look at my calendar and see eight hours of not being with you. I don't want you to feel the ramifications of that, now or later. I have the chance and support to have total integration instead, and I am trying to own this is how I am a mom today.

~~~

My mom used to tell me the thing she was most proud of in her life was being my sister's and my mother. I realize now that I never really believed her. I saw that title sitting next to everything else she did in the world and could not imagine that we ever trumped her career and passions. I could not have told you this fact ten years ago, or even one year ago, when you were six months old in my belly. I'm startled to learn it now.

I feel like I need to re-examine every thought I had about my childhood. And it's not my dad's love that I question or need to recast. It's my mom's. I feel desperately far away from her and her way of being my mom. I am unsure how to get closer without hurting her. Because sometimes to ask your grandma for details on the past is to push in too close for her.

"How did you leave me?" I want to ask her. "How did you not feel heartbroken when you came home and saw us but only for a moment? When you came home, did you sink into us? Did you sink into me? Did you cover yourself with us until you had to let us go to sleep, or did you say hello and keep going?"

And that is the heart of it all. Because I say hello and get smothered *and* keep going. I put away the groceries and make dinner and vacuum and put away laundry and make sure your monitor is plugged in and your changing-table toys are ready, adjust Anna's schedule, make a grocery list, put everything away, and more. And I feel guilty that I do all of that versus just *being* with you. And then I see Anna with you making silly noises on the floor, just being with you, and I want that role. Do I want it enough at the cost of chaos in the house? Perhaps this is my question to myself.

When you look back on your childhood, I want you to know that you were loved and you came first. Everything I read says it's good for kids to see their mothers having other roles, other identities, other priorities. I would have made that argument too. But now, I realize, I wish I could have known in my heart that I was Mom's number one.

March 16, 2017
Audio Journal | Eight-and-a-Half Months Old

Today, I lied to perfectly good people. But before I did that, I went grocery shopping. I wandered around my favorite local market in Portland, Maine, ninety minutes from our house, and felt like an imposter. I have not been there since before you were born. I used to go there all the time, to stock up on airplane snacks like Honeycrisp apples and the brie I was not supposed to eat when I was pregnant. And before that, I went there as me. Just me.

Who am I supposed to be now? I know the pregnant person, and I know the person I was before I was pregnant. But I don't know this person. This person who is me, the person who is a mom.

I gave my first speech since having you today, at Bates College. It took two questions for me to get to the lie.

"What does your typical day look like?" a student asked.

I stared back at her. It would have been so easy to give an answer based on who I was before I was pregnant. But that was a lifetime ago, or maybe three if I count it as your two lifetimes plus my own.

"It's more of a typical week," I said, launching into a description of balancing climbing and running Legado. Then I stopped. I looked at the young woman who'd asked and the young men and women in the room, and decided they deserved the truth.

"Actually, lately, my typical day involves my eight-month-old twins and learning how to be their mom and work and climb."

I am not sure if I fell in status or gained it. Or maybe I fell in status today but will be remembered in the future for being honest.

———

To tell these college students or myself that who I am now is the same as who I was before you two existed in my belly would be absurd. That time was the fulcrum. Being pregnant with you was such a totalitarian assault on my body and my mind and my abilities, and it was so different from anything else I had done, that it changed me forever. And then there was the act of bringing you into the world, and the past eight-and-a-half months.

Who am I now? What's my true north? I have a vague idea that in two years I will be in some new equilibrium—I will know my center again. But I can't see that now when my body is still deeply intertwined with you two other creatures. And I don't want it not to be intertwined with you. I want to nurse you forever, and I get why women would do this until their children are eight, but of course I am pretty sure I am not going to do that to you, but god, who knows? I sure love it.

It blows me away how much I love nursing you. It's the rawness; it's being your person. It's being the only person who can give you that, and it's like finding my puzzle piece, finding my two little puzzle pieces all the time, every time. And just this utter knowledge that it's where I am supposed to be. I have never felt like that.

———

I have this idea that all I want to do is be a mom.

Wait, is that true?

I don't know. I don't know what I want to do right now. I don't know if I want to work full-time or work half-time or not at all. I just know I want to be with you guys, and if I spend the day away from you, it's too much.

Sometimes I wonder if I could ever become a stay-at-home mom. That just made my breath catch and my stomach flip. What do I think about me being a stay-at-home mom? I wonder if that reaction in my body is because it's something I truly need to look at or because it's something that so truly repels me—which also means I need to look at it.

I grew up adamant that I would kick ass in the female form. Seeing that in my mother, being told I was strong, being told I was special, and following in the footsteps of a woman who was fighting for it all, always. It never crossed my mind that I would (or could) just be a mom. I have to unlock this because there is something loose and interesting and tethered to my concept of womanhood and femininity, but then totally upended by what I feel like when I am around you guys. Something is off.

I can see how, as a mom, I could get so entwined in your lives that I'd just walk away from everything else—because I am central, because I am the most important thing in your world. And then, when I am no longer the most important thing in your world, because developmentally I shouldn't be, because you grow up, because you have friends, because you have things going on, how I would feel a profound sense of loss and sadness.

Does this change miraculously after a year? Is that why the Canadians have it all figured out by giving women a year of maternity leave? Am I going to feel that different in three-and-a-half months when you're a year old? I don't know.

I wonder if it was easy for my mom when she went back to work. I sort of hate her for doing it. I sort of love her for doing it. I wish I could go find her and say, "How did you do this, what do you feel, what's in your heart?"

I feel profoundly changed and awed by the amount that I love you. I feel it viscerally—I want to eat you up, I want to kiss you, I want to be slathered with you.

Did my mom once feel like this about me? Did she feel like she could never get enough of me? If so, how can she be this far away from me now? How can she sometimes be so mean to me? How can she be so mean now if that is how she felt then?

Does love for your kids mirror love for your spouse? I once loved Peter so much, and now I see that love replaced with so much resentment and exasperation. Does it follow that I could love you two this much now and have that love also diminish or even spoil? Is that what happened to my mom?

Why wasn't I important enough to hold her energy?

But then there I was, last night, playing with you while absentmindedly texting on my phone to coordinate a photoshoot.

I fucking don't get it.

March 16, 2017 (Later)
Audio Journal | Eight-and-a-Half Months Old

Irenna-bear, are you going to hear this? Kazaroo, are you?

I want everything to be remembered and quantified.

I want to remember that I started sleep-training you at five months old and you still slept in your own cribs in separate rooms. Irenna, you had a sleeping chamber in the laundry room, and your "mattress" was a padded piece of cardboard. You should get points for that forever.

Kazaroo, you're the one who always wakes up earlier. We make you stay in bed from five to six.

I just peeked in on you from the back roads of Maine, grabbing just enough service to load in your baby monitor across the airwaves.

You and your dad were piled on the couch together, each of you tipped into his sides with his big, strong arms encapsulating both of you—as if three could become one.

"Purple cat, purple cat, what do you see?" he read, and, Kaz, you squealed with delight.

I watched all the way through the nighttime tickle session. Is it creepy or good to spy on your husband and see him be the dad that he is?

I cried while you laughed.

I want you to remember, little girl, that when you were tiny, your dad could jiggle your whole body with one hand splayed over your full belly. When he does that, you have a deep and full laugh you save only for him.

"Papa loves you, little monkeys," I heard him say, and then the monitor went into night mode as the lights went dark. I wanted to keep listening and crying, I wanted it not to stop, but I was already delayed getting home.

I want everything written down and charted and captured and put somewhere, and I don't want my time with you to pass me by, not even incrementally—like I am a time stamp. I want to do something with this time, create something more with it.

Maybe I'll write a book about my time with you. For you.

March 20, 2017
Audio Journal | Eight-and-a-Half Months Old

The selfie of the four of them gets to me. Bike-helmeted up, sharing exclamation points of joy and exploration with the world. Or the social media world.

Kate and Gilbert, along with their partners, Mark and Jason, are all climbing and biking in Cuba. I am the one from our friend group who first went climbing in Cuba, on the limestone walls of the Viñales

Valley. I sound psychotic even in my own head—as if I own the market on climbing and exploration.

"Cuba looks fun," Peter says from the living-room floor, where he does leg lifts while scrolling through Instagram. He already knows I know what he's talking about.

I should be happy that my husband is such good friends with my friends and climbing partners. I used to be.

"You know I have been there, right?" I say.

"Did I tell you that Silas has filled up eight weeks of guiding in Europe?" Peter goes on.

Yesterday he told me that your Uncle Richard—who's also a guide—had just landed in Iceland.

It's not lost on me that Peter's two best friends and reflection points are both childless and plan to remain that way.

"Is it hard for you to see them doing all that?" I ask Peter.

He shrugs. "Right now I just want to get my knee back to one hundred percent."

I don't ask him what he thinks is coming after. I don't want to hear his answer and see how nonaligned we are about our mutual and independent futures. And besides, he didn't ask me how I felt seeing Kate and Gilbert out in the world. His unkind came first.

March 27, 2017
Audio Journal | Eight-and-a-Half-Months Old

Newborn clothes are scattered around me like a supernova radiating out from where I sit. I'm in our loft trying to organize your clothes so we can give away any you've outgrown. There is no way you were ever small enough to fit into these clothes. I lay them on top of my belly like I did to try them on you when you were inside me.

Tomorrow, you're going to be nine months old. Nine months is how long they say pregnancy lasts, but we all know it's really ten.

———

My friend Sarah Garlick just came back from being in Europe for work. She was gone for eight days, and when she came back, her four-year-old son refused to hug her, retiliating against her and saying he now only wanted Dad. Like he needed to punish her for her absence in his life and for her presence in her life.

This is a woman who, before kids, used to be gone for months at a time climbing and doing geology fieldwork. The friend with whom I started what would become Legado, who first quested up Mozambican granite with me in 2011 searching for cracks to grant us safe passage up Namuli's face. A woman who then could not come back with me to savor the fruits of our labor in 2014 because she had her own labor instead—for the son who now hardens his heart against her when she's gone.

How can any of us put this all together? This week your new au pair, Florencia, arrived because Anna's term was up and she had to go back to Germany. And today, I feel guilty because I did not get enough work done to justify having someone else working full-time to take care of you. On the plus side, I finally have an office with a door, having moved Florencia into our full guest room downstairs and claimed the room with a closed door off the loft as my own. I can still hear you from there, but there's separation in concept and reality. If only there were also a bathroom.

I hate it when you cry. I hate it when you're not satisfied. It's so hard to be in the house and to hear you having a difficult time and to not feel like I need to swoop in and get involved. But I understand that I am probably making it worse if I do. But also, to sit and listen as others struggle to soothe you? It's excruciating.

Maybe taking you to a daycare is a better plan. Maybe being able to walk away, shut the door, and not know what is really happening will be better for all of us. I am sure that Florencia will do great. I am sure that if she doesn't do great, we will somehow find someone else. I am sure that we have it within us for this to be some sort of great solution. Yet, at the same time, right now it feels insane. It all feels insane.

On the one hand, I feel so pulled to you and compelled by you and tethered to you. On the other hand, I feel so fraught with how I am supposed to be spending my energy. I'm trying to figure out the right mix—to be present and not trying to work on my phone when it's family time. I feel guilty that it takes two people for me to manage you sometimes.

What I do is what I do, and I am making good parenting choices. I need to keep telling myself that, and at some point, I should probably start believing it.

—⁓—

Your dad and I—we're okay. He is our chef who cooks and bakes and is already planning our summer garden. On his biggest days in the mountains, he comes home and bakes the most, starting bread while making dinner and sliding a pie in the oven before we all sit down to eat. A long time ago, your dad's brother, your Uncle Jim, told me Peter shows his love through food. I see that now when I'm able to focus on anything but you. I think I show my love through organization. We could be a perfect team. Except we don't feel like the teammates I remember from school, who supported and encouraged each other. Right now it feels like we're teammates who only tolerate each other.

I'm also mad at him—a lot. I feel like no matter what job I do, I am doing the harder job. If I spend the day guiding, when I get home I want the recognition because I spent the day guiding and then came home and was a mom. And if I am at home all day and your dad is guiding, when he comes home I want the recognition that I have been at home all day and not out in the mountains working or playing.

Yes, it's not logical or fair. I know that. I can't want recognition no matter what I do, but maybe that actually is the thing I want recognition for: that no matter what I do, it feels like a lot. In my friend Janet's marriage, her husband is the one who needs appreciation. What creates this need in us? Can I keep it from being created in you?

I want to be happy. I want to be proud of the way I am mothering you. And damn, sometimes it's just hard to have two of you. It has to be okay to say that. It's as if every hour we're together is two hours of parenting, but even that is not right because it's not just double. It's more.

Maybe what I need to do is take a break sometimes and say, "You know what? I'm taking one of you and we're out of here."

No major epiphanies today, team. Just living this life.

March 30, 2017
Audio Journal | Nine Months Old

Wanting something and starting it is not the same as having it and finishing it. The last time I tried this hard at anything, I ended up leaving a marriage.

Did you know I had bunk beds back then? Or the space carved out of a straw-bale house for them, to someday have Eddie's and my hypothetical children sleep there? I built that house and life when I was twenty-two—as if I could will a physical and marital existence into being if I just stacked the straw and troweled the stucco on top of it. I put down roots in a mountain town as a mountain guide with a mountain man but ended up throwing it all into the air like a game of pickup sticks and driving away.

Nine years into being together, Eddie and I went to a wedding in Vail. He drove and I tried to get him to talk to me. I was twenty-eight by then, and had been convincing myself to stay in my marriage through a series of two-week experiments that had gradually woven themselves into a seven-year tapestry of marital unhappiness. *Try to only say nice things to him and maybe he will be nice back. Try to not ask him to make love and see if he responds. Try to smoke pot with him and see if he stops sneaking outside to get high.* The wedding weekend was my newest experiment. *Be extra nice, ask questions,* I coached myself.

"Where were you the summer you were twenty-eight?" I asked my forty-year-old husband.

Eddie told me about his VW van and its dented door that he both loved and hated. About climbing in Joshua Tree and Yosemite for months on end.

"Maybe we can do that," I had said.

"But I'm not twenty-eight anymore and I like our house," Eddie said.

The highway was half-closed for repairs, and we were stuck behind a slow-driving Indiana tourist on the one-lane road. When Eddie swerved around the cones into the closed-off lane and sped around a corner to pass the tourist, I closed my eyes. I opened them to flashing lights and sirens. I closed them again through the whole $750 ticket and traffic violation, all while mentally calculating the impact it would have on our insurance costs. The reality of how we were tied together had never seemed as clear before as it was in that moment, pulled over on a mountain road on the way to celebrate someone else's love.

I spent the whole wedding caught between wanting to sneer at the nuptial bliss and wanting to believe in it. Back at the motel, Eddie peeled down to his boxers and watched TV while I took a walk on blacktop pavement through town, wondering if I could finally get away from marriage and love forever.

A week later, I took the bravest step I ever took and left it all to be me, just me. Me, traveling and climbing around the world.

———

Three weeks after that, while I was climbing three hundred feet off the ground and three miles deep in a desert sandstone canyon, a microwave-sized rock cut loose from the wall and used my left foot as a trampoline. I hobbled out with my climbing partners' help and thought I'd escaped without serious injury—until we pulled up to the hospital and I confidently opened the door to stand, only to crumple to the ground. Adrenaline is funny that way.

Would I feel differently now if I could have attended my divorce mediation meetings via a Skype call from Yosemite instead of limping into an office in Boulder, Colorado? I'd wanted to run so badly I ended up being unable to walk for eight months.

It took me four years and your dad to even consider love and marriage again.

April 4, 2017
Letter | Nine Months Old

This week my mother arrived. Her visit spanned from eleven thirty A.M. on a Tuesday to three thirty P.M. on a Wednesday. Twenty-eight hours.

A third of the way through her visit, the kids were asleep, she was upstairs lying down, and I was typing away. I was writing about how I didn't feel connected to my mother, who was upstairs. So I went upstairs and joined her.

As I crawled in the twin foldout bed, she automatically lifted the covers and moved over on the pillow. No hesitation—as if it was the most natural thing. As I lay notched against her, the weight of her left arm on top of my waist and shoulder, I realized that she did love me as much as I love you two.

Today, when you two cry, I hold you tighter, rock you harder, catch your tears with my thumb. But one day you will cry and I will instead hold you and not ask why, not change the position of my arm on your side, not even flinch when you suck the snot back into your nose. I will lie with you until your breathing regulates and your tears cover the half of my pillow I ceded to you without pause.

"We haven't done this in a long time," my mom says. And it's then that I remember all the times we have done it—when any early morning I wanted to, I could creep into her room and she'd welcome me with a pulled-back sheet making a tunnel to the warmth of her belly. My sister would sometimes already be on the other side. "My girls," my mom would say. "Me and my girls."

Today, I lie with the weight of her arm on my side until I feel my breathing slow and regulate. I watch the fan lazily *thwap* along the ceiling in the house she helped me select from my hospital bed the day my kids came into the world, and I realize that what I've needed for the past three months was to know how much she loved me.

"Tell me about when I was little," I say.

"I thought we were sleeping," she says.

I snuggle back into her a little more deeply and try not to notice that she feels smaller than me for the first time.

"Did you really only have three weeks with me before you went back to work?"

She tells me about how I was so late that she used up half her maternity leave before I was born. "It was a different time," she says. She hand-pumped at work, came home with the milk in one arm and a full briefcase on the other, and then re-entered her world with us. She'd pull out the papers and reports later at night when she needed to, but not when we were awake.

"I loved it just being about you and nothing but you when I got home. Being with you was the most important thing to me," my mother says. I think of her working full-time, and see a contradiction in her statement that I've finally come to understand. Because I realize I feel exactly the same.

April 7, 2017
Letter | Nine Months Old

Last night I stuffed a load of foul, dank laundry into the dryer, three hours afer I'd asked Peter to move it over from the washer. Then I cried for my ex-husband.

"I ache for you," my mom used to say to me when she could not fix what was wrong.

I picture a couple trapped in the entropy of an unhappy marriage who were marching toward its end all along. They had no idea. How to fix this. How to be this. How to change this. I ache for them—that faraway version of Eddie and me.

I promised Peter vigilance when we married. Or rather, I demanded it, and he gave my previous marriage a wide berth. "The only way I can think to protect us," I told him back then, "is to never protect us from talking about what matters."

I thought that vigilance would keep Peter and me from getting to this point. Now I realize it is going to have to get us through it.

April 10, 2017
Letter | Nine Months Old

Kate called today. She was driving home to Bishop, California, from Ventura, home from the airport after climbing in Cuba, in Kenya, in Patagonia.

We might see each other in Montana when I am visiting my family with the kids if she can buzz up there from her summer location of choice in Jackson, Wyoming.

"Wait," she says. "The only thing that might conflict is if I go to South Africa."

As she starts talking about the variety of logistics and questions that are part of her decision-making process, a series of thoughts, each less rational then the next, washes over me.

How dare others go there without me?

I know South Africa best from my monthlong trip there nine years ago. Why didn't she or anyone else ask me if I wanted to go?

Why am I even having this conversation if it makes me think all these things?

I tell her the trip sounds cool, and then we're cut off as Kate zooms in her truck over the folds and layers of California.

I recognize I have been the person Kate is being to me to other friends when they were fresh mothers.

I recognize that I will not be in this exact position—with nine-month-old twins whom I nurse eight times (each) a day—happily, lovingly—forever.

I recognize that in some not-so-distant future, I will be ready to go somewhere for some amount of time.

I recognize that thirty days of rock climbing in South Africa without my children or my husband is not what I want now.

I tuck my phone in my pocket and pick you up, Kaz. You're hungry. You're always hungry. I nurse you. I don't like the collision of emotions. I don't like not liking to talk to one of my closest friends. I want to be a better person than this.

Perhaps I thought I'd be immune to the working-mother pitfalls and paradoxes and typicalities because I have an alternative career. I'm constantly surprised when I face them. When you've made a career out of pursuing your passions, connecting seemingly unconnectable passions into giant projects, you think you can pull anything off . . .

I thought you would tuck neatly into my life, alongside my plan, merged easily into anything I wanted to do. Sure, I would miss you at times—when I was ice climbing in Norway or at a bat conference in Ethiopia. But we would figure it out. I never thought much about it beyond the unconsidered notion that I've been able to pull off most things in my life up until now. How could this be different?

And then there were two of you.

For me to do this—to keep this life up—this life will have to change in the way that makes the most sense for me. For us.

—⁓—

Two months ago I was guiding when my pump started to fail in five-degree weather that bitter winds had reduced to well below zero. I soloed—unbelayed, trailing the rope—up nearly vertical ice because my client had never climbed before, and I decided they were more likely to pull me off the ice than keep me safe with a belay, a not-uncommon scenario for mountain guides. My long underwear and fleece and shell all fit wrong on their own, and abysmally together. I ignored my discomfort and tried to go as fast as I could to earn myself time to pump while my client ate after seconding the pitch.

Normally I never sit down or stop when I'm guiding. But I have to do both to pump. I modified my tops at the start of the winter—slicing a zip-up turtleneck to my navel with orange scissors and following suit with a thicker top. Under all of that was a nursing bra, and below that, lassoed around my stomach for when I needed it, was a pumping holster.

On that cold, raw day my body shrank from the freezing, stiff plastic of the pump's cones even as I threaded them through the zippers, my bra, and finally the holes of the holster to my breasts. With numb, shaky fingers, I put my gloves back on and tried to enclose myself in my extra jacket.

I sat with my back to my client with the wind whipping around us while he smacked his lips on a peanut-butter sandwich. I pumped nine-and-a-half ounces out of my breasts to match the pace of you two eating at home. By the end the pump whined from the effort, the batteries straining against the cold.

I spent the rest of the day climbing with the pump's battery pack full of its eight AAs tucked next to my chest to keep them warm so

I could pump again. I came home with a day's wage and twenty-six ounces of milk.

—⁓—

Six months prior, while learning how to field two two-month-olds, Peter and I had discussed the idea of a family trip to Patagonia.

"We could all go," he said. "Rent a house, be there as a family. I could climb and you could . . ."

He never finished his vision because I never let him. In my head I envisioned myself in Patagonia that upcoming season—our winter, but the austral summer. And I thought of my body still ravaged from pregnancy.

I thought of ice climbing close to home and saw possibility. I thought of Patagonia alpine objectives—hiking nine miles into the mountains, a glacier bivy, and being away from the kids for three days—and saw nothing.

I flipped to the next option. I saw myself being a full-time mom in a mountain town at the southern end of Patagonia as all my climbing partners and contemporaries clocked in and out of El Chaltén on the way to various objectives.

I knew then I was not a generous-enough person—largely to myself—to undertake that trip. Patagonia was off the discussion table for a while. Or at least, in our family it was. And now I know I will have to learn how to talk about the climbing I am not doing—or I'll need to find new friends.

April 13, 2017
Letter | Nine-and-a-Half Months Old

When I was twenty-four years old and had been married for three years to Eddie, I put together a barbecue for a group of climbers at our mountainside house. Our house was always hosting climbers and guides, and I loved filling my table with food for our ever-growing, ever-fun community. All the climbers at that night's gathering were taking a guiding course with Eddie, and among them was Jana. Years later, Jana, by then a longtime friend and fully certified international mountain guide, told me that on that night in Estes Park all she could do was shake her head at the thought of me. "I had heard you were a badass woman climber, and instead you sure looked like a housewife," she told me.

I'd thought hosting a group of climbers made me seem welcoming. Jana had thought it made me seem pitiful. We never know anything about anyone.

And now both Jana and I are mothers to two children each.

I thought being married was to be absorbed together. Eddie and I even had the same email address, an amalgamation of our first names. How could I have been that person then but be so determined to be myself now? How could I *not* be this determined now, having worked so hard to untangle myself from an faltering marriage?

....

April 15, 2017
Letter | Nine-and-a-Half Months Old

Last night I told your dad I wanted to list out all the domestic tasks we each do on sticky notes, and then workshop them together and redivide them. He got yellow notes, I had blue.

"Ready?" I asked.

He nodded, and I put my head down.

Write a weekly childcare schedule, wrangle hand-me-downs, pay bills, coordinate any work needed on the house, make appointments for cars, manage doctor appointments, create a system for washing poop-covered clothing . . .

By the time I looked up your dad had two notes, covered in his elegant handwriting. I had thirty-five splashed in my rapid-fire diagonal scrawl.

"What do you have?" I asked.

Peter picked up one note and read, "Shoveling snow or mowing the lawn, grocery shopping and cooking . . ."

I wanted to explain that the point was to list one job per note and that it wasn't fair to list joint work. Instead I shared one of my notes: "All night feedings."

Peter picked up his second and final sticky note. "On this one I wrote what I know you are doing," he said.

"But that wasn't the point," I said.

"But isn't it kind?"

I couldn't catch my breath.

I don't want to talk about being kind. I want to talk about all the work that seems to fall to me without anything looking like it's changing. I want to stop being the safety net for our family. I want to be married to a sociologist who understands that if this keeps up, we will go under—and when we come back to the surface, we might each be alone.

April 27, 2017
Letter | Nine-and-a-Half Months Old

My dear baby girl,

Today you forced a break from work upon me. You woke up early from your nap for no reason, so I tucked you next to me on our bed and you fell back asleep.

I almost didn't notice your slumber—I was focused on getting to my next thing. But your hands were what stopped me. They grasped and released, flexed and extended, puckering the dimples that will one day be your knuckles. And then they went still. And I waited, and you slept.

You are my marvel. You are long and lean and tough. And recently, you've even grown a belly. I think we are both equally proud of its round arc above your hips and below your ribs. "Look at this belly," I say to you every time I change you. And we jiggle it together—me with my hand, you with your laughter.

Your fingers are narrow and strong. You do tricks with your tongue. You give me wet, open-mouthed kisses on my ears, my cheeks, my nose, and my mouth. You flutter your arms like a bird when you want something, when you like something, when you see me.

Today, lying with you as you drifted back into a nap between ten thirty and eleven A.M., I reminded myself that I only get a finite number of these moments with you. Sometimes I wish you (or your brother) slept with me every day, every night. That we were that type of three-some. But your sleep, my sleep, and our sanity became more worth it, so we are on a plan. And we're also on that plan because I work.

One day, if/when you become a mom, I wonder what choices you will make—or that you will be able to make. I am conducting a grand experiment wherein I am near you almost all the time, but only *with* you for part of it. Instead of daycare, we have an au pair. I go up to my office, turn on the noise machine I put outside the door, put my earphones in, and talk about private-sector linkages and water trusts for conservation agreements upstream on Mount Namuli. I come back down to nurse you, to hike with you, and then go back up and return to the panel of my computer screen.

Some days, this feels like the worst possible idea for my work, my sanity, and my general desire to complete things in life. But then I get a day like today. A day when I get to lie next to you in your green overalls with my hand engulfing your hip but your body and breath strong enough to push it up and down, up and down, as you breathe yourself back to sleep.

"This is how much I love you," I say. "This, this, here." I don't want to forget it. I don't want to miss a moment of it.

You, at ten months less one day, crawl and pull up and look out the window, into the oven, and at the poodle. You especially like to pull up on a couch/chair/leg and laugh at your brother. You have your toys stolen quite a bit. And you're learning to take them back. You make pops and gurgles and *da-das*. You love your papa. You wake up at five thirty A.M. You try to fall asleep in your backpack on our morning hikes, but we don't let you. You eat like a fountain fish coming into attack for just the bite you want. You have blue eyes—I still hold out hope for them turning brown so yours will look like mine. Your hair is fine and straight but may be about to curl. Your toes are skinny. You don't like hats. The poodle licks your fingers. When you wear overalls, Kaz treats the shoulder straps like Irenna handles. You like salmon and yogurt. But not together.

April 28, 2017
Letter | Ten Months Old

This week, the last winter snow melted from our garden and the crocus patch bloomed and closed just in time to escape your attempts to eat its purple petals.

I spent our first winter together pulling you on cross-country skis in a tandem sled that gave me independence while keeping me tethered. The woods outside our front door were the hat trick: my exercise, your naps, and our collective sanity all in one. Together—always together—the three of us did a five-month in-depth study of our backyard-ski-trail snowpack. We broke trail in two feet of powder, snowplowed through rain-soaked crust, and swooshed perfect tracks through ankle-deep corn, all in equal measure. And, when things got desperate, we snowshoed.

Your father and I have a combined fifty years pursuing the vertical for life, work, and most everything in between. Together in the mountains, we were a well-oiled machine. So when, childless, I envisioned parenthood, I saw your dad and me with a version that was light and fast with lean, efficient systems enabling endless, flexible adventure. Snowshoes—and the gaiters and post-holing that accompanied fifty percent of my "ski" outings with you two—were never part of my picture.

Then again, having two of you was never part of my picture.

———

Back when you both lived inside my growing belly, I fielded questions about my future climbing plans with noncommittal shrugs. I didn't want to under- or over-commit myself. Then it was suddenly January 2017, you were six months old, and I was shifting my weight back and forth on stemmed-out mono-points and wondering if I should place another ice screw. Now is a good time to tell you that your mom's always liked gear. And it's also probably a good time to tell you that, ten months into your presence in the world, I seem to like it even more. All winter, as you learned to crawl, I climbed higher and farther with two new rules: I'd place one screw for just before the moment that mattered and one screw for after. "Twins," I would tell my partners, my clients, myself. "I am the mother of twins."

But don't be fooled: I don't think and talk about you all the time when I'm climbing. And that is good—for all of us. We all need time apart, just not too much. This winter I felt utterly myself when climbing and when with you. It wasn't hard to know this meant I was supposed to be doing both. What was hard, however—and might always be—was the knowledge that I wanted to do both well.

Sometimes I wish I could make it easier on all of us and want less. I wish I could take climbing and the elation and craving and risk that accompany it out of our family picture. In our newfound time we could make kale cupcakes, hand-sew your clothing, and maybe even remember to brush your newly emerging teeth. But instead we are learning how to manage vertical passion as a family.

Will we all go climbing together? Will we move as a rope team over glaciers, up aiguilles, and through icy notches? I think we have to wait and see what you want and what your dad and I can stomach as you become the extension of ourselves we cannot control.

For now, and for at least a little while longer, I can pluck you away from danger and into my arms. I can go climb at eight A.M., come home at four P.M., and be devoured by double kisses and four sticky hands.

Not everyone will think I'm making the right choices. This March, I taught a thirty-year-old man named Shimmy how to ice climb over the span of four days. On our first day he learned I was your mother and he asked me what I was doing guiding him if I had you at home. On our second day he told me, as if commiserating, that he understood that I could guide near home but could never take a climbing trip. On the third day he announced that perhaps I could take a climbing trip, but never one with your dad. And on the fourth day, as I pumped milk from my body sitting two feet from him on a sunny belay ledge four hundred feet up Mount Willard, he asked me where your dad and I were planning our next expedition.

Today, ten months into knowing you two, I can say with certainty that our life together is like those four days with Shimmy—but stretched out yet also compressed in an endless, beautiful loop. There will be limits I don't want; there will be understandings I don't expect. There will be climbing. There will be plans that change for the better and for the worse. And, if I have my way, the four of us will always be both tethered and independent.

April 30, 2017
From the Notepad | Ten Months Old

"Ueli Steck died," Peter told me from the corner of the couch tonight. "In Nepal."

The Swiss machine, I thought, Ueli's nickname, given for his super-human speed in the mountains and constant pursuit of performance at the edge of possibility. "Where?" I ask.

"Nuptse," Peter answered. Then he sighed, thick and heavy.

"In so many ways the pinnacle of pushing it—and pulling it off," he added.

I lay on the floor and looked sideways at Peter scrolling through his phone as he talked. Neither of us knew Ueli personally. But you didn't need to meet him to know he was a superlative. Ueli was undoubt-edly one of the best climbers in the world. Sprinting up harder and harder climbing routes, with less and less gear at higher and higher altitudes—often without a rope. I stayed quiet because I could tell Peter wanted to say more.

"When you have ultimate ability *and* you keep pushing it and trying things that are harder—and stacking it all up—is this just what hap-pens? What can be expected?"

Neither of us said anything for a while.

Irenna let out a wail. I waited, then Kaz joined in. I got up and started down the hall.

What do we all expect?

Grandpa Roger—Peter's father—took one of his motorcycles out of the shed last week when we were visiting. "Vroom, vroom," he said to Irenna.

"Oooh," she said eagerly back.

"That's enough of that," I said, swooping her out of reach and sight of the bike.

"Really?" Roger asked. "Do you really want to go there?"

This is a man who collects 240 gallons of sap to make six gallons of maple syrup a year for his family, and replenishes our Mason-jar supply of it via his motorcycle whenever we need it.

"What if we said that about climbing?" he presses.

"I don't like motorcycles," I say.

"Think of it as another version of what you do," he offered, shrugging. Then he went back to his garden.

"What do you think about my going to Patagonia by myself this winter?" Peter asked me tonight. "I really want to go."

What can you expect? I think.

May 2, 2017
Letter | Ten Months Old

Kazaroo,

Today, I learned how to catch your vomit in your shirt by pulling it up to form a trough the moment I hear you starting to retch. You're sleep-nursing on my lap, which might have been the wrong thing to do, but withholding the very thing that gives you comfort—even if you puke it up—is beyond my capability.

Irenna is asleep in the backpack after I walked her around the house in it. Meanwhile, I took care of you and caught your vomit. We're already four episodes into this, just today. How many more before I call the doctor? I squeeze your fingernails to make sure your capillaries fill back up with blood.

I have been moving a black hair tie from wrist to wrist for twenty-four hours a day since you were born. I change it every time you nurse so it sits on the wrist—and corresponding breast side—Irenna is due for next. If I break from protocol and assign you only my right side today and keep Irenna on my left, can I keep her from puking too?

May 9, 2017
Letter | Ten Months Old

Today, we signed the contract for the big grant with the new funder.

Today, I also wrote the US ambassador to Mozambique saying that no, I would not be going there this summer after I'd spent a year chasing him down with emails and calls to have that meeting.

On a roll, at the post office, I also told Ben—a fellow climber in the valley whose respect I feel I'd just gained—that I was not going to Africa this year after all.

"Because of the kids?" he asked, raising his eyebrows, shaking his head, and sending me down six rungs of esteem in one moment.

What a douche, I texted Garlick.

You might have said the same thing to yourself two years ago, she replied.

Good point, I wrote back.

May 11, 2017
From the Notepad | Ten-and-a-Half Months Old

"Have you talked to Gilbert recently?" Peter asks today as we trade ends of the climbing rope so it can be his turn to be lowered down an open-book granite corner below, one I'll belay him back out on. He's almost one hundred percent recovered from his surgery, and we're back out climbing together on Cathedral Ledge.

"Nope," I say, swapping his end into a belay device.

"She's going to Alaska soon," Peter says as he leans back on the rope.

"I know," I say. I just don't know what I am supposed to do with that knowing. I can tell he wants to talk about going to Alaska himself. "Ready?" I ask instead.

I send Peter over the edge. This is our new way to climb together: attacking the cliff from the top and lowering each other down all two hundred feet of rope to get the most climbing in the shortest amount of time. Other climber parents I know chose mountain biking. Others chose bouldering, where you don't need ropes and one parent can always have an eye on the kids, others choose new spouses who don't climb.

When Peter gets back to the ledge, I hand him his approach shoes, to clip to his harness.

"We're done?" he asks.

"Florencia only works till two today," I say.

Peter unties from the rope and heads above me to get away from the edge. By the time I join him, his sneakers are back on and he's packed his pack.

"Okay?" I ask.

"I just wish we had more time," he says.

"Huh," I say. "I want to be grateful for the time we have."

May 19, 2017
Audio Journal | Ten-and-a-Half Months Old

"I don't know how to be a parent and a climber in Chamonix," your dad said to me today.

"Neither do I," I said. "But I want to find out."

I could have gone to France by myself, high-fiving your father in passing at the airport as he came back from his own trip to guide somewhere. He could've gotten off his flight, hopped in the car, and sped back to you at home with Florencia as I got on a plane and flew away. But even though your dad told me he's supportive of a solo trip, I could not say yes as the me I am now.

It's not that I can't imagine a trip. I have built my career around envisioning and executing trips. But what I imagine feels empty because there is no desire there, no immediacy. I am not on that timeline right now. Because I am on your timeline, at least for now—nearly eleven months in, the three of us tied together eight times a day.

It took us a month to decide that it was a good idea to travel en masse to Chamonix—you, us, Florencia. Alaska and Patagonia lost out, and Chamonix seemed like a better fit for our family.

But first your dad will start traveling more for work again. Two months of him back and forth, enough to earn me the offer to go to France by myself. But instead I choose to somehow pull this next version of us—the full traveling circus—off instead. The last time we did this we came home three days into the climbing portion of our Minnesota-Banff-DC-Kentucky rodeo disaster. This time it's only a climbing trip, there will be one destination instead of four, and I've already reserved two bassinettes for you to sleep in the whole way there. And I know. You won't really do that. But I can always hope and pretend.

June 18, 2017
Audio Journal | Eleven-and-a-Half Months Old

Today, serving as Legado's proxy for me, Eric, our program manager, landed in Maputo, the capital of Mozambique. Peter landed in England. And I am here in Jackson, New Hampshire, with you two. I don't want to be somewhere else. Correction—I do, until I understand it means not being with you.

I wrote Eric an email, timed so he'd receive it upon landing in Mozambique. "Thrive in your expertise, in your knowledge, in your passion and creation of this program. Enjoy the discussions, the partnership creation, and the buzz of making this work as you move through the next weeks," I wrote.

"Disfrutas," I continued, in Portuguese. *Enjoy it to its essence.* "All of it."

And then I hit send and cried.

———

I've never not been the one running this ship. And yet I know that Legado has reached a point where I cannot be the only one leading. I think of Eric landing, jet-lagged, neck kinked, roughed up from customs, and electrified by the stranger-in-a-strange-land hyperawareness that makes your skin jump at every pore as you step onto foreign soil.

I was addicted to that rush. I used to arrive in new countries days before my expedition teammates so I could soak it all in. Once, my first time to South Africa, I landed in Johannesburg and got in a manual-transmission rental car on the wrong side because I'd never driven on the right side of a car before. Then, after not sleeping for eighteen hours, I proceeded to learn how to drive on the left side of the road during four hours of nighttime highway driving. Each time I drove past a CAUTION: CARJACKING sign, I considered the wisdom of my choice. But I kept going because what were those signs to me except reasons to do just that?

Yet here I am now. At home. With these two. Trying to keep Kaz from biting when he doesn't mean it, stopping him from steamrolling his sister, who is seventeen pounds to his twenty-two, chasing them both, loving them both, and wondering constantly if I have the mix right.

I'd like to be more zen. I'd like to be more certain. Not knowing if you're doing it right? People laugh and say, "That is parenting." But that's not the glib answer I want. Okay, it's parenting, but how do you do it *better*? How do I make this world your best world?

Right now, you are eleven months and twenty-one days old. In ten days you will be a year old. People tell me this is the hardest time—the first year, getting through it, surviving—but I don't know anything different.

I want to be with you anytime I am not. I want to cover you in kisses. And then when it's difficult I want to scream. When you are both screaming and writhing and it's only me, or worse when it's me and your dad but he doesn't seem to be pulling his weight, I want to scream too.

June 21, 2017
From the Notepad | Eleven-and-a-Half Months Old

Irenna, if I pull you away from your brother's kicks and slaps, am I making you less resilient?

Kaz, if I don't intervene, will you just learn how to be a brute and get away with it?

June 28, 2017
Letter | Twelve Months Old

Today is your first birthday, and I got you life jackets so you can ride in your grandparents' canoe up on the lake. No big party, because you would not remember it and I could not imagine it. Life jackets and strawberry shortcake seemed perfect.

I am 365 days into holding you, and what I want most is to go back in time. For a slice of a day, for each week I was pregnant, to feel you kicking, to feel your butts, your knees, and your hiccups inside of me. It's gone. It has vanished. I want to hold your hands for the first time, have your fingers wrap around mine, have your eyes struggle to stay open and your withered lips alternate sucking and mewing into the world.

With every day that passes, I lose more of those memories, lose more of my sense of how it felt, how you smelled, how I felt. I am not sure why this matters to me so profoundly, why this brings me to my knees. But it makes me sob. Perhaps this is why people have more and more children. I want all of these tastes again. I want them in a hermetically sealed chamber where I can just keep them in pure, distilled essence. Maybe I want them with one of you at a time—even though I'm not supposed to say that.

Is this mortality? Is this ephemerality? It's devastating. Slow it down; give it to me in smaller doses. Let me capture it all to revisit again and again and again—and give me time to do so. Each year there will be more memories; each day there are more firsts and lasts. And maybe it is the lasts that have taken me down. Because I always knew there would be firsts, but I never knew there would be lasts. And it's this fact—that I will never hold your fingers for the first time again, or have you both fit in the palm of my hand—that I was utterly unprepared for.

Of course, the better attitude would be to cherish what is to come. But right now I can't seem to get beyond the leaving-behind. Because, of course, this means that one day an even larger leaving-behind will take place. Capture it, snap it, video it, and scratch it into my heart so I can always access it.

I lay in bed at night and go through what I'm grateful for. Each day, my list gets longer. Each night, things inevitably fall off the list because I cannot remember them all.

Right now, you two want to be with me at any cost. Your Mom-seeking radar is ever on. You crawl up me, over me, and onto me, grasping at my shirt and my ears and my hair, and you each have an unspoken agreement that you will get to me and keep me. One day, I will not be able to hold you both. As it is, I get stronger each day as you get bigger, and together we can still stand up from the floor, become one, and go forth as I carry us all. One day—any day, any minute, any moment—you will walk on concrete floors, around a stone fireplace, and I will watch.

———

How am I ever going to survive this if I feel this much?

"What's wrong?" your dad asked from the blue couch last night, surrounded by spit-up and sippy cups and more.

It's not sadness, it's not happiness—it's just feeling. And a sense of *wanting* to feel this. Wanting to capture it and hold it close, because if this is not the feeling of life, of true life, the kind you're supposed to pay attention to, then what is?

Here's what I like the best: Seeing you master a new play activity, move, or toy. Hearing your lips smack when you have a new taste you like. I love your curiosity. Yesterday, Irenna, you crawled up onto my chest while I lay on the floor, inserted your thumb into your mouth, and took a catnap on top of me, your head in my neck the way you nestled it into Kaz's neck when you were in my belly. Kaz, when you hold me around my neck, I feel you as my growing little boy, the love in your kisses. Irenna, we rub noses now.

What I wish I had an easier time with? Having both of you at once. I don't even feel I am supposed to say that. As if the universe will take one of you away if I admit it. I feel no one gets what they need in those moments. And they are not moments—they are our constant state.

Yesterday, I took you, Irenna, on a walk to the post office. Just you and me. You kept flinging your left arm into the open space in the double stroller where Kaz normally sits. "Ooh," you'd say when your arm was met with space instead of your twenty-two-pound brother.

Your dad and Kaz played crawling obstacle games on the floor the whole hour we were gone. "Best time ever?" I asked him when we got home.

"Best," he said. "It's a whole other world."

We need to do this more—so we have more space to slow down and remember.

It's time to stop writing to you today because your dad is almost home. It's time to nurse you and go to Gramgram and Grandpa's house. You'll don your life jackets, we'll attempt a boat ride, and we'll celebrate whatever happens with the strawberry shortcake.

July 2, 2017
Audio Journal | Twelve Months Old

> *Doooo doo doo dooo.*
> *Bluuuub dooo doo doo.*
> *Blubdoo.*
> *Duuuub . . .*
> Irenna—the whole day long.

July 8, 2017
Audio Journal | Twelve Months Old

Today, I am single-parenting you. Your dad is in Wales, guiding, for the second time in three weeks. Which means I get to watch the BBC drama series *Call the Midwife* on TV. Which might not be a good idea.

Last night, I went to bed crying after watching yet another woman give birth. Or at least act like she was pushing a child out of her pelvis in a beautifully simulated vaginal birth. My friend Elizabeth told me I am not allowed to watch anything about babies being born until I fully heal. At forty-six with decades of working in conservation spanning over fifty countries, she just now decided to become a mom. She has sworn off the show herself for the next nine months. I text her today and tell her she might need a longer hiatus. I'm nowhere near ready.

Here is what I remember:

We went to the hospital in the morning. We said goodbye to my mom and the poodle at our home on Skyline Drive. I took a walk with you two and the summer sun that morning—down the driveway, to the left, and out Rachel Lane. My shirt didn't fit over my belly—then again, almost no shirt had in over two months—and I didn't care. Over half of it—of you—jutted out proudly into the sun and the world. I wore a skirt. The day was heating up. It was Sunday.

We could have had you on Thursday (or started the process), but that was two days earlier than thirty-eight weeks, so your dad and I opted for one day past the deadline. Those last three days, when I knew I could already have you in my arms, were the toughest. Every move you made, every extra ripple of four heels across my belly, made me wonder if you were about to start things on your own.

Did you know that for months (yes, months) everyone thought you might be coming? No one thought I'd make it to thirty-eight weeks because I had contractions all the time. I went over and over to the birthing center, and they'd strap two monitors around my growing belly and find each of you. You stinkers never stayed put.

They had to count so many movements, crescendos, and accelerations to make sure you were okay. And one of you would always move. They would check me to see if I was dilated, which sometimes took several nurses and a doctor. They had to get their fingers up and around and back to god knows where my cervix was, clenched shut in order to keep you two in. It was always a no—not yet.

On June 26, your dad and I finally went to the birth center knowing we'd come back with you in our arms. Maybe when you have your own kids, things will be different, but for me, the doctors would not let me carry you in my tummy after thirty-eight weeks. I wasn't sad to go to the birthing center that day—I was ready. It was a relatively unceremonious start, with a nurse inserting half a Cytotec pill inside me to induce labor. Then we waited.

After one hour the contractions I'd already been having with you—the "unproductive" ones, as the medical staff labeled them—came on harder and faster and stronger. Even though they'd only given me half a pill, they decided that this would not be the route they'd take anymore. It wasn't safe for you, and this was all about what was safe for you, and me, and us.

Pitocin was next. That meant an IV and being hooked up to a monitor continuously. All I had wanted was to be able to move around freely with you two. Instead, the need to track you took over. I wish they'd told me this—had told me that I might not be able to go anywhere. In birthing class, they had touted the amazing trails on the hospital's grounds that I'd be allowed to walk on while in labor, the whirlpool tub I could use, and the single mobile fetal monitor—all amenities that are entirely useless to a woman birthing twins.

I had to pee all the time, which became a six-step process. I'd get up, your dad would help me wheel the IV tower and Pitocin over, we'd unhook the monitor, I'd pee, we'd go back to the bed, and we'd plug it all back in. And usually by then, one of you had moved. Then we'd have to find you all over again.

It's hard to believe that any movement was possible then. It's not as though you had much space. Kaz, you were having a harder time.

They didn't want to let you off the monitor as your heart rate would go up and down.

More Pitocin.

That day is fuzzy in my mind. I know my water broke while your dad and I watched *Game of Thrones*. I had finally moved to sitting on an exercise ball, and we could keep you visible on the monitor if I bent forward just enough. Bounce, bounce, bounce. And then, amniotic fluid rushed out of me—covering the ball, covering the sheets on the ball, covering the room. More fluid than I could have ever imagined.

More Pitocin.

Faster and faster contractions, but still no dilation. Well, nothing beyond a half-centimeter or one centimeter. (We'll have to ask your father. Maybe we got to one centimer.)

I got an epidural. By the time the anesthesiologist showed up to give it to me, I was in more pain than I have ever felt or hope to ever feel again. Crashing waves of contractions and a feeling that they had nowhere to go. Squeezing tight to your dad's hand, to Carol the doula's hand in pain and in total fear that I might not be able to stay still for the epidural.

Six years ago, after two back surgeries, I swore I'd never let anyone near my back again—but here we were. Me with a tube being inserted along a spine I'd worked so hard to protect. I hated giving up moving, getting a catheter, lying down. But I had no other choice. The pain was too much.

Kazzer, you were still having a hard time. I think you were pretty smushed. Your head was so far down that my cervix was way behind it. By then, checking me was almost impossible for the doctors and nurses. They had to prop me up on my fists, tilt me, and reach far behind you. Somehow we all hoped my body would shift and catch up with you, Kazaroo. In the meantime, you only liked it when I lay on my right side—your side. Your heart rate would drop way too low if I tried anything else.

Then I got an infection—a fever of 102 (or maybe 103?). More meds.

We kept going. Dr. Lauren would come in every three hours and check me. Still no movement. She swept my membrane. I got to four centimeters.

Four.

Four.

Four.

Four.

Again and again. At ten P.M. on our second day, thirty-eight hours after arriving, we decided we'd wait one more cycle. And then that time passed too.

Each interval between checking, between draining the catheter, I'd tuck in my earplugs, pull on my eye mask, and think of what I was grateful for. I always started with twenty toes. Twenty toes, twenty fingers, four hands. I'd count each part of you in tandem and take myself away from the pain. We tried propping my legs apart on a giant, peanut-shaped pillow. Then we tried taking the peanut away.

Once we all decided on a C-section, things happened quickly. More meds for me, then the too-bright lights of the hallway. Then the operating room, the brightest place I've been in my life. It felt like Mars. I could not see, and I could not keep my eyes open.

—∿∿—

Do you want this story to only be the good things? So do I. So do I . . . so much. I want it to be like the woman who came in after me. She was induced, delivered a baby, and held her in her arms ten hours later. But we were forty-one hours into the process and you were still inside. Until Dr. Lauren released you from the drum of my belly. I want to say that you were inside until I gave birth to you, but that doesn't sit right with me yet. But it will need to one day, for me.

Kaz, you came first. You were a bit roughed up from the contractions, and they had to give you a bit of oxygen. You were blue, but you recovered quickly. Irenna, you came out second, one minute after your brother, at 2:24 A.M. But you were first on top of me, rooting around with your precise mouth and eyes—and just like that, you were nursing. Like a piranha, because you had some ground to make up. You were five pounds, fourteen ounces, and Kaz, you were seven pounds, fifteen ounces. Irenna, you were on my right, though you'd been on the left in my belly. Kaz, you joined her shortly thereafter. You tucked in, a bit more tired, but just like your sister, you moved your mouth to me and latched on. They wanted to take you from me to move me to a different bed. I would not let them. For the first of what would be thousands of times, I grasped both of you tightly and refused to let go.

Then we were all together. You had to get big IV needles in your tiny, little paws, wrapped up just so. The needles delivered medicine two times a day in case you had a big infection. You didn't—they tested my placenta—but you could have. All three of us were a bit banged up. But we were here.

<hr />

You both just woke up from a nap while I told you this. First you, Kaz. And now you, Irenna. I was done anyway. I got to the part of your arriving. It's your story now.

July 11, 2017
Audio Journal | Twelve-and-a-Half Months Old

Motherfucker.

I'm leaning over the plane's fold-out bassinet, which is rated to twenty-two pounds against my 22.8-pound boy. I'm adding my weight to it as well by using it for support as I drape and dangle my breast above Kaz for him to nurse. We are hurtling through the air, somewhere over the Atlantic, and my shirt is hiked up to my armpits. My jeans have stretched out and slid down, exposing part of my ass to anyone who wants to see it.

And for what? For why? For me to have the life I want in concept. But if this is reality?

Kaz had a fever for fifty-two hours coming into this trip: 103.3, 102.3, 100.8, and finally 99 three hours before we left the house. We survived driving the van to the bus terminal, riding the bus, navigating the airport, and getting to the plane. Or *almost* to the plane. The flight was grounded because of weather in Boston. You ate puffs off the airport floor while we waited.

Fly to Geneva, find the shuttle, take the shuttle, get to Dad, who is already in Europe guiding in Italy. Break it down, I kept telling myself—just as I used to when I ran to train for volleyball and track in high school and made my way around the lakes. *Past Jonny's house. Past Anna's. Keep going.*

—⁓—

I have spent twenty years refining my system of international travel, devising a set of tricks that I now realize are wholly irrelevant when you're with your twins.

When to take an Ambien. Not an option.

How to sleep sitting up. Not an option when your kids are definitely going to roll off the seat if you take your eyes off them.

How to go to the bathroom. Also surprisingly irrelevant when you can't leave your kids unattended anyway and have to come up with a whole new system.

Regardless, fifteen hours after leaving our house, we're driving up the Arve Valley to Chamonix. Memories of previous journeys to this region are washing over me while you finally sleep. Corsica, the Verdon Gorge, Chamonix . . .

Oh, how I have been craving the high of stale, recirculated airplane air, being locked in an aluminum tube with 147 strangers, the rush of a foreign landscape upon arrival, and the pride I feel vaulting myself into each new experience.

I used to be so proud of myself for it all, almost as if I had been the one flying the plane. Taking the leap to go seemed almost as important. The reward is to be somewhere for the very first time, making sense of whatever I could—a word I recognized, the name of a shop, the road sign for merging, a donkey, a lake. This I know; this is new. It makes me feel alive.

So that is why, less than two hours after getting off the plane, I am already starting to think it's worth it. But maybe it's also because you're both asleep in your car seats as we speed along the highway in the Chamonix shuttle and because I have no one pulling my hair right now.

Sunshine and a mountain landscape do wonders.

We keep winding our way toward Chamonix. I see the Dru, the Aiguilles, and Mont Blanc, and I am filled with the knowledge that I know where I am. Every mile—kilometer—that passes fuses me with my former self—my *current self,* dammit—sandwiched between Kaz on my left, Irenna on my right, and Florencia in the back row of the van behind me.

July 15, 2017
Audio Journal | Twelve-and-a-Half Months Old

Today I walked past the restaurant on rue du Docteur Paccard with the wicker and rattan chairs where I announced that I wanted babies. Back when I was overcooked on traveling back and forth to Africa and my climbing time was so precious to me. And then I suddenly could not function as a climber because of a hole in my toe and promptly went into a tailspin of climbing angst. How silly, how stupid, how shortsighted I'd been.

And now, it's two years later, and I am here in Chamonix with twins. Dodging tourists and climbers clad in boots and lime-green long underwear as I weave my double stroller along the cobblestone streets. "I am one of you," I want to announce to the climbers I navigate around, but they don't even give me a passing glance.

Was I that standoffish? Maybe I was worse. I feel so removed from that life where the next vertical objective was everything. And yet I'm still so hypercompetitive—despite my protestations that I'm not—and desirous of being in that life with that focus that it hurts.

Tonight, Peter, Silas, and I sit around the table playing pass-a-twin between our laps while we finish dinner and plan the next few days of climbing.

"Do you want to go tomorrow, or should I?" Peter asks me.

"Come on, Majka—it will be great," Silas says. "It's the perfect day for a big, long, proper route in the mountains." Silas knows this is exactly what I have been craving. He is game to team up with either of us even though he's Peter's longer-term climbing partner.

Irenna nose-dives into my armpit. Kaz, bouncing on Peter's knee, sees her from across the table and tries to project himself toward me to do the same—narrowly missing the table with his head. Peter scoops him up and deposits him on me directly.

"Climbing," I say to the twins. "Can you say *climbing*?"

Irenna pushes her face further into my side. Kaz grabs a gnocchi off my plate, then cones his fingers as a sign for more.

"What time would we have to leave?" I ask, even though I already know the answer.

"Five in the morning," Silas says.

It's 7:45 P.M. now. I do the math and come up with my having had a total of ten hours of sleep over the past three nights. Tonight, if I am lucky and with that early wakeup, I might get five hours. *Might*.

"I want to, but I can't," I say. "I shouldn't."

Silas turns to Peter. "Five?"

"Done," Peter says.

———

Ninety minutes later Irenna is fast asleep, Kaz is up crying for the third time this evening, and Peter is packing. I swoop Kaz out of his French travel crib and shield his eyes from the lights from town that illuminate our rental. I take him into the windowless water closet to see if I can get him to sleep there.

I sit on the toilet with him in my arms, nursing and rocking and singing. I listen to Peter racking the climbing gear for tomorrow, the metal clinking. Our gear. My gear—all those carabiners are mine, from an equipment sponsor.

My legs fall asleep from the toilet seat pressing into my hamstrings. I wait it out all the same, and by the time I slip Kaz back into his crib, Peter is in bed.

"If you have to leave gear tomorrow, you have to replace it," I say as I lift the duvet up and crawl into bed.

"What?" Peter asks.

"It's mine," I say.

"I thought you wanted me to go climbing," he says.

"I knew I wasn't supposed to go climbing," I say. "That is different." Peter doesn't respond.

"You can't just wear out my things while I am sustaining your children," I go on. "That's not the way this is going to work."

I wait. Then I realize he is sleeping. Something I cannot seem to do right now.

———

Mad. I practice saying it in my head over and over. *I am mad.*

I also know that in my exhausted state it's not safe for me to climb a huge route tomorrow. The way to get our kids ready for me to be gone all day on long climbs is not by taking off for fourteen hours tomorrow when we're all still cranky and travel weary. It's just not time yet. *Yet. At all? Ever? For now?*

I don't expect this to be easy. I do expect grace. At least some. At least some moments when everything feels even and on course—moments of equilibrium.

July 17, 2017
Audio Journal | Twelve-and-a-Half Months Old

It's eleven thirty P.M. Our sixth night in France. And Kaz still can't settle.

Actually it's only 10:53 P.M., but he's been crying for sixty-five minutes and I feel broken. I'm responsible for his tears because we foisted this trip on our good sleeper. We took something that had finally worked and turned it ninety degrees in the form of a six-hour time change.

I lie in bed listening to him cry and think of all the things we will not be going to because of our sleep routine. Barbecues, late-night dinners that start at six, sunset hikes across the Brévent.

I lie in the dark, the glow of my phone illuminating a little pocket around me. I Google "cry it out maximum time" and come across article threads about reduced brain development.

Sixty-seven minutes.

I read about the woman who sleep-trained her baby in one night and never had to do it again. I'm happy for that woman. Maybe. But my reality is that it's a readjustment every time Kaz gets sick, he needs me, or we travel.

No one told me just how much it hurts. To make a minute-by-minute decision to not go and help your child. I've felt like puking the whole time, and then the real clincher is that there comes a point at which you can't turn back, when you know that the heartbreak you've just endured has to keep carrying you forward to the other side. Because if you go get him now, everything you've done is for naught.

Seventy minutes.

If you're going through hell, keep going. But that's also not easy if there is a poop or a tooth or a sad boy.

Seventy-two minutes.

Quiet maybe?

Seventy-three minutes—not yet.

The whole goal is for us both to sleep—so I can be the mom he and his sister need during the day.

That is what I wish someone had told me: that sleep-training would mean seventy-four minutes of crying.

Seventy-five.

Maybe not.

July 20, 2017
Audio Journal | Twelve-and-a-Half Months Old

I'm climbing cracks on the Aiguille de Blaitière. The spire's namesake glacier cleaves and crashes off my right shoulder, thundering down rock and ice while I jam hands and feet in the fissures to go up. I started today's climb with my mitts frozen stiff by the alpine air, confirming I was on the handholds via sight versus feeling the granite and knowing I was secure. After that rocky start, the second lead felt more like me—climbing, moving, venturing up, stretching out the rope between pieces of protection, making moves that were hard enough to demand my full attention.

Maybe this is why we like climbing so much—why *I* always have: because in the moment of fighting with a wide crack, it's the only thing on my mind. I shove my knee into the offwidth and smile when it holds me just long enough that I can move my arms higher. I feel the rawness of the climbing and the power of my body—as me. I feel it all the way until I stop climbing and belay Peter up, when the power

I feel is displaced by contemplation. When I start to think of you and Florencia four thousand feet below in town, all I can feel now is selfish.

When I ask Peter if he feels the same, he shrugs in response. I ask him this while I use a hand pump to harvest milk for you—I cannot escape my biological purpose for very long these days.

We're perched on a two-foot-wide ledge hip-to-hip to fit together, with a thousand feet of rock below us rearing over another thousand feet of dirt-strewn glacial snow. While I pump, Peter alternates feeding me bits of a salami-and-pickle baguette and taking bites for himself. We've done the same with different sandwich ingredients all around the world. Since you two arrived we've had fewer of these moments, but we've had them all the same. It's unspoken that we use a portion of our childcare time for this, and at home we text each other to find four-hour chunks of time to go play together. Today we're on France time with a full nine-hour window and more granite than we could ever get to.

Part of me wants to go back home to you early. Instead, we finish the sandwich, tuck my pump and your milk into the backpack, and keep going.

July 23, 2017
Letter | Twelve-and-a-Half Months Old

I'm lying when I tell you I took this trip only for the climbing. I also wanted to be closer to Mozambique. I rationalized that two weeks of sharing a time zone with the continent would make for a practical work solution and offset some of the insanity.

Our Namuli team is growing—tripling our field team, bringing women and other new hires on board, buying motorbikes to access the mountain, and setting up to interview more communities on the back of the mountain. All of a sudden, the traction is immense. But of course it's not all of a sudden. It's taken three years. I feel so close and yet so far away from it.

I write emails to contacts in Maputo: "Yes, I am still not there, but I will be there next August." I type those words out and then erase them, worried that my certainty about the future will serve only to make my absence look even more pronounced.

July 26, 2017
Audio Journal | Twelve-and-a-Half Months Old

Today's shining moment was lying on the floor of the plane with my head next to the bathroom as you, Kaz, nursed yourself to sleep. My left arm was numb, and I breathed through my mouth to avoid the smells. I winced every time someone clicked the door on their way in or out.

Before you, I had a system for these trips. I had my neck pillow, eye mask, earplugs, noise-canceling headphones, Ambien, a footrest, water bottles, and a special meal. Twenty years of flying had finally culminated in airline frequent-flyer status and know-how. But both have been eclipsed by the more immediate task of holding forty-two pounds of baby in individually perfect sleeping positions at the same time.

———

We are in the car heading north to New Hampshire from the Boston, Massachusetts, airport. It's hour eighteen of our journey home from France. You've finally fallen asleep, your dad is at the wheel, and we are still three hours from home.

This is when I tell you I won't do this to us again. I will not take you two, freshly learning to walk, into an institutionalized, confined tube flying across the Atlantic Ocean ever again. But of course I won't—because we will never be in this same position together. You are changing every day.

I'm not convinced trips like this are the way to family happiness—or individual happiness, for that matter. Will you even remember France? How you ate croissants and raspberries in the shade of the Alps? My parent-friends who are further along the journey tell me this will make you better travelers later. But I suspect this is a trick we play on ourselves to justify what we want versus what you need. You're resilient. Clearly more so than me.

August 9, 2017
From the Notepad | Thirteen-and-a-Half Months Old

Eric is leaving Legado. I'm at the ranch in Montana, he's in Mozambique—and he will not be there for much longer.

I beg off of Skype, claiming a bad connection before he and my friend turned colleague Elizabeth can see me go to pieces.

He has a right to move on.

It's not about him.

I pull up a new window and search for tickets to Nampula, Mozambique, before I even admit I'm doing it. Because—why? I'm going there?

I would have before.

Before what?

My family.

I would have fixed it myself. Stepped onto a plane. Changed the course of my life to save this. It is what I have always done with Legado.

Now, though, I have to find another way.

August 13, 2017
Audio Journal | Thirteen-and-a-Half Months Old

Chamonix was one thing. Going to Patagonia this winter is another.

"I'm out," I told Peter last night.

"Maybe when you're done nursing," he said.

"Maybe," I said.

The last climb I did in Patagonia was our ascent of Fitz Roy ten months before I was pregnant. The whole route took sixty hours, basecamp to basecamp. The plan for me, Peter, and Gilbert was to do it more quickly, but a meter of freshly fallen snow changed that plan overnight. The Supercanaleta is supposed to be a three-thousand-foot moderate ice climb followed by fifteen pitches of brilliant, dry rock climbing. The three of us wanted it badly enough and knew it was safe enough to do in poor conditions anyway. We spent our first night at the base of the route and the second huddled together on a three-quarter-length sleeping pad just below the summit.

And while I remember every hour of our ascent, these days my memory gets stuck on replay for the one hour I spent on the route with the speed climber Chad Kellogg's body dangling directly above me. He'd been killed by rockfall while descending Supercanaleta eleven months before we climbed it. We knew there was a chance we'd see Chad's body, left there because logistical and safety complications had, thus far, made it too hard to bring him down, but when I took over to go first on the last thousand feet of ice climbing, it never occurred to me that I'd climb until I could see his corpse frozen into a position no living human could ever maintain.

The early-morning light felt as brilliant as the climbing that morning on the Supercanaleta. I belayed Gilbert and Peter to me and focused on looking down, at where we'd come from, instead of up to where Chad's remains served as a constant reminder of how he never came home from his climb of the same mountain, killed by an errant rock dislodged by the rappel ropes.

Peter, Gilbert, and I didn't mention Chad or his body to each other that day. Instead we shielded our eyes and stared at anything but a destiny we firmly were trying to fight and forget.

Today is no different, and I don't bring up Chad when your dad mentions Patagonia. Not now.

Will I feel differently about going back when I am not nursing, when you are four years old, or ever? Should I?

....

August 29, 2017
Audio Journal | Fourteen Months Old

It's 4:10 in the afternoon, and though I have childcare and time before dinner, I can't figure out what to do, so I settle for a hike. I am going on my eighth week of waking up in the middle of the night with Kaz, first for his fever, then for France, then for the post-France payback. Then for Montana, a cold, his teeth, and him. I don't feel whole in any aspect of my life. Meanwhile, I am trying to jump into the running of Legado and be present as the leader of our team. It's getting harder rather than easier to pull this off. I hike and breathe and slam my pole into the ground as I go uphill. Maybe it's time to be done. Maybe this is not worth it, realistic, for my life.

A bumpy red-and-gray frog jumps across the trail. The size of my big toe. It hops onto a downed pine branch, and I stop and watch. *Fucking frogs,* I think. *They suck me in every time.*

I'm not supposed to be pushing paper. My work in the world was never supposed to only be about emails and proposals and reports. So why am I limiting myself? Why is this the work I am doing? I see it in that moment: that I've cut myself off from anything that feeds me.

In three weeks my whole team will get together in Gurúè, Mozambique, for a twelve-day training on how to inspire people to change their behavior with the organization Rare, a leader in the field of behavioral science. I want to be there with them. I do the math, count the days. Can I get to Namuli and back in six days? I suspend reality for ten minutes to plan it as if yes is the answer. I miss seeing this mountain, having context, having access to people and hearing them. I am relying on secondhand and thirdhand details; I am becoming an administrator. But I am not an administrator.

Elizabeth told me about twin baby gorillas in the Congo—one of three sets ever documented. A mother gorilla takes her babies at three hours old into a tree, using one arm to climb, one arm to hold a single baby. "How does she do it with two?" I asked Elizabeth, but she said none of the scientists knew. No one had seen her climb with them both. What they do know is that twin gorillas are thriving.

September 9, 2017
Audio Journal | Fourteen-and-a-Half Months Old

Today I'm flying away from you. I'm going to California to meet the Patagonia athlete crew and be part of a climbing-advocacy summit. I'm putting thirty-five hundred miles and four days between us when we've never spent more than ten hours apart. And while I conceptually know it's all okay, I'm mortified that this is happening.

—⁓—

You started walking. Kaz went first—big and brash with booms galore. Irenna, you started a month later with precision and persuasion. Teeth are crashing through your pink gums, and syllables are spinning out of your lips to form words against the new white orbs.

I write with my head and my heart upside down. Right now I don't want to be away from you, but I am afraid that I'll turn into slush if I don't start grabbing these opportunities I used to be drowning in. I want to do this all. And I want it all to feel good and right. I want to make the correct decision in the moment that's good for the moment *and* for the long haul.

Sometimes I work above you, hear your squeaks, and want to be with you. Or we are at the park and I check my email because I need to work . . . that's bullshit . . . because I *want* to work. I want to have that relevance. I want to be wholly in either place, but I'm forever split.

———

You're fourteen and a half months old. I'm nursing you six to eight times a day. It's the best and most favorite thing I do in my world. So now I fly with a suitcase of ice that's packed into plastic bags and Styrofoam to carry my milk back to you. Who knew this would be the thing I hold onto the hardest?

I didn't birth you. I will let that sentence stand. I'm supposed to correct it—contextualize it. You came into the world through a slice into my belly, and nursing gives me back that connection. Nursing repairs it—every time.

I love you so much it hurts. My mother took only weeks off work, stopped nursing me early, and left for work every day. I am lucky for her sacrifice and what it enabled in my life. And I am haunted by it.

Do this right.

Do this well.

Make it count.

··

September 9, 2017
Audio Journal | Fourteen-and-a-Half Months Old

Day 1 in California

I'm sitting in the hotel room in Oakland, shared with my friend Kate, getting ready for the DACA march. I'm know I'm technically here as a climber—for that Patagonia athlete meeting—but I saw a flier for the DACA march and needed to go be with people—not just climber-people—for one hour today.

I've been away from you for thirty-three hours. *Is this worth it?*

I can't catch my breath once I have had that thought.

I've also realized that I've stopped washing my face. My bags are full of milk and my first pair of Spanx, and when I joined the group of other climbers in the hotel conference room two hours ago what I wanted to talk most about was how each parent in the room survives their own personal vortex of climbing, parenting, childcare, and partnership, not what their next big trip will be. This is in part because my ego can't handle the climbing-trips conversation yet; it's too daunting. The DACA march sounds better.

September 9, 2017
Audio Journal | Fourteen-and-a-Half Months Old

Day 2

I spend my free time at breakfast checking in with my coathletes who don't have kids, Brittany and Kate. Brittany won't; Kate not yet or not at all. Tommy, Josh, Dylan, Steve, and others have kids of varying ages.

At lunch, Josh, Dylan, and I sit eating pizza in the Dogpatch neighborhood after a session at the bouldering gym where I did rehab in the back forty because my abs are still not knit together enough to climb anything steep or jump off high things.

We talk about climbing plans, our Treadwalls. Josh tells me that on the weekends he goes climbing and has a "dad day" on Wednesday.

"What's a dad day?" I ask.

"A day with just me and my girl," he says.

I want to ask if all the other days are "mom days," but I don't. I am trying to fit in.

Being a dad, Josh says, is working out for him since he can still work on his climbing projects. Dylan agrees.

"Peter and I are still trying to figure this out," I say.

They nod.

"Except," I add, "we both are trying to climb."

Josh and Dylan are quiet for a moment.

"I dated a climber once," Josh said. "It didn't pan out—too hard for us both to want it."

I laugh painfully. "Right? Can anyone think of examples of both members of a couple getting after it, and doing so after kids?"

Dylan brings up Chad and Lara. "But don't be like them," he says.

"Did they fight about it all the time?" I ask.

"Yeah," he says. "But I meant don't end up like them—dead."

I think of Chad's body, hanging two rope lengths of rock and ice above me on Fitz Roy. In my mind he had blue and yellow on, but really I can't remember. My friend Bernd joined two other climbers, Jess and Ben, earlier this year to honor Chad by taking his broken body from the bottom of the icy sluice of the Supercaneleta, where it had fallen after another climbing party detached it from the ice above, and moving it to its final resting place on a nearby ridge.

I think of Lara rappelling off the ends of her ropes on Mount Wake seven years before Chad left the world. When she died, I mourned her as a contemporary but not a friend.

I think of how they did not have kids. But over pizza today, none of those distinctions matter.

—⁓—

Two winters ago, when I was barely five weeks pregnant and sitting on that athlete panel at the Banff Centre Mountain Film Festival, the panel moderator and climbing journalist Ed Douglas asked Tommy

Caldwell and Sonnie Trotter what it was like to bring kids along on
their adventures. And then he asked them what they thought about
pushing new limits with children. All I wanted was to stand up and
say they were great and awesome dads, but that the question was
unfairly biased for only being posed to them.

I have even more to add now. *Don't ask them,* I'd say. *Ask a woman
who gave her body over to pregnancy, who still has a fissure four fingers wide
in her abdominal wall, who nurses and* then *comes back to climbing. Ask
her about pushing limits.*

Ask her; find her. I want to hear her answer too.

September 19, 2017
Audio Journal | Fourteen-and-a-Half Months Old

Yesterday, while climbing back at home, my partner for the day, Brian,
asked me what I wanted to be when I grew up.

"I want to do this," I said. And by this I meant climbing and
motherhood and all of it. But especially, I want to be the best at
being your mom.

Will everything else magically fall in line? If I give everything
else one hundred percent too, is that a recalibrated one hundred
percent? So that "all" means something new and possible for each
pursuit? I feel like I am in a macroeconomics course at McCosh
Hall at Princeton, trying to fit this into a logical model when there
really is none.

Today, my young climber friend Michael drove past as I pushed forty-
eight pounds of you, plus the mail, plus a stroller full of apples and
water bottles uphill to our house.

"Aren't you supposed to be a mountain climber?" he said.

"You're looking at just that," I told him.

"Your hands sure are full," he replied.

Everyone tells me this.

They've never not been.

....

September 25, 2017
Audio Journal | Fourteen-and-a-Half Months Old

Today starts at 5:53 A.M. because I can't wait any longer through the crying. The idea that sleep-training is something that happens once is a total fallacy. I'm barely down the hall and nursing both of you when Peter tells me he wants to talk about two things before he leaves. In three hours he's due to walk out the door for fourteen days of work in Arizona, followed by twenty-seven days of work with three days off at home, followed by eight days of work in Germany. And now he proclaims that he wants to climb in the Alps for a week after Germany *in addition* to a three-week personal climbing trip in Patagonia after he guides in Frey for the eight days following Christmas.

I chase Kaz around the room. He likes to hide by Irenna's crib in the triangle sliver it forms with the oblique outside wall of their room. He's naked, and usually if he stays that way for more than a minute in the morning, we're cleaning up pee for the next quarter hour and smelling it for days. I chase him down, he squeals with delight, and I wrestle a diaper onto him. Then I ask Peter if he really thinks this is the best time to talk about this.

For two people who have talked about logistics and climbing for almost ten years together, we have not yet sorted how we're going to handle what used to be a normal—and not emotinally charged—discussion in this new version of our life together.

When I was pregnant and Peter went to Patagonia for three and a half weeks, I told him I wanted that time in credit for when I needed it. I'm still not clear if we ever confirmed that, but in my head it's there—plus for all of the quick two-day trips he's made since. At Peter's current rate, I'll have three months of personal climbing trips saved up by the time I'm actually able to use them.

When we first met I liked that I was a stronger and bolder rock climber than Peter. I especially liked it when I saw how he could blow me out of the water on ice. Now I'm nearly fifteen months of kids and nine months of pregnancy behind. And that is how it feels. Like I got pinned in place and then lost ground.

I know I'm conflating it all—my wanting to be him, to walk away so easily. But I can't go on a multi-week climbing trip right now, even if I wanted to.

—⁓—

My mom is in town on an impromptu visit—just her style. I last twenty minutes after Peter leaves for Arizona before telling her about the conversation.

"What are you going to do?" she asks.

"I just wish he hadn't asked," I say. "Or that he'd warmed me up by first telling me how grateful he was for what I was about to undertake."

If I could write Peter's script, I think, *we'd get along so much better.*

"You can't accrue the days, Majka," she says. "That doesn't seem right."

My mom, one of the most competitive, successful, and forceful women I know, is telling me to stand down.

"You are doing what you want," she goes on to say. "You're home being a mom and working, putting it together in a way that feels good. If you're storing up days for later, that's not right."

I don't know what I'm doing. This is my choice insofar as I don't want to take off for weeks at a time right now, but it's not as clear a choice as having beef or turkey on your sandwich. It's not an option for me to leave for multiple weeks right now anyway. Not with our childcare, two kids, my nursing, or my way of being a mom. I don't want to be punished for my approach in my marriage, in my partnership, in the world.

And I don't want to punish myself by sabotaging my happiness or Peter's and my togetherness.

Later, I cook toddler and grown-up tacos for dinner and wonder if I should have done things differently. Maybe I should have stayed on the mountain-guide career track myself. Then I too would have a schedule full of work trips to cool places. But how would that help us? It would just mean Peter having to watch the kids while I worked or us having to spend more on childcare while we were both out guiding—and thus less money and more stress overall. I never knew I was building this other career to account for motherhood, but it sure works better for that than being a full-time guide.

I just can't seem to wrap my head around Peter still being a full-time guide, even though we never talked about another option. I concede that. I am trying to support him as his career grows, even if that means more travel. However, what I can't, and won't, roll over on is his seemingly incessant desire to tack on time away. His personal climbing is what niggles at my brain and my soul. And I know, personally, that guiding is not climbing, and that we mountain guides face an eternal struggle between having enough energy to work in the mountains but also stay fit and sane for our own personal climbing—the thing that brought us to this world in the first place. But still. Am I envious of him or enraged by him? Can I be both, while staying content and sure that my decision to be with you is the correct one right now?

How can Peter and I navigate his side and my side of this but still end up in the same place as a family?

September 30, 2017
Audio Journal | Fifteen Months Old

At 9:35 A.M., after thirty-two minutes of his crying, I can't take it anymore. I pull Kaz from his crib, and we lie down on the couch. We stack together, his head on my arm, my chin on his cheek, and he settles. Each time I try to pull away he wakes and cries until I let him nurse again.

I lie there, missing a meeting with our lawyer to finalize our will and have a plan for what happens if . . . what would happen next.

Instead I lie here, my phone far away, trying to listen in case Irenna needs me at the other end of the house. I oscillate between breathing in the sweetness of my little boy and the warmth and perfection of his body coiled toward mine, and thinking of what I could be accomplishing with this time and how behind I will be because of it.

My phone, my work, my ability to say yes or no, is in the other room. In this moment, I am only Kaz's mom.

October 2, 2017
Letter | Fifteen Months Old

Today, we switch you two to one nap—something that feels like the largest project I have ever undertaken, even though it will likely be something I cannot remember one day.

Irenna, you want to sleep; Kaz, you do not. I've been forced to make a choice that is better for one child and worse for the other. This likely won't be the last time.

While everyone is discontent, I get an email with a link to a new song about Mount Namuli written and performed by our team in

Mozambique. I press play on my computer and listen to this lyrical beat masterpiece and start sobbing. Partly because I am proud of what I have helped accomplish, and partly because I am envious of my team, who get to be there doing the thing while I'm still here in New Hampshire.

———

Today, you wore mittens for the first time, looking at your patterned hands quizzically as if I'd removed them instead of covered them. Yesterday a frost blanketed our high hummocks, while the garden hollows were spared. This morning, as we played outside, only your cheeks were visible—still plenty for me to kiss.

I am overcome with love for you. It washes over me in great waves, and I cry with it. Maybe this is why I pushed myself over the edge to get to you. Because this is what I receive in return.

October 10, 2017
Audio Journal | Fifteen-and-a-Half Months Old

My phone pings. The preview on my lock screen shows it's my dad. And a quick glance across the message tells me I don't want to read it.

"Do you feel threatened?" I ask Peter. "Because I do."

My father is asking me to talk about the young alpinist Hayden Kennedy's death. Today, news tore through the climbing community and rippled through the mainstream media that Hayden had taken his own life two days earlier. Some time before that, he and his partner, Inge, had triggered an avalanche in the mountains of Montana that had buried and killed Inge. Hayden had searched for her in the snow for hours, but to no avail.

What are you supposed to say? What am I? What is anybody?

It's as if we're afraid we will jinx ourselves and our partners, so instead we barely touch the subject or the specifics of our friends' deaths. We celebrate life instead of mourning the loss. But what if we've missed something? Passed it up? Part of me feels like I've failed—we've failed—Hayden.

To me, Hayden was human to be that sad inside an unfathomable situation. I hadn't seen that in him the last time we'd climbed together, three years ago. Now, never again.

I'm filled with an acute rush of anger at Peter because of the situation his job and passion put us in, even while being aware that his ability to evaluate risks and pivot around them is better than anyone's I know. In this moment, it's the fact that he still climbs that is the problem, and I want to use Hayden's and Inge's deaths as a way to get him to question how or why or if he even should. I know my dad also wants to talk about their deaths because he hopes they will get me to reconsider my lifestyle as a climber too. Yet I refuse both conversations. They are not the way to get Peter or me to stop or modify our climbing.

I know that if you keep making the decision to climb, you will eventually find yourself in that same environment and situation—not clipped in on a descent in the Tetons and slipping off a ledge, skinning in to climb with a loaded couloir above you, stacking rappels against exhaustion and a ticking clock.

Not me not us not this time, we say. And then we get away with it.

Hayden couldn't take the grief anymore of any of us dying—even at age twenty-seven he'd already lost too many friends in the mountains. And then he lost Inge before his very eyes.

My phone lights up again; this time my dad is calling. I ignore him. I looked to Hayden's parents, Michael and Julie, as leaders for how they raised this big, bold, beautiful boy into a man. All of us in the climbing community did. They were evidence of what was possible. *We are climbers, so we can do this too.*

What have we been missing?

October 13, 2017
Audio Journal | Fifteen-and-a-Half Months Old

The shuttle I am riding pulls onto campus, and I look up from my book the minute we cross into the sea of beauty and green. The Princeton boathouse, Terrace Club, Woody Woo. All these places I know but don't know.

I didn't ever really want to be here, I think about my alma mater. But then, I don't know if that is true. I don't know what is true today.

I have hours before my speech, and I walk campus like I am wiggling a tooth to make it hurt and feel good at the same time. With every step, memories come back: walking into the anthropology department at Aaron Burr Hall and asking Professor Hildred Geertz if I could study on my own in Nepal; and then, upon my return, seeing the manila envelopes, unopened on her desk, stuffed with mimeographed copies of my field notes. Whenever I have thought about anthropology since then, I can almost taste and smell the dust and oldness of that office.

I remember getting into a four-hundred-level course my first semester at college and using that as a measurement for myself—if something was difficult, and I could pull it off, it meant that I must have wanted it and that it was right for me.

⁓

Does anyone understand what college was to them twenty years later? Does everyone cry when they return? I stuffed this place in a small box so far away from myself when I took a year off that when I came back, I could not figure out how to fit in or what to do. I left to climb first, and then in the process of following climbing around the world I met someone—Eddie—I wanted to share my heart with as I chased after the vertical. So when I came back to these hallowed halls, which never felt like mine, and tried to stuff myself, bursting and new, back into the mold, it felt impossible. I remember being happy and settled in myself . . . until I returned to Princeton.

I wish I could go tell that young woman . . .

What, what would I tell her? Tell *me*? That this would be my life? That I will always push and grab and stack things together that don't appear to fit or even be related?

Now here I am at forty-one, with fifteen-month-old twins at home, breasts aching, tears streaming down my face in a hotel room, calling to say hello to the psychologist I saw when I was in school here.

"Hi, Dr. Lindman," I say on the message with too much cheer. "It's Majka Burhardt. It's been such a long time. Anyways, I am in Princeton of all things and thought, hey, maybe you're still around. It would be fun to say hello."

I hang up and lie on the floor of the dark room and practice breathing, but the tears roll sideways from the corners of my eyes instead of down my face.

My phone beeps with a text, and I sit up. It's Dr. Lindman: *I would love to talk to you—but I'm in Florida now. Send me some times and we can talk on Skype.*

I take a breath and let the tears come unabated. I ache. I cannot stop thinking about Hayden. Yesterday on the way to the Portland airport, I talked to Kate. She was driving to Hayden's memorial.

"Are you coming out?" she asked.

I drove loops in the parking garage searching for a spot. I thought about changing my ticket from Newark to Denver, driving west through the Rockies to Carbondale, where Hayden's parents live. "I can't," I say. "I can only be gone until tomorrow."

"I'd love to see you," she said.

"Maybe . . ." *When can I see everyone, really?* I think. "Another time," I say.

Maybe I should have tried to go to Colorado. Maybe I should have let myself. Because now I am alone in this wood-paneled hotel that smells like old, moneyed privilege, and I can't stop sobbing.

We failed Hayden as a climbing community—and as a human community—when we didn't give him the tools to properly navigate this loss that is the all-too-often-ignored dark side of our endless thirst for adventure. How do you make sense of losing so many people you love—people you know, people who are identical to you in your pursuit?

I feel so confronted by this. I know it's because I have Irenna and Kaz and Peter, and each of them adds to the unknown of my actions and his and theirs. And together this is our life. We're that ever-adjusting and-collapsing wooden figurine that stands upright until you toggle its base and the string and hinges all flex and together make the little figure buckle and wobble, until you let it be.

I feel vulnerable to the world—vulnerable to all the loss and death. To see the real cost of the climbing life—Hayden committing suicide because he was not able to bear the grief anymore—makes me understand how you could simply decide you've had enough.

I stand up. I check my calendar and write Dr. Lindman back. *The eighteenth or twentieth at three p.m.?*

I start the shower. It's time to pull myself together. The people who are coming tonight have signed up to hear a professional climber tell a good story. So right now, that's who I have to be.

December 1, 2017
Letter | Seventeen Months Old

Dear Kaz and Irenna,

It's not you I want to write to. It's your dad. Or maybe it's your dad and me. Or maybe it's all of us.

I'm mad. And it's not that I don't want to be with you—because I do want to be with you. And I also want to feel freer. To have time. To not feel like I must choose every day to cross items off our never-ending to-do list or risk being crushed by the demands of our busy life.

Elizabeth tells me it's a lost cause to try to change someone else's behavior. So what can you change then?

———

If I write you this letter, dear husband, will it help us? Or will it hurt us? I feel like I am choosing to disrupt us now in the hopes it will make us healthy in the long term. One month ago you fell climbing. Mistook a foothold, slipped from a handhold, fell (only) ten feet, and landed on your side below a mere periphery of cliff you'd been using to teach clients. You stood in front of the sink with a gouged hand full of mud and pebbles, and we both knew the right next step was to dig it all out. To agitate the wound, to debride it, bracing for more pain before healing. It's no different with our collective heart.

Everywhere around me marriages are breaking up. People are getting past the furthest point of possible return. I don't want to get there. I've been there.

We don't always talk about my history, the fault lines in my geography that led me here.

I know what it's like to finally find the person who will listen to you and validate you. To lean into them and see them lean into you. To have them listen. To have them share. I want to be that person with you, and when I ended my marriage twelve years ago, I promised I'd never marry again without having that ballast.

And here we are. Ten years into knowing each other, on the precipice of leaning away. And my bringing up what's hard seems to push us farther apart.

———

There is goodness here too. It happens when we swap "craziest twin" stories while we're driving or hiking together. It happens when we make love. It happens when we both slow down enough to stop and see what we've created—like when we're with your parents at their house up at the lake and our eyes meet across our babies' twin heads as they sort puzzles with Grandpa or make custard with Grandma. But the bad will eat this goodness for breakfast.

What am I angry about? I'm angry that I have found myself here—that I am an educated, world-wise, divorced, therapied woman who is working full-time while also doing the lion's share of the housework, the mental work, and the childcare. This alternative life-style we have kidded ourselves that we are creating? There is nothing alternative about this division of labor. Perhaps it's so shocking because I'd prided myself on being different—living by and making different rules, building a straw-bale house and having a non-traditional career of climbing and writing and traveling. But our current domestic scene feels so damn normal it pisses me off.

I don't want to have dinner with my female friends and colleagues only to discuss tips for doing laundry. I want us to admit that we all read that trending article on rage and that we feel it too.

Right now I feel less like a climber than I have in years. Because while it is December 1 and the ice has come in in New Hampshire, I am not climbing it. I am not even making plans to climb it. Because right now our childcare went belly up and our kids need me (or you) around more than I need to climb. And that makes me know I'm a good mother, but makes me feel like a fake as a climber.

"Well I know the solution," my sister says.

"Really?" I say.

"It's time to get another job. You've had your go at doing it differently."

I abruptly tell her I have to go, and hang up not much later.

The hardest time to do what's right for you is when it seems wrong.

Maybe if I pretend Peter is someone else I could actually tell him what's wrong. He can be my Polish Peter—"Piotr"—instead.

Dear Piotr,

    I'm married to a good man. I am a good woman. But we're not having a good time.

December 4, 2017
Audio Journal | Seventeen Months Old

I am hiking straight uphill on this trail right now. I need to sweat because I'm so damn angry, and if I don't sweat, I'll scream.

I have been really, really angry and frustrated lately. I've become this person I don't want to be inside of my skin and outwardly to your dad.

I'm angry at what we've done—how we've replicated this massive cycle of inequity between men and women—as if we are cogs in some gender-role machine. I have never wanted to be that. But how much of my anger should be directed at your dad for his part, or at me for my part, or at society?

Every day, I am trying to figure out how to be your mamma and how to be myself. How to be a dedicated mom, the executive director of an international NGO, and an athlete—all at the same time.

And I think that has been my understanding: that if you just push hard enough, you can do it all. Because I have always, mostly, been able to push hard enough and make the really divergent pieces come together in my life. Right now, it's dawning on me that maybe I *could* do it, but there is a cost, and the cost is my rage. This body-shuddering, hands-shaking rage.

I don't want to be that person. I don't want to carry that. I don't want to give you that legacy.

By the time I was seven, I was demanding that people say *humankind* instead of *mankind* and pinching them if they misspoke. I challenged all the boys in sixth grade to push-up contests and won. I asserted I was no different than them. But I can't change the larger story. Today I am bringing up a little boy and a little girl for their first two years amid a political culture dominated by a president who has sexually harassed women again and again. In case after case, episode after episode, moment after moment, men in power reveal how they have so abused their privilege, their access, their control.

It's scary to think about raising you two in this world. I have always thought that I lived a different kind of life and that different rules would apply somehow. I thought that because I wasn't in the corporate world, because I was not wearing nylons, because I did not have business suits, that I wouldn't have to deal with glass ceilings or corporate misogyny and harassment. But the outdoor world has its own heritage of sexism and inappropriate behavior. When I first became a sponsored climber, one of my new athlete managers shot a video of me eating a martini olive off a toothpick and played it on repeat to the whole bar as a joke. And I laughed. I hate writing that here; I am ashamed. When people told me I was doomed as an athlete for being pregnant, I said something neutral like "We'll see" or "That is not my plan," when I should have said their statement was inappropriate and indicative of systemic bias. The unwritten code always seemed to be we were climbers first, business associates second. It's what made us "a climbing tribe."

Of course, we've been naïve to think there was not real work to do to make things better.

How can I acknowledge this and have it fuel me and not destroy me with fury?

December 10, 2017
Audio Journal | Seventeen-and-a-Half Months Old

Yesterday.

I lean back in my ultralightweight harness and feel it hold me—to myself and to the mountain. I debate pulling my pump out of my pack, assembling it, unzipping four layers of clothing, unhooking a nursing bra, and affixing the cold plastic to my breasts. But I decide against it. I watch your dad move deliberately and gently, and note that if a six-two man is moving like he is while ice climbing it means there must be very little ice to speak of up there. I stomp my feet again to warm up and wish I'd built a three-screw anchor instead of a two-screw anchor.

It's my second time ice climbing this season, but since your dad spent last winter in a knee brace, it's our first time out on ice together since we had you. Cannon Mountain sits on top of Highway 93, and I watch a Camry whiz south below me, its inhabitants safe and sound twelve hundred feet lower. They're surely barely aware of the peril above, a boulder field of chaos on a mountain that yearly, even season-ally, delaminates huge chunks of bedrock affixed to a veneer of ice so thin you need to be thankful for the clouds lest the sun melt it away. Up here, tethered to your father, it feels like we could both get pulled from this mountain, from you, from us.

Peter has been on lead for been sixty-five minutes and is halfway up the climb. My hands are cramping. My left foot feels like a block. I shudder, moving my shoulders in and out like a penguin. It's almost one P.M. At home I'd be nursing each of you to sleep, one by one, each with a belly pressed against mine, eyes closed, singing to you as you go down for your nap. I want the warmness of you. I want our connection. Instead I try to shrink smaller in my jacket as freezing water drips onto me from the icicles above.

Last winter, when I ice climbed, your dad was recovering from knee surgery, so I climbed with other partners. I wouldn't subject myself to two-hour belays for anyone else. Because each moment longer is a moment longer away from you. But I'm not sure it helps to think of you, at all, when I'm anchored into two screws on Cannon.

I check my systems. I do it again. I praise auto-locking carabiners in a way I never did before. Your dad stops above. It's my turn now.

I get home to your feet rushing to the door, four arms outstretched, two smiles, fourteen teeth going on sixteen.

Twenty minutes later, at dinner, you protest and only eat blueberries. Each of you. I don't know why as per seventeen-month-old twin logic this is to be my punishment, but I take it, offering you pasta, broccoli, yogurt, and then back to blueberries. I give in to how you reclaim me.

December 22, 2017
Audio Journal | Seventeen-and-a-Half Months Old

I have a fellowship opportunity that will float our team for one year waiting for me, but today I instead spent my best brain time looking at Pinterest pictures of how to organize my pantry.

Legado is about to accomplish a goal we've had since the start—hand our work off to a large conservation organization to take forward. We created the momentum; now they will take Legado into the future. And here I am, with Kevin, the head of a large foundation, asking me to tell him more about how that comes together.

Twenty minutes into our phone call, Kevin says he has to get in his car, but we can keep talking. And then he promptly steps in dog shit and tells me he has to call me back. By the time he does I'm nursing Kaz, but I pretend to be at my desk with all the time in the world.

"We need to know you're all in—you're full-time, you live this, you dream this," says Kevin.

I toggle the phone off mute to answer him. "Absolutely, this is my total priority."

I alternate between muting and talking, and I nurse throughout it all. I thank the universe that Kaz is the longest, quietest nurser I know, as if he's been training for this moment all along.

"Tell me more about how you want to scale," Kevin says.

I lean back on the couch, tuck Kaz's body around me tighter. We sigh together.

I see it all unfold in front of me—securing more partner orga-nizations on Namuli, the fellowship, growing Legado to multiple mountains. Travel between New York, San Francisco, DC, and Mozambique, and then France and Malawi. I know what that will feel like. I have done it before. I have done it by myself. I have done it six months pregnant with twins. It feels electric and self-important. I used to love coming back from travels and stopping at the store for a slice of salmon, a yam, and greens and cooking them when I got home, eating the leftovers the next day, and then getting back on a plane again the next.

<center>~~~</center>

Days later, Peter and I drive up Route 302 to ice climb in Crawford Notch. It's windy, and the trees are snapping and billowing on each side of the two-lane mountain highway. The blacktop is crusted white from a squall, and we are twenty cars deep behind a plow.

"Is that what you want?" Peter asks.

We peer up at the ice at Frankenstein as we drive by. Is Bragg-Pheasant in? Is the tendril of ice on X, Y, and Z formed enough to climb, or is it already too big to be of interest? Peter promises me he can drive and look at climbs at the same time, but I know better. I remind him—the father of my babies and my long-haul mate—to keep his eyes on the road.

I know the life the fellowship would demand, and I cannot imagine having it now. Wait. That is not true. I can. It's just that I wouldn't enjoy it. I don't see any margin there. I want to live on a sailboat with Peter and the twins for a year. I want to canoe the Thelon River in Canada as a family. I want to take off in our camper van with just Peter on two-day climbing trips when the kids and grandparents are ready to be without us that long. I want to be on the Jackson school board. And I want to be a climber who's still a professional athlete. Would the fellowship leave any space for that? Besides, Florencia is back home in Chile, we are patching together childcare with short-term local babysitters and a Montessori program, and it all feels *just* possible.

Can I even afford to say no? Is this the watershed moment in my career when I lean in? *Act as is*, the thirty-four-year-old CEO of another foundation I am trying to woo tells me as unsolicited advice, and I can almost hear his lecherous wink.

Am I all in? I have not called Kevin back about the fellowship in over a week, yet he says he's available anytime. I am all in to my life. To my family. I laugh and tell Peter that this is it, this is the balance piece I am trying to find.

—⁓—

I grew up seeing my mom live in this world of high heels, planes, suits, and electrifying relevance. And there is a part of me that wants that. But dammit, what I want more is to pull everything off. *All* of it.

I will push back to the fellowship organization. I will tell them I don't need to do this 100 percent of my time to be all in. That I am better if I don't.

December 30, 2017
From the Notepad | Eighteen Months Old

It's minus fifteen degrees outside today.

I'm guiding tomorrow.

Peter flew business class to the Canary Islands yesterday for work because his clients bought his ticket.

Irenna just puked all over me.

It's two A.M. and I've already gone through three changes of clothes since I got into bed.

She wants to nurse.

Kaz wants to nurse.

Kaz does a power nurse.

Irenna pukes again.

Kaz spills water.

No one is here but us.

I was ready to tell the fellowship that I'm in the game, and we decided to talk in two weeks.

What game am I in?

January 1, 2018
Audio Journal | Eighteen Months Old

I'm standing in the kitchen scrubbing jam off the underside of the counter, watching my mom play and laugh with you.

I don't remember her as that mother for me. She always did other things.

What will you remember about me? Because I have things to do, always.

My stepdad tells me I have my priorities right. But I'm not sure how to take that from a man who worked his way through his family of six, with a full-time housewife at home minding the kids all the way through their early years.

Mom, who traveled often for work, tells me she respects that I don't want to travel the way I could. But what does that mean?

They both tell me I am doing a great job.

Why? What do they really see? And what do they really know?

January 10, 2018
From the Notepad | Eighteen-and-a-Half Months Old

"Anger is not getting what you want," I write on a Post-it note by my computer while I talk to Dr. Lindman.

"Figure out what I want," I write below. Underlining it, twice.

January 14, 2018
Letter | Eighteen-and-a-Half Months Old

Today, you are eighteen and a half months old. One day I will stop counting the weeks, the half months. But right now you change so quickly that I have to mark them. Maybe all of us change that quickly but we only see it in children, holding adults to a forever inaccurate, static representation of themselves.

We are nursing together. When I hold you close to me, when you are a part of me, I love you so completely. I ache from loving you. I have never known that ache before. It's as if I am being completed and torn apart at the same time.

But there is another side to this love. Another side to being full from you, which is that I don't have space to be full of anything else.

When you, Kaz, cry at night, pulling me from sleep, and then your father emits a single snore, I roughly shake Peter to tell him to stop. I hiss at him. I cannot take one more thing. He does not get any generosity from me, because it's all gone to you. And I know that cannot be sustained.

"I don't know what to do," I say to your dad, swinging my legs over the bed. "I really don't know what to do. If I go get Kaz he will do this again, but he is sad."

There is no formula, no sense. Nobody told me how much you, my boy, would cry and how much each rage-filled scream would tear at my heart, eating its walls and ripping the tissue inside. All that I have left is an open wound, constantly abraded.

———————

There was a rainstorm here for two days straight that dropped three-and-a-half inches of rain. Rivers broke their ice and flooded. Culverts filled and washed. The hospital flooded. And then the cold rushed back in, turning everything into a frozen vertical playground. Climbers, if they paid for much, would pay for this. But I just ignored it—I had to for my sanity. I focused on training a new person to help with you two, and I hoped she would stay long enough for my efforts with her to be worthwhile. Today I taught her how to put on snowshoes so she could play outside with you in the deep snow while I wiped out the trash can and scraped moldy food out of cracks in your toddler counter towers. Meanwhile others sank tools into newly formed ribbons of ephemeral ice.

January 15, 2018
Audio Journal | Eighteen-and-a-Half Months Old

I have a little girl who's sleep-nursing in my arms for the second time in nine months, and then her brother wakes and cries.

All I want to do is give her all of me.

But then what does Kaz get?

———————

January 16, 2018
Audio Journal | Eighteen-and-a-Half Months Old

I just listened to myself, two years ago, predicting what will be hard. So much for saying I made these recordings for you.

In some ways I was dead-on, others dead wrong. It is not even about the work or the climbing; it's about having the bandwidth, energy, and desire to build an unruly and unconventional career above everything else.

There are so many more steps to even return to my *wanting* this career, let alone actually doing it. Will that change? I imagine it will. Perhaps. Maybe when motherhood gets easier it will.

Maybe. This must be why women have to crawl their way back to work. How can you achieve in your career and build tiny humans at the same time? Right now, work seems like yet another thing to do well, and really, I only get two or three things that I can do well. Actually, two things.

Kaz and Irenna are those two things.

Adding more things just so I can do them poorly seems wrong.

January 16, 2018 (later)
Audio Journal | Eighteen-and-a-Half Months Old

Irenna is in a fleece that smells like mildew because I forgot to dry the clothes or clean the washer or wipe it out or something.

She is asleep with my nipple in her mouth. My left side bowed to her like the moon. My leg is numb, my arm is aching and numb, and I am unwilling to shift.

Today, I'm trying to find new childcare, again, and I have a grant report to write. But instead of doing those things, I sink and slither down in the worst posture ever and look out the window at the coming snowstorm. My boy is sleeping by himself, and my girl is sleeping on me. They are yin and yang. At least this time I am pinned down by the lighter one.

"It turns out that you've already gone ahead and done it before you realize you couldn't possibly do it, not in a million years." Anne Lamott told me that last night in her book *Operating Instructions*. Or wrote it. Her words keep ringing in my ears.

January 24, 2018
Letter | Eighteen-and-a-Half Months Old

If I had a third child, I would not let them cry. I can't take it anymore. My nerves are frayed from hours of anguish while Kaz cries himself in and out of sleep. It's too much crying for a nineteen-month-old—I know this because I have a carbon copy of him sleeping just ten feet away.

You hear about these parents who don't let their kids cry. *What wusses,* you think. *It's okay for kids to cry.* That is, until you have a kid who cries and whom you cannot keep consoling indefinitely. *I can't keep making this better for you,* I tell you in my head. *I can't survive it.*

When do I start and you stop? When do I care for myself above caring for you so that I *can* care for you?

We're trapped in some purgatory that comes in two-week cycles, in which each time we get you to sleep well something else sets us back—a tooth, four teeth, molars, a snot-filled nose, a cough. And just like that we're back, with you and I wrestling each other while your will and vocal cords strum my heart and the very essence of my being. I've never questioned any choice in my life as much as I question now, nightly, what to do about your crying. Is it time to respond? Is it time to ignore? Is it time to fix? Is it time for you to solve it by yourself? Add these to the list of questions I was not prepared to answer.

Contempt. It's number one on the list of marriage destroyers. I feel it for your father. Or for what he represents to me right now. *The other*—the one not in it at the level I am in it. The one who snores just loudly enough to make it sound like the start of your cries, just loudly enough to thread its way into my sleeping subconscious. His snoring wakes me up because I am always sleeping at attention, wondering who is about to cry. So now I trade slumber for vigilance, waiting, listening, and giving up precious minutes before I realize you're silent and it's the man lying blissfully aslumber next to me who not only woke me but will keep me awake for the hours to come. And then I convert my exhaustion into contempt.

I don't want to be this person. But I don't know where to put these feelings. They don't belong to you two. I know enough to know that it's not even a sliver of an option. But the emotion, the questions, the uncertainty, the exhaustion, the upheaval, need to land somewhere. I want to find a new place or space. Is this when I take up kickboxing? Or can I swing at the ice hard enough to have it absorb my contempt so I become a more serene mother and partner?

Last week I was driving home from giving a speech, listening to the news. Sleet pelted the New England roads. As I tucked through Crawford Notch and surfed the ice for half a second, a story about the passing of the American Foundation for AIDS Research founder Mathilde Krim came on the radio. The reporter spoke of her importance in the world—saving hundreds of thousands of lives because of her activism and commitment. I waited for each sentence of the memoriam to give me something more. It was not until it was finished that I knew I was waiting to learn if Mathilde had been a mother. The next morning as I lay awake, wondering what to do about Kaz crying at 4:15, I scanned articles until I found my answer. There, at the end of her obituary, was what I wanted to know—survived by a daughter.

I wanted that story to be about her as a great woman *and* a mother. I wanted to hear these things threaded together inseparably. But they were not. Because how do you tell the story of a mother? You can say someone was a geneticist and virologist who changed the global stigma of AIDS. Do you follow that with a sentence about her being a mother who woke up at four o'clock every other morning with her daughter until her child was two years old? Just saying someone is a parent is not enough information. You can be any sort of parent. We eulogize based on facts. I wanted to know how she did her work and balanced motherhood. I want to know how I will do these things too.

When I was growing up I would see my mom being honored—maybe as chair of the board of regents at the university—and listen as they read her biography out loud. At the end they always said she was a mother to two girls.

I remember thinking it was so odd that this fact—my sister and I—would be in her biography. *That's not important to her,* I remember thinking. And I knew this was complicated for me, and for her, and not fair, even as I thought it.

"Being your mom was the most important thing in the world to me," she's told me several times. I've never believed her. I saw the other pieces so much more clearly. The plaques. The articles. The briefcase full of papers. The nylons. The suits. The cars. The gold pins accessorizing the lapels. This—all this—so much easier to hold up and count. But what of her markers as a mother?

Raising my sister and I was *one* of the things my mother did in her life. Not the most important, if you asked me. *The* most important, if you asked, or ask, her. Now, in my own life as a mother, I'm at a loss for how to build my own formula. Everything right now seems to revolve around being a mom; it's the lens through which I see the world. To survive now—these years, months, hours, days, and even minutes—I must let motherhood cover me completely, in rainbows both dark and light.

February 1, 2018
Letter | Nineteen Months Old

"Figure out what you want. Then ask for it." Dr. Lindman tells me it's that simple. But what I want doesn't seem to present itself as simple.

"Give him ownership of tasks and let him be. Be exact about what you need. It will help," she says.

Why should I have to do this all and *then* figure out what I want others to do also?

"What if there's more to it?" I ask her.

"Keep it simple," she tells me.

More is the rush of anger feeling good. More are the venomous words I feel building in my mouth, then swallowing back. More is the feeling that this is not only about the present. This has to get solved now for us to have a later.

February 8, 2018
Letter | Nineteen Months Old

My ascent of the testy mixed rock-and-ice route Remission Direct on Cathedral Ledge was anything but direct. Three years ago I tried my best on the pitch, only to come flying off the ice after the crux overhang. I was uninjured, inspired, and determined to get back on the next week. The New England weather, however, wasn't having it—delivering a warm-up that melted the climb, and my chance at redemption, away.

Next winter, I promised myself. Except that the next winter I was pregnant with twins.

Yesterday, I not only pulled off the lead, but did it in what alpinists call "full conditions." Faceful after faceful of spindrift pummeled me each time I looked up to swing, tap, or hook. It was a long lead on not a very long pitch—only ninety feet or so. It took extreme patience and generosity from Gilbert to belay me. There was downclimbing, there was encouraging self-talk, there was whimpering, there was being pumped out of my mind, there was the hunt for the strategic resting positions that allowed on-route recovery. And finally, there was the top.

Ice climbing is a brilliant and absurd pursuit. I am so glad it is a part of my life, and I'm so thankful to be here, the day after Remission Direct, with forearms still aching as I type. I'm warm and dry in my home having just tucked my nineteen-month-old twins safely in their beds. Here's to going big when we can, and sometimes even pulling it off.

One day someone will ask you both if you are competitive. Kaz, for you this likely will be a compliment. Irenna, for you I hope it is too. Know, also, that it might depend on who is asking. Is it competition that I felt when I watched Gilbert chart upward on the route French Canadian Reality in Evans Notch, Maine, the other day, climbing farther between her ice screws than I have ever been able to, all while telling myself that the climb was surely "easy"? That I felt when I followed her lead, which my internal narrative had not only made "easy" but had also rationalized had been softened by the sun's rays into a simple joyride up the pliable hero ice that takes reliable tool placements—only to realize, as I climbed, that the sun-baked ice had instead become iffy and shearable?

I will have to deal with my ego, clearly. Is it competition or ego? I obsessed about which as I fed out slack while Gilbert steadily moved up each climb she led during her visit to New England. It probably doesn't matter which it is, so long as I don't let it consume me.

My life as a climber has been anything but a trajectory. Long ago, I pretended to stifle any competition out of me because I knew I'd lose. It was clear to me that I was not likely to be the best climber in the world. Back when I was a full-time professional athlete, the only time I took away from climbing was when I was injured. But injuries are temporary; injuries heal. The difference now is that you two are staying with me.

Today I was covered in strawberry-and-avocado vomit at 6:50 A.M. Then I nursed alternating needy kids until nine A.M. before I'd even had breakfast myself. Yesterday after we were done climbing, Gilbert headed to our loft with a yoga mat for two hours of stretching. I nursed, I hammered out a grant budget, I juggled you both as you fought over the one orange crayon. What is the recovery from motherhood if you're permanently inside it? It's not a recovery, but a cohabitation. I knew how to rebound when it was just me. But this is unlike anything I have known.

—~~—

When I was twenty-six, I started a writing program with five other women between five and fifteen years my senior. The oldest, Bonnie, told me one night over wine in a hot tub that one day I'd feel what it was like to no longer be the prettiest one in the room. Or the smartest, or the one everyone wants to talk to.

"It will shock you," she said. "And that's being in your forties."

At the time, I was more fixated on how adult and real it felt to be surrounded by writers instead of climbers, drinking wine instead of beer, in a hot tub instead of around a campfire. I shrugged Bonnie off. *Whatever,* I remember thinking. *She seems bitter.*

Now I am the forty-one-year-old avoiding the mirror, pulling out fistfuls of hair with my rubber band each time I twist it from my scalp. Now I watch younger, bolder, stronger climbers pull up even to me, and then pass on by.

Mentally, I can understand this. I know what I'm coming back from physically. I understand that barely sleeping for twenty months straight cannot be good for my recovery. But emotionally, being surpassed mainly serves to piss me off.

The pharmacist just called to go over instructions and payment for Irenna's custom-made ibuprofen suppositories because she spits out every medicine we give her orally. Sometimes her fever is so bad we have to rotate Tylenol and ibuprofen to get it down. Because I'm her mom, you can damn well be sure I found the nearest compounding pharmacy so we'd have this option.

Now it's minutes later and I'm staring at the cursor where I left off.

February 11, 2018
Audio Journal | Nineteen-and-a-Half Months Old

Dear Peter,

I need to figure out why I am so mad.

I constantly feel like I have the shorter end of the stick; I am the one doing more, I am the one we've all created to do more, who steps up for more, but doesn't get the credit. And I feel like part of this is something that I need to fix in myself, and part of it is something that we need to fix in our marriage.

I am beginning to think that the only way forward for us is for me to tell you how angry I am. And that some of that anger is with you. I am not angry with you all the time, but on a daily basis I have to coach myself out of contempt and toward compassion. Out of frustration and toward friendship. I come up with alliterations, I come up with jingles, and I come up with declarations, but frankly, nothing is working.

I want to be the person nursing our children. I don't necessarily mind the responsibilities I have. But it is unworkable for me to have these responsibilities without recognition. Is there something wrong with me because I want all of that? Possibly. I need your help to work on it.

I need your help to sit and hold this open for me, to hold appreciation for me, to help me see where to push and where to let go.

This morning at 7:20, when you took the kids into the gear room, I spent that whole time cleaning up the house, putting away clothes, getting their pajamas organized for the next night, finding the bath toys, tucking them away, looking for the crayons, and transferring the laundry. Meanwhile, all I could think was that if the tables were turned and I was in the gear room, you would be scrolling and texting on your freaking phone.

I think I am ninety percent correct about that. You might do some of it—you might do a couple of dishes. You might do all the dishes. But you wouldn't wipe the floor. You wouldn't put the PJs away. You wouldn't take a big-picture look around the house and work on getting things organized.

And that's what makes me feel like I'm drowning. It's what's making me so angry. I know you're at your max. We both are. I know we're different, that we pay attention to different things, and that I want it all done now. But instead of me feeling compassion for you being at your max—the same compassion I know I want from you—all I want to say is: "Are you fucking kidding me? You are not doing anywhere near the amount that I am."

But the thing is, Peter, you *are* a really good dad. You give more every day, which is good because they need more every day. You've taught the kids to jump in time to "Thunderstruck," you wear their pajama bottoms as a hat when you read them bedtime stories, and you almost always have an even voice that sounds like the kind of love every kid deserves when you talk to them.

You're amazing when you're engaged. And maybe my judgment about you is actually about me. I'm not sure, exactly, except I *am* sure these things are tied up together. And I'm sure this emotion that I feel, and this anger I feel, is ultimately not healthy. It's not healthy for me personally, and it's not helpful for us.

I don't know how to fix it. I am really scared to tell you how angry I am. I am scared for you to really hear me and maybe be angry back.

March 1, 2018
Audio Journal | Twenty Months Old

We are on the floor playing our new favorite nursing game—Kaz or Irenna pointing to me and then themselves, so I say, "Mamma, Kaz!" or, "Mamma, Irenna!" And then they point out into the air and I say, "Papa." They like to try to stump me. "Mamma, Mamma, Mamma, Kaz!" I say. I take in the moment, following their hands, seeing their eyes light up with a smile, watching their lips focused on the task at hand.

I never understood smiling eyes before, but now I know them so well.

I greedily nurse you by yourselves, efficiency be damned, at least once a day. I get to look at just you, fold my body around one of you in your entirety, brush your cheeks and ears.

My mother used to run the outside of her thumb up my cheek, scuffing it, in tenderness, even though it never felt physically soft. I do that to you now and wonder if you will also remember it as love, roughly.

Over the past few weeks, you have started to hug each other. Holding your arms out for one another and intertwining. You stand there, engulfed and engulfing at the same time. I have never seen anything more sweet and true. Sometimes only one of you wants a hug. One day, I hope you will figure out when it's a good time to give a hug and when it's not, but for now I work to separate the skeptical from the hugger lest it turn into the biter and the bitten.

In the mornings, you are starting to talk to each other when you wake up. I listen closely to a whisper of it before the crying begins, and I savor your trilling.

You have words coming every day, and we walk hand in hand up whole staircases. You love the poodle and take time-outs to hug him and drape your arms over his body as if he were a pony. So far he lets you.

Kaz, you soothe yourself while nursing by twirling your hair. You can sleep-nurse like this for over an hour. You have lost chunks of it already to this practice, your curls torn asunder by your need. You've started to reach for my hair too.

Irenna, you look for your dad every morning the moment you're done nursing with Mom. "Papa? Papa? Papa?" you say, wobbling like a drunken sailor down our long hallway. By the time you're in the kitchen, your walk gets straightened out right at the moment Papa lifts you into his arms for your morning communion.

Neither of you likes to have your pajamas put on at night or taken off in the morning. My hair is still falling out by the fistful, my belly is still not the belly I once knew, my body is still tied to you with nursing and hormones.

Last week, I went to Boston by bus. Standing in line for the ladies' room at South Station, I watched women peer at themselves intently in the mirror, spray their hair, and adjust their lipstick and makeup. I pass these opportunities for self-reflection with only a glance in the mirror so quick my likeness is blurry. I dry my hands on my jeans, which have the twins' boogers entrenched in their weave. I console myself by knowing the jeans look good on my backside.

I take pictures of you while you nurse singly—grateful for these sweet, inefficient moments we have together. I write you these letters by typing a one-handed email to myself on my iPhone.

I work upstairs just out of reach, sight, and sound. You tempt me, always, to return to your giggles and shrieks. You concern me with your cries, give me relief when I hear the door close and I know your new babysitter, Amelia, or your dad is taking you on an adventure. Then I can slink back downstairs to pee, drink water, and eat ham, and then go back to work.

I realized today that the start of my traveling life will be the end of our nursing. Right now, when we're together, we cannot make it more than thirty-eight minutes bombarding me to nurse. We have a long way to go before I can get on a plane and leave for two weeks and come back and not have that key tool of our togetherness. Of course you can go without nursing—you do it daily if we are away from each other for four, six, or eight hours. But when we are together, it is part of our language. I know it will have to change, and that it will change, but I am loath to force it, to introduce another reason to cry and be upset into an already-fragile armistice.

Will this bond give us something stronger than I ever had with my mother? Is that why it matters? For the past twenty months, I have been trying to figure this out—not judging and blaming her for going back to work and stopping nursing, but trying to understand the impact of her choice. And I know, alongside of all that, that I am trying like hell to do this my way. And that one day we will stop. But not now, I say today.

Not now. Irenna is getting her lateral incisors.

Not now. Kaz has a shark tooth coming in.

Not now. You both have colds.

Not now. Daylight saving time, new childcare, poor sleep.

Not ever, you seem to say.

March 1, 2018 (Later)
From the Notepad | Twenty Months Old

"I had lunch with my ex-husband the other day," my mom says.

I'm talking to her and scanning the internet on a break from work. I close my eyes, track her words. I decide to feign a similar nonchalance.

"How was it?"

"We made eye contact—something we haven't been good at in thirty years, even though we used to love each other."

I am trying to hold and treasure each word she says, and then I realize halfway through her talking that there are not enough breaths going into and out of my body—as if we're enthralled in some spell and I might break it.

I didn't have parents who liked each other. From an early age, I would dance between them to keep them separate.

"It was just the two of us, so very long ago," she said. "What could have been?"

I don't want to give this more attention than my mom does, except it's the largest news I might have ever heard. What if? What would have been different other than everything?

March 3, 2018
Letter | Twenty Months Old

Today, I got to play with just Kaz for a whole forty-five minutes after his nap. We played with the dolls. We have a blue doll and a pink doll, whom I used to call the boy and girl doll and whom I now call the doll wearing blue and the doll wearing pink. Kaz likes to carry them both around, and I told him that's what we do in our family—carry two, two, two.

I have happy babies, whom I love. Whom I am writing to instead of being with. And that is why I decided not to go to Europe this summer—to give us all more space and time together.

What if I seek balance differently? What if instead of seeing balance as a larger life objective, I see it as something to have in a day? For my whole life I have thought that balance was something to achieve broad scale and when found would offer large swaths of ease. I thought, and still think, that if I had balance then I'd feel even and equal at every moment, as if I was always living in harmony, in perfect equilibrium with my ambition, love, passion, and responsibilities.

It strikes me, today at 3:55 in the afternoon on a Saturday—having played with my kids for the morning, worked on budgets for the midday, and writing now—that maybe I need to look at the smaller picture. Today I have touched each important part of me. I even went on a hike with my kids.

Maybe appreciating today and gathering it up with recognition for myself is what I always seem to want from Peter.

March 6, 2018
Letter | Twenty Months Old

Today, I'm sick but you're not. We've been swapping coughs and sore stomachs every month it seems.

In the middle of my turn throwing up last night, I got an email announcing that I won the Mulago fellowship—it's from the accelerator for social entrepreneurs. It comes with flexible funding to cover almost a year of our team, or whatever we need, plus a six-day workshop in California. I burst into tears when I read the email and was still crying when I told you and your dad. You all seemed equally confused.

Fifteen minutes ago I sat down to contemplate what this will mean in my life and in ours. I blocked out the days of the workshop on my calendar in yellow, my color-coding for travel. I stared at the long line of away time, stretching more than a week. Then I started Googling how long kids can pause breastfeeding without stopping completely.

I'll be the first to tell you you're amazing eaters. Nursing is not about survival for you. Rather it's about the deeper, human connection part of survival, of slowing down, of just being together.

Right now, every day that I am home, I pause to nurse you four to eight times a day. I sit, I contort with you both, I scoop with one. I notice your cheeks and the taper of your eyes into your nose. I think of sixth-grade portrait class with Ms. Ball, where we learned that the eyes are in the center of the face—something most novices get wrong.

I am not a person who pauses that often. Adding up the days away from you, I feel as if I am going to trade you for my career in one fell swoop. I had been planning to do that on a scheduled trip to Mozambique—my first since I've had you—but this new opportunity is only six weeks earlier. And it feels like a lifetime too fast.

I am not ready to give you up. And I know, intellectually, that this is just us in a new expression. But this connects me back to those first minutes after you came out of my belly. This is our tether. I don't want to let it go.

Can I pump in California, and will you want to nurse when I get home? For what? For six more weeks before I go to Africa? If you stop nursing, will you wake up with me and snuggle me in the mornings, or is this the end of you feeling like my babies?

Here I am again, work and motherhood up against each other. Or maybe I need to think about them in a new way—up *next* to each other.

I am not ready for you to not be my little littles. I want more of you. I want to be able to hold you as little forever. I have never been that good at understanding life's shifts and continuums. I want it to stop so very badly. And now I hear the garage door opening, telling me you are home from the park with Amelia and about to come through the door, so instead of writing this here, I will love you in person.

....

March 20, 2018
Letter | Twenty-and-a-Half Months Old

Hand, foot, and mouth disease. Way to go big, team. You both have it all over. The worst are the sores on your left hand, Irenna, where your thumb-sucking has created blood blisters on and around the other blisters, both on your thumb and the fan of fragile flesh below.

We just had a tandem forty-five-minute crying session rolling on the kitchen's concrete floor. You are inconsolable. I would take double projectile puking in a heartbeat over this. I have dealt with that, and it seemed to be easier. Explaining to you in a language you can understand that there are blisters in your mouth is so much harder.

Peter is in Chamonix skiing for fun—a trip we agreed for him to take now and for me to take down the road. For both our sakes, for all our sakes, I want it to go well—but instead I'm sideways on my own at home with two sick kids.

I pick up my phone and text him.

I need to be able to tell you how hard this is right now. Just as you need to be able to tell me what a great day of turns you had. I'm not looking for you to feel badly, and neither are you. But we have to be able to share the reality of our experiences.

Ask me what else, I write to him. *Write: tell me more, and then what else?*

These are the phrases I want to hear. I need to hear. I am not sure if this will work, but I want him to be like a friend in these moments. I want to pause the partnership and the guilt and shame and anger and go back to being friends who can commiserate.

I have had eight nights of single parenting, and I have three nights to go. We have never made it past four A.M. This morning, I tucked us back into my bed together at 5:40 A.M. and pretended we were somehow blessed to be there at this "later" hour. I work to match your happiness.

"Say, we did great last night, didn't we?" I say. I'm telling you what I appreciated about the night the same way I say I appreciate you using the spoon to eat your yogurt instead of just throwing the spoon across the room. Maybe all of us can ascend to this new level, if it's the only one we're focusing on.

March 27, 2018
Letter | Twenty-and-a-Half Months Old

Yesterday, I filled out an online survey for the fellowship. "What do you most want to gain about impact at scale?" it asked.

I sat in my office listening to the two of you chortling underneath me while Amelia watched you, trilling and saying, "Apple, please, do do," for thank-you. We had just spent an hour nursing after your midday nap and making a fort out of pillows.

My answer was easy: I want Legado to grow in a way that fits the values I have around balance in my life.

I answered as if I have these values engraved on a mission plate. As if I am not throwing an ever-evolving list of values against the wall and trying to make some stick.

Will they kick me out of the fellowship for this? Why would I want it, then, if they do?

I press submit.

———

I've been poring over photos of another mountain in Mozambique, riddled with suspended caves that no climber in their right mind would ever want to enter. This morning I got an email from a chiropterologist named Jen confirming that she'd love for me to put her in one of those caves. "I'd do roost searches in the larger crevices during the day, mist-netting on the upland plateaus, and set triple-high nets near rock faces that have narrow crevices," she wrote. I read her email on my phone at 8:30 after dropping you off for your morning at preschool, and started to laugh with excitement. Eight years ago I didn't know which species I'd find where, and which scientists I needed or where to find them. Growth and learning are magical.

May 5, 2018
From the Notepad | Twenty-Two Months Old

Hey, I write to Gilbert. *I hear you're going to Alaska soon . . . Do it up, babe. Be safe, have fun, go big, and come home.*

I press send and feel like a better human.

May 31, 2018
Letter | Twenty-Three Months Old

Dear Irenna and Kaz,

Today is my 703rd day of nursing you. I didn't set out to nurse you or *not* nurse you. When you were growing in my belly, I told myself I'd have no expectations for this—that I'd let our path be our path. Back then I never dreamed our path would take us this far—to you being one month shy of two years old, and us still attached this way.

I was that woman who, before I was pregnant, said I'd never nurse my kids when they were old enough to verbally ask for it. "That's just weird," my former self confided to others. My current self is the mother of twins who have been announcing "I nurse" for months. I find it to be the most endearing statement you make. Parenthood, it seems, provides a continual opportunity to eat the words you spoke before you knew better.

—⁓—

Back when we started nursing, I told myself I'd continue as long as it worked. It worked through feeding infants every two hours around the clock, double mastitis, two winters of pumping and ice climbing, six business trips to four states, and thirty-two new teeth. Whenever I thought of stopping, the only thing that made sense was for it to happen organically—the natural end point for the as-long-as-it-works strategy.

Tomorrow, I'll nurse you in the morning for our last time. And then I'll get on a plane and spend ten days away from you. Is that a natural end point? Inasmuch as my career creates one, yes. But for us as a three-pack? That I do not know.

What I do know is that this basic, animalistic connection has given more peace and certainty to my life and my soul than anything I've ever done. When we are with each other like this, there is no doubt it's what I'm made to do in that moment. And for a person who multitasks most everything in her life and almost never slows down, it's given me singular focus and breath and ease.

Intellectually, I know we're on a trajectory that has us all growing and changing together. Emotionally, however, I don't want anything to do with this trajectory. I want to keep you here tucked next to me so that I can forever keep you safe, me safe, Dad safe, and all of us fresh and new. But life is about movement and change, and the two of you so perfectly embody what it means to be alive. So today, instead of resisting this change and what it brings, I'm going to celebrate what we've done together.

Here's to you, Irenna and Kaz, and here's to us. Thank you for letting me be your mom and giving me a chance to share my love with you like this every day for the past 703 days. Thank you for grounding me this intensely for this long. Maybe it slowed me down long enough to really teach me that this new life—the one with you in it—is the life I was headed for all along.

June 7, 2018
From the Notepad | Twenty-Three Months Old

Crushed it! I text Gilbert. *So proud of and inspired by you.*

I sent this text off even before Peter told me she and Chantel succeeded on the Slovak Direct route on Denali. Some 9,000 feet of technical ice, rock, and mixed climbing all the way to the Alaskan giant's summit at 20,310 feet. I already knew it because I'd been checking for the news myself. First women ever.

One day it might not matter that two women did this route, because enough of us will be climbing at every level in the sport. But that is not the case right now, and right now it matters so much.

July 26, 2018
Letter | Two Years Old

I didn't stop nursing you in California after all. I gave in after not pumping for eighteen hours. I kept pumping, I told myself, just in case. *Maybe they won't want me,* I said to myself.

Five minutes after walking in the door, after ten days away, I heard you, Irenna. You were waking up from your nap, and I told Amelia I'd get you. Your arms and my arms were reaching for each other from the moment I opened the door.

"I nurse?" you asked.

"Oh, baby girl, nurse away."

—⁓—

Now, five weeks later, today might really be my last time putting you down for a nap while you're attached to me. I leave for Mozambique in three days. "Am'bique," you call it. Your dad is in Italy now, guiding in the Dolomites, and then we have three days of overlap at home before it's my turn to fly away and work.

—⁓—

July 28, 2018
From the Notepad | Two Years and One Month Old

Our country is on fire, literally and figuratively. I'm making the choice to go halfway around the world to work when I could be just as effective here. We live in a time when our country is building to war, when our leader is anything but, when I can't listen to the news without doing deep-breathing exercises to regulate my blood pressure.

July 29, 2018
Letter | Two Years and One Month Old

About eight minutes ago it hit me: In three days I am leaving. Not just you. Not just both of you. But this life I have had for two years. Leaving this iteration of myself for another. We are always changing, but sometimes the changes are abrupt. Like giving birth to you. Or stopping nursing.

I wonder, will *work* be a dirty word in our family? Garlick said it was in hers. Work took her dad away from the family. What about work as laudable? As a pursuit of your passion and primary expression of self?

Today, while playing with the kids on the side of the Saco River, I told Peter I am going back to Mozambique in 2019. "Next summer," I said.

"Next summer? Again? You never told me," he replied.

He might be right. I am not sure. In my head, I'd told him. In my head, he knows the conversations I have had with the nine people who will each contribute significantly to Legado and go with me to Mozambique. But Peter and I are not as aligned in my head as we used to be. He used to be the person I talked to about work—my sounding board, the person who knew the most.

Now it almost seems he is the person who knows the least. This must be why people have affairs with their co-workers: that tantalizing combination of both understanding your work and seeing you thrive within the context of it. In our marriage, we triage without even knowing it—prioritizing the kids, their schedule, and which sponge to use where to clean the house. The minutiae I choose to tell him. The things you can easily share in three breaths while you run referee between two twins fighting over the squirting zebra and the elephant bath toys.

At the river, I reminded Peter that I run an international conservation organization protecting one of Africa's critical mountain watersheds. So it stands to reason I should go to Africa every now and again. I moved my feet carefully, rocks slippery from a week of New England rain, rocks turned almost soft by a layer of algae. In my mind, I pictured myself convincing Peter that my work was good and true and necessary for me, but then I bit my tongue. I don't want an uphill battle with him, too, because some days I am already trying to convince myself.

I'd booked this trip to Mount Namuli last year, committing myself by committing to others—the one hundred people taking the training and the sixteen people who fundraised with their hearts and souls for it. "If you are there, I am there," I told them. And so, in two days, we will go.

I am restocking my medical kits with meds that expired in 2013. Back in 2015, two years past expiration seemed okay to me—but now they're five years past, and I'm not so sure. I pick up the kit—pink Pepto, aspirin, Keflex—meds I will use and meds I don't want to use. I set up my tent in my living room to make sure it's still functional. It's been three years since I've been to Africa, three years since I put away my compression socks for the plane, the water filter, my bed liner, not for a moment thinking it would be this long.

I know I should be proud to be going back. But I don't have one emotion.

"Are you excited?" my sister asks.

I am everything. I am mournful. I mourn the end of this life with my kids. I think I am celebrating a return to another life, but I also know there is no return. There is forward, there is new. I try to tell the kids we will have new ways to cuddle when I come home, but I don't have the heart to talk to them directly about no longer nursing them.

I don't know if I want to say goodbye to them or slip off during a nap. I am packed in full: one bag at 50.5 pounds and one at 49.9 pounds. They sit ready at the door. Waiting. I have never been packed this far in advance. But somewhere inside of me, I knew I needed to so I could clear a way for something else to take over before I go.

The kids show me every day that nothing is static. I am not static. I need to embrace this change. I need to be ready and open and stand like a superwoman in front of it. I need to believe I am creating boldness every day as a mom and as a woman.

August 1, 2018
Letter | Two Years and One Month Old

Leaving you broke my heart. I had to be Mom. I had to not cry. My desire for you to be okay in that moment had to be bigger than my tears. Your dad was going to take you to a friend's house to play to ease the transition, so instead I said, "Have a nice time at Tommy's."

I did not say goodbye. I said that I would see you in fifteen days. But after I closed the doors on the van and walked behind it where I was sure you could not hear me, I told you, "Mamma loved nursing you, every minute." And then Peter gave me a hug and I sobbed.

I am not really sure this is what I want to do or am supposed to do right now. I can see, somewhat, that our lives will change one day, and I will need this central expression outside of you. But right now all it does is take me away from you. Peter told me I could work on a conservation project in Poughkeepsie if that would make life easier.

It has been three years, almost exactly to the day, since I was in Mozambique—three years of growing you in and outside my belly. I pulled over three times on the drive away from you to Portland and sobbed. At JFK, I walked out into the sun, going from Terminal 5 to 4, and cried the whole quarter mile. When something is not feeling right, do you turn around and go back?

My flight was canceled, and instead of being whisked away from you in a series of barely caught flights, I sat in an airport, only 350 miles from you, for eighteen hours. That also made little sense.

Other moms write to me and say this matters. That I am showing you me—I am showing you passion and commitment, which is far more important. Or they tell me they let their careers and passions slip away and had to fight to find them again six years later when their kids started school.

I want the perfect balance of it. And for my whole life I have assumed that if I were in balance it would feel good all the time—as if I'd have an intrinsic meter for knowing exactly how much time to parcel out to motherhood versus career, to staying at Mom's house versus Dad's, to being in the mountains versus being at school. Maybe I had it wrong. Maybe balance is not achieved or felt as bliss. Maybe balance is achieved with heartbreak and yearning at the margins. Yearning to be with you when I am gone, yearning to go climbing when I am not, yearning to feel more satisfied in the moment. But I am the only one who can create that.

I've spent my life trying to get this mix right. When I was a kid I worked to make my dad and mom both feel loved enough, to streamline my life as a child of a divorce. Now I wonder if I were to split my attention the right way, could I climb hard and run Legado and make enough money to support my family and pay for a nanny? But that's not all, because I also need to go to Africa with my team and be as cool a mom as I am a CEO, to give my toddlers a life of happiness and joy.

I'm going to Mozambique. I'm in the airport swapping stories with other weary travelers. I'm back in the mix.

August 5, 2018
Letter | Two Years and One Month Old

The Queen of Namuli and I are trying to remember how long it's been since we've seen each other.

"Three years," I say to her. "A very long time."

She nods.

"In those three years I got *very* pregnant and had two babies." I pantomime a huge stomach, two babies.

It's only later when I show her the photos of the twins and she asks who they are that I realize how much of what I said was missed by our twenty-five-year-old male translator.

—***—

Namuli hides itself well. Murrabué Mountain, which cloaks it to the south, is similar enough in shape to taunt you into believing it's Namuli herself. The first time we came here I drove up the tar road and saw Murrabué and came back to tell Garlick I had seen Namuli. It was not until ten hours later, rounding a corner into the blue gum trees, that I realized the real Namuli was everything Murrabué was not—Murrabué is covered in vegetation, and is dwarfed by Namuli's soaring two-thousand-foot granite cap, twin summits, and long, arcing flanks that cradle the landscape below. It is not different now, seven years later.

Namuli has changed—how could it not?—but not fast enough for those who live here. "Where is our hospital, where is our secondary school, where is a cell tower? What should I tell my people when they ask me this?" the queen asks.

"I hear you," I say. "Change takes time. We are here to work with you to protect your mountain's biodiversity. And I understand you want these other things. We have heard you."

I sit in the district head's house and make sure to keep my back straight, to nod at the queen while she talks in Lomwe, to nod as one of our team's field technicans, Dias, translates to Portuguese, and to take it in when our agriculture intern, Anthony, turns the Portuguese into English. I speak and try to look at her and at everyone in the room. "I understand you are frustrated. We are here to work together. We are here to do this work in collaboration with you," I say.

It's not that I did not expect the meeting; but how does one answer those questions? I understand that the Namuli communities have a list of needs they want met. I would have those same needs if I lived here. But those needs are not what our project can solve. They are not what our funders will pay for. I try to share the context—that together we have elevated the profile of Namuli. That together we have worked to catch the attention of the government of Mozambique and the international donor community, and that the reason the international donor community has been on board is because of the biodiversity. "The forest," I say, "is what has captured their attention and their commitment."

My answer is unsatisfying to everyone, including me. "I will keep working to make this about more than your forest," I say. "Will you please do this with me, with us?"

The queen and the council of community members discuss. I wait. I nod. I breathe. They say yes. Now I have to make it happen.

—

My friend Raimundo, who lives with his family at the base of Namuli's southwest face, has a Suzuki motobike. It revs to thirty-five miles per hour, and he coasts it expertly to save gas downhill. It's also missing the right passenger peg. My foot instinctively kicks for it and hits the exhaust pipe instead. Then I look to see a jury-rigged peg—a modified lug nut sticking out a half-inch from where the peg should be. Raimundo and I ride together, always. I don't even debate—just affix my right foot onto the lug nut, smearing my big toe and promising myself I will not get burned. The tea fields and their red soil pathways come first, the air cool and the driving easy. Out of the tea fields we climb, over packed dirt glistening in a five-inch strip created by all the motos traveling to and from Namuli. But motos are not the only thing driving into Namuli anymore—higher, a twin track of textured concrete spirals up the hardest section of road, switching back and forth to gain the saddle that protects Namuli from the south. Other areas have been scraped and widened. Bridges that used to be clusters of logs that would often go missing are now more-permanent concrete arches. Even this remote mountain is changing.

August 11, 2018
Letter | Two Years and One Month Old

Dear Irenna and Kaz,

I summited Mount Namuli today. By the Queen's Route.

The queen herself gave me a present before I went up the mountain—two kilos of butter beans. I cried.

Seven years ago, when I first came to Mount Namuli, the queen told me she wasn't sure if she trusted me. "We will see what you can do for my people and Namuli," she said.

Yesterday, during the ceremony she conducts with all who attempt to journey up the mountain, she made her own mountain of nshima flour by pouring it handful after handful off her fingertips like a river as she emptied the five-pound bag. It's a ceremony I've seen her perform a half-dozen times, but this time she handed me the flour and had me help make the mountain. She asked for me to share with the ancestors what I wished for Namuli, and introduced me to them as a protector of their mountain and their home.

Today your dad told me you seem to be missing me more every day. And that wake-ups and naps and any time you are sad is hard. He says you want Mamma. I want you too. I'm not sure technology is good for my heart when I'm away from you like this. You patch in and out over FaceTime, and you each want to carry and hold Mamma on the phone. Right now that mainly means you hang up on me.

Last week I learned that the US ambassador to Mozambique wants to come to Namuli. I can't believe we've gotten this work to this stage, and I can't believe it means I'll leave you again for Africa in less than two months to liase with him. But the queen has introduced me to the spirits, and I need to do my job.

People tell me that one day this will be good for us. That you will like to know what your mom did. But what I think these people forget to say—and what I am beginning to know—is that this will only be the case if you are my central focus when I'm at home, if you are more with me than without me if I am to leave again. It has to be quality time—a phrase I hate but somehow also need.

I'm in Mozambique with a large group of people young and old. One, Jacquie, is a self-described workaholic. Her goal is to retire in a year. Her twenty-seven-year-old son talks about how she works till ten P.M. I don't want that for us. But then again, they have one of the best bonds between a mom and son I have ever seen.

We have so much in front of us together. Like coming home to new cuddles and snuggles. I had a dream that you, Kaz, were lying on me and tried to nurse, but instead pushed you head into my chin and snuggled in tight. Then you, Irenna, did the same. In my dream we're all lying on the floor, the two of you on me, *of* me, just like you've been for almost three years. We lie there balanced together, breathing together, happy together.

When I stood at the top of Namuli today, looking out on layers of forest and mountains, homes and fields, I thought of you—and how from the moment I took my first step down the mountain I would be on my way back home to you.

I'll be home soon, my bugs. My loves.

September 5, 2018
Letter | Two Years and Two Months Old

Dear Irenna,

This one is just for you.

One day, I want you to have a girl of your own so we can talk about how to raise strong girls together.

You like pink and purple. More so than if you did not have a brother. You won't wear Kaz's hand-me-downs. No matter what color they are.

I say "young man" to him and "young lady" to you—at least, that's what I say when I am not thinking. Why does he get to be a man and you a lady? Why not young gentleman and young woman? I am trying to shift this. As much as I would like the shift to be complete by the time you have children of your own, I think we will still have work to do, together.

September 13, 2018
Letter | Two Years and Two Months Old

Dear Irenna and Kaz,

Irenna, do you know that I try to make sure I put your name first as much as Kaz's?

You're twenty-six and a half months old—an age at which I'm not supposed to count in months anymore (in public).

"No milk, Mamma," you both say before diving in to snuggle me. Kaz, you snuggle hard. You cover my face with my hair. "Hair down!" you demand, hugging my face, my head, and grabbing my cheeks with each of your hands so you can plant an open-mouthed kiss directly on my lips. "Kiss hug," you say. "Kiss hug *now*."

———

Every day—every hour—I think, *Well I never knew . . .*

That naps would be so hard at two years old.

That I would cry every time Irenna says, "No milk, Mamma."

That I'd let you put on your own diaper ointment.

That I'd learn to decipher a whole new language—yours.

———

"Whoopsie daisy," you say, Irenna. Something my grandpa would say to me. Did I teach you that? Did Montessori? We're all hard at work making sense of each other.

Locations are big for you right now. Papa is in New York. "No, Mamma, Af-ka," you say. Your cousins Jeannie and Sawyer are in "Sota" (Minnesota). We chant these words daily, updating locations and confirming the whereabouts of each person in our extended network.

I've been talking to you about how we need to be a pack. "When it's just me, just Mamma," I say, "I need you to stay together." I am that woman at the park and farmers market who is trying to give you space to explore independently until I'm suddenly running after both of as you're heading for the parking lot. When you're both safe in the moment, I suddenly have nothing to do but check my texts and email; when it's total Armageddon, I usually lose my phone.

Your dad and I are okay. We are not great. I was two-and-a-half years old when my parents separated. Four months older than you are now. I don't remember them together. But I sure remember them apart.

Does that mean we have four more months to figure this out? To have conversations about who is working when and who is with the kids when? To get along with levity and love instead of tension and accusation? Or will you already know that sometimes it was hard for us, and have we already etched this fact into your psyche?

What I don't get is if we can't talk about it in front of you, and if I go to bed before nine because I'm exhausted, while Peter stays up later, when *are* we supposed to talk about it?

On a daily basis, I try to imagine what percentage of the world has children. Seventy percent? Eighty percent? How on Earth can this feel so difficult when so many people do it? Or is it that I just haven't had any actual understanding of or empathy for parents?

Amelia moved on to another job last week, done with childcare and ready for something different. Would it be easier to find longer-term help if we lived in a city? Lately I have looked around at my friends who live here in this small mountain valley, feeling like we tricked ourselves. When we were young we thought we could pull it off—that we could have alternative careers, be athletes, and do it all while living in a yurt. Then life and kids came in, and we were not prepared for this collision with normalcy. When two parents' careers are built on flexibility, travel, and long hours and days away, these things are no longer so accessible with two little ones to take care of and seemingly never enough childcare in sight.

September 25, 2018
From the Notepad | Two Years and Two Months Old

I don't know if writing you is really helping me to be a better mother. I spend most of my time thinking I should write to you. Thinking I should catch more of what you say and bottle it up in pen strokes and keystrokes, on video, and in photos. And then try to organize those videos and photos. I wake up in the middle of the night and tell myself that tomorrow I will not drink wine; instead I will stay up past 8:45 P.M., and I will stretch and do my pelvic-floor exercises. But then the next day starts all over again.

September 30, 2018
Letter | Two Years and Three Months Old

You run and play hide-and-seek in the garden with your dad while I put things away. It's not always like this, but it's like this enough that I notice it and worry about our pattern. And the pattern of what you see.

Am I supposed to let it all go? Stopping will mean the world crashes in on me even more.

"Have your boys babysit," another mom says. "Talk to your boys and girls about consent starting at five years old."

All we do in our family is talk about taking turns, taking care, what "no" means, how to share, and how to understand if someone else is sad. Kaz, you cry if Irenna does not take the cow puzzle piece you offer—as if the ultimate way to hurt your feelings is to refuse your generosity.

In the morning you both now run to the bedroom door and knock on it, and when I crouch down to catch you, Kaz hurtles first into my arms, screaming, "No, Irenna!" Each day we make up songs about team cuddling; we make a pact that the next morning will be different—that we'll learn to share Mamma. But then each morning we start the same. What are you, my daughter, learning when you see me holding your brother instead of you? When you throw yourself down on the floor and scream and I cannot pick you up, or worse when you sniff and sigh and walk down the hall looking for Papa? Am I making a resilient woman out of you, or one who feels she gets second dibs on love?

—⁓—

Today my new plan is to alternate the color of the glowing light in your room—yellow for Irenna day, green for Kaz day. And then I want us to go live in a cave somewhere where none of this would matter—though even there, it would. The problem would be who gets to sleep closer to me, on me, next to my belly.

"I want nurse," you say, Kaz. I say I do too. It's been two months now since we stopped, and I never knew when I was nursing how much easier it made our morning reunions. Now we all have words and hugs and the power to push each other away and say no. And each morning my heart breaks a little more with each no.

October 5, 2018
From the Notepad | Two Years and Three Months Old

"If you start from the proposition that there is something good in everybody, it is a lot easier to get along with them even when you disagree vehemently."

Justice Sotomayor said this to me and a crowd of thousands tonight during a panel discussion at Princeton. Maybe she should be my new beacon of hope when I feel like I'm viewing my marriage and our country otherwise.

I wait for the moderator to ask Justice Sotomayor or Justice Kagan about kids. But of course she doesn't—was that a deal they made backstage? "Focus on the court, being a woman, Princeton," I imagine them deciding.

Kagan tells us there are very few fatal mistakes. We're all on the edge of our seats waiting for one of them to touch the live wire of the Kavanaugh confirmation taking place at that very moment. Instead they tell us to get involved.

How much more involved can we be? I think about tossing out everything and going into politics. Fighting against lecherous, power-hungry humans like Brett Kavanaugh. But then I see my time with you disappearing even more.

I'll be on stage tomorrow morning with Julia Boorstin from CNBC, who will interview me about leadership and risk. When I left today to be here in time to catch the justices, the two of you were practicing going to work and coming home. You did it on the lawn, with one of you disappearing over the hill for work and then running back down it in glee when you came home.

Did I do that? Was my mom there to notice?

October 9, 2018
From the Notepad | Two Years and Three Months Old

We've been working on team snuggles—still. And we need more work.

"No, Irenna!" Kaz still screams when I pick him up, focusing on what he doesn't want instead of what he has.

"We snuggled as a team the whole time you were in Mamma's belly," I tell them. "Do you remember? You were on top, Irenna. Did you feel Kaz kicking you?"

"What was it like in Mamma's belly?"

"I saw a nopa," says Irenna. In our house, tomatoes became nopas.

"I saw a strawberry," says Kaz.

I ask again the next morning and get the same answers.

Then this from Irenna: "And then, peekaboo!" She starts laughing. "Big peekaboo."

"Mamma cried," Kaz says today. "In Mamma's belly."

I don't know how much of any of this is about their life now versus their life inside. But he is right. I cried. And I still do.

October 18, 2018
Letter | Two Years and Three Months Old

This week, you discovered you can wake up and sing together in bed.

"Hi, Kaz."

"Hi, Irenna."

"The Itsy Bitsy Spider" is regularly a top choice. Kaz, you sleep on a mattress under Irenna's toddler bed. I had been thinking Irenna looked crumpled in her bed until I realized this morning that she's in that position because she's sleeping with her hand through the slats to hold yours.

Before we had twins, everyone told me you two would have your own language, be each other's best friends, mirror each other. I wasn't convinced—you are boy/girl twins (why is it always boy/girl?), not identical, just siblings who were inside my belly at the same time.

But now I see it.

When Kaz gets a sliver on his left palm, you, Irenna, announce you have a boo-boo on your hand. And if you, Irenna, poop and we ask you if you did, you say, "Kaz pooped." (I think that one is less about being a twin as it is an attempt to delay the inevitable.) At lunch you two face each other—your evergreen meal date—across the table and hide plates and forks under napkins for endless laughs from each other.

You have only just begun.

———

If the temperature dips low enough tonight, tomorrow your dad and I will go ice climbing. It will be October 19. Most people don't go ice climbing this early in the season or want to, I suppose.

"The early-season ascent of the Black Dike is a stunt," Peter says—usually climbers do the route in winter, when the ice sticks around long enough to thicken up. This time it will be a flash freeze only.

That may be, but it's an ascent I want. I want to go and place my picks delicately into barely frozen water to see if it will hold me. Rock climbing is my partner, but ice climbing is my lover. It's more exciting, more freeing, and it makes me feel strong and appreciated. But climbing what is basically a giant heap of poorly bonded granite that routinely sheds smaller pieces of granite when it's barely frozen might not be the the best choice around risk for Peter and I anymore.

"It's debatable that we should even go together at all," he says.

I don't know if I should consider his point or be looking out for a trap. Does he hope I'll instead cede him a personal climbing day—or should I say, "I have to go to the bathroom," and furtively text my climbing partners to find another rope mate? We've been making a family vision with the help of my mentor, Susanne Conrad, who helps people be their best selves and with whom I've been working for the past eight years. I should know how to act "above the line," dammit. I tell myself to stand down.

"But if we shouldn't be doing it together," I say, "isn't the logical extension of the argument that we shouldn't be doing it at all?"

As a lifetime climber who's been asked about risk, and now a lifetime climber plus mother who gets the question constantly, the last thing I want is to be having a conversation about this in my marriage. Except it's the only safe and real place to have it. With this man who is my partner in marriage, in parenting twins, and in risk.

"It's some of the riskiest climbing we do," Peter says. "So maybe we should just not do it together."

I picture raising the two of you by myself.

The wind howls. The poodle barks.

"We can make the call when we're there," I say, opting to postpone the bigger question and make it an in-the-minute risk calculation. Something far simpler, far more familiar. One day soon we need to have the rest of this conversation. For now, I tell myself that the two of you will not have to learn that one day you lost your parents in a stunt. But then again, to some people, *all* climbing is a stunt. To others it's a passion, a lifestyle, a religion, a livelihood . . . it's some version of all of these things to me and your dad. The pendulum swings, and we try not to look too closely at what it all means when it lands in the wrong place.

October 23, 2018
Letter | Two Years and Three Months Old

My last letter to you was weak sauce. Or at least the ending was. I'm not a superstitious person, yet I did not want to write down what the outcome of a "stunt" gone wrong by your dad and me would mean to you. Sitting at my desk fourteen hours before delicately placing ice tools in the freshest frozen veneer seemed the wrong time to visualize, memorialize, or even acknowledge any outcome other than coming home to you safe and whole.

We play a game as climbers, as parents, as people. We constantly rationalize risk. We do it checking text messages on our phones while we drive. When turning left across lanes of traffic and trusting that the oncoming driver with a blinker signaling right will follow through on her plan. Because if she doesn't, she'll hit us. To be truthful, I don't trust those drivers much. Certainly not on the mountain roads where we live, when many times they are distracted by the beauty, the ice, or finding their vacation lodging or their next burger. I didn't used to distrust so many people. Including myself. Having you changed this in me. When you were three days old and I carried you between the bedroom and hall, I suddenly saw the hard corner of the doorjamb as lethal to your still-soft cranium. Now I see accident potential everywhere, and while it used to scare me that something was wrong in my head, I now think it must be a parenting instinct that lies dormant in all of us until we need it.

Your dad and I are not doing so well. Climbing is a part of it. Yesterday we all went to get our flu shots and then scrambled to get you back to our latest childcare partner, a new au pair named Monica, so we could enjoy New Hampshire's granite for a five-hour window. We're lucky to have a cliff nearby—so lucky that it feels precious. Too precious, which is part of the problem.

Did you know I could have been a full-time mountain guide like your dad? That I was? That it was that life and that same passion that landed me in Mozambique, just as they did writing grant proposals and balancing budgets between Skype meetings at home? I never thought I was heading for an office job punctuated by wild journeys. But wild journeys, how I want to be your mom, and how we need to support ourselves are all jumbled together right now.

———

Here is the thing about climbing: it goes better if you do it more often. And it takes up an ungodly amount of time. The trick as a parent is to get hyperefficient with climbing. I knew that even before I was your mom. But what I did not understand was that the shift in energy—going from holding your hand as you bravely watched the needle go into your thigh and the flu medicine dispense to pulling on small granite edges I deem reliable amid otherwise friable rock—is too much for me.

There, I said it. It's too much.

—⁓—

"I think I'm jealous of Peter," I say to Garlick on our hike.

"Of course you are. I often wish I could be a man."

Just like that, she's already thought the thought and made peace with it—a woman younger than me but ahead of me in her mom life. Back when she was pregnant with her second child and I was debating having a family, I told her, "I just don't see any examples of women who do it well." Garlick had one baby in the world, another in her belly, and two books and one National Science Foundation grant under her belt, and yet I'd callously missed all of it. At the time, I did not see the disrespect or obliviousness in my comment. I was searching for a model of parenthood and climbing and being a woman that looked exactly like the one *I* wanted.

Good friends, Kaz and Irenna, will get you through those moments. They will sit you down and tell you you're being an ass and explain why. And then, years later, when you're crying while hiking uphill with them on a forty-degree autumn day made colder by twenty-five-mile-per-hour gusts, they will gently remind you that you didn't get it either.

—⁓—

Last night, Irenna, you stalked me in the bedroom in your dinosaur fleece pajamas—making eye contact from across the room and then sneaking up without looking at me. You took twenty strides to reach me and plopped down on my chest. "Mamma time," you said before plunking your left thumb in your mouth.

You've taken to putting your face on top of mine, your index finger curled up around your nose and your pinkie hooked around mine as if to create a private tunnel through which only our breath can pass. We breathe in and out, in and out, your hands smelling sweet despite your bath. I want to breathe like this with you for always, but I also want to take a shower, finish my dinner, and have a moment with your dad.

I envy the co-sleeping families in this moment. I want to shift our family routines and stay in bed with you and Kaz and fall asleep sweetly together. Except we've tried that. And, Kaz, you usually end up sleeping on top of my head like a cat. I am nearly one hundred percent certain that your thirty-five-pound frame draped over my face is not the kind of chiropractic adjustment that will help my chronically aching neck.

So instead I ask you each to pick a hand to count with you through each of your five "kiss hugs" goodnight—what we call it when we shower kisses on your cheeks and lips while holding you close—and your dad and I pepper you with love until we all say our final goodnights and I walk away from your snuggles.

November 4, 2018
Letter | Two Years and Four Months Old

We climbed the Black Dike after all. I'm sure you're not surprised. Climbing, however, is a bit of an incorrect term for what it really felt like to leave the ground and journey up last week—on October 26, when we left you two with Monica and did the climb. Early-season ice can often be more of an exercise in levitating; you're not pulling, not pushing, just alternating your weight back and forth between your limbs in a generally upward direction.

"Do you think about your kids when you climb?" people ask me.

I did last Friday. I did when I saw the clear expanse of intermittent ice rearing up the black, water-stained granite above me. We'd followed crisp footsteps through the snow to the base of the route, winding up through a hobbit forest of tiny, wind-twisted trees into an unstable boulder field then finally to the ice. Those footsteps then seemed to have kicked once into the fresh ice lens and decided otherwise. In that moment I thought of you two, right up against the absurd energy rush that confirmed Peter and I would be the first to climb the Black Dike this season.

Climbing has to be personal in the moment of execution. I looked at the fresh terrain in front of me and tried to temper my elation with the knowledge that others had chosen otherwise—had decided *against* this climb today. But for me, it felt right. And it kept feeling right for the first eighty meters—tapping and breathing with very little protection, with very little likelihood of falling, but very high consequence if I were to do so.

"I don't free solo," I tell people emphatically. And yet. I thought of you two as I tapped my pick through a six-inch pillar of ice to make a hole just large enough to thread a sling, to make a protection point that was less than just-so, as if to protect my psyche in the moment if not body in a fall. Above me was a series of ledges and edges, rocks not fully adhered to themselves. Or maybe only adhered for the moment thanks to the early winter.

Ice climbing holds my attention because it is always different no matter how many times you do it. A twenty-foot section on October 26, over not-quite-cold-enough rock and flash-frozen ice, took me four times longer than it would've taken me in the depths of January, with thick, well-bonded ice. Last week's choice was sketchier—if I'm being honest.

I don't know what climbing will be for me going forward. I don't think either your dad or I know. You bluster a lot before you have children. But the reality is that weeks on end of 4:30 A.M. wake-ups, double pink eye, and croup that has you coughing every time you lie down will beat the desire to do anything clean out of a parent.

I didn't understand before that climbing is a total luxury.

November 6, 2018
Letter | Two Years and Four Months Old

Do you both know that when you have babies of your own, you're going to live next door to me? It's the only way I'll get to have them again. Because I want more. I want more of the intoxication of you—but I also know that if Peter and I did have another child, I'd have less of the two of you. I want to be able to have each stage again—perhaps for not as long this time, but enough to feel your rumps scraping the sides of my belly, your syncopated hiccups, your nursing lips.

"I missed you, Mamma," you say, Kaz. "How was the day at work?" And then you run up into the field in front of our house and tell me, "I'm going to work," and that you will be back later.

Your turn, Irenna: "I'll be right back," you say to me now, holding your finger in front of your face as if asking for or announcing one moment.

If either of you wants something from the other, "maybe one minute" is the affirmative answer. Though recently, "maybe now" has made an appearance as well.

November 16, 2018
Audio Journal | Two Years and Four Months Old

I told my mom that I don't feel respected or valued as a mother.

"What is wrong with you?" she retorted. "Work! What do you mean you want to be done at 4:30? I was never done at 4:30."

Mentioned by my mom in the same conversation, "My mother told me, 'Don't even dream of coming home from school with a B.'"

"I don't ever remember you saying that to me, but it was implied," I said.

What is generationally passed down? Without ever saying it?

December 11, 2018
Audio Journal | Two Years and Five Months Old

I watched Tommy Caldwell's film *The Dawn Wall* today. I had been avoiding the movie.

Tommy; his ex-wife and the climbing prodigy, Beth Rodden; Eddie; and I pressed go at the same time in the late 1990s, diving into marriage with our vertical soulmates.

I remember so acutely the feeling of being different as a climber and charting my own way. And then meeting someone whom I could pursue that passion *with*—on any mountain, any rock face, in any tent in the world. I remember thinking, *If that total alignment is not something to base marriage and a life upon, then what is?* People have built lives together with so much less. My parents did it with a different amalgamation, and it did not work.

What are you supposed to base a life together on?

It's not like dating in a city where you see someone now and again and don't have to immediately think about moving in with them. In climbing, you're with them 24/7 in a tiny tent peeing next to their head and emptying their pee bottle alongside your own. At that point, marriage doesn't seem like much of a stretch. Watching Tommy and Beth in the film today reminds me of how I thought I was doing something so different—and that having a partner in this alternative lifestyle might have been something I did to normalize that difference.

Of course, that makes you dependent on the marriage and that person. And when they let you down, or when the marriage does, you're all alone on the largest climb of your life, without any backup.

December 16, 2018
Audio Journal | Two Years and Five Months Old

Kaz screams in the dark. My decathlon between our bed and his tonight involves a stubbed toe on Irenna's chair and something sticky and wet on my heel. I glance at the clock: 3:33 A.M.

I try to secure Kaz from thrashing around while attempting to be a ghost in their room. Was that a catch in Irenna's breath? Only god knows how many nights I've been up with them. I will do anything to have one of them stay asleep.

Irenna likes "skin skin"—yanking my shirt down to touch her cheek to anything on my chest. Kaz wrestles my head with his whole body as if to absorb me into his being.

"I love my mamma," Kaz says. "I love my family."

—⁓—

"Nurse Buddha?" Irenna asks one morning at breakfast, pointing to our Buddha statue, which sits above the table. I look more closely, and the Buddha has a slightly swelling chest.

"That looks so nice, baby girl," I say. "So nice."

—⁓—

When we put ornaments on our Christmas tree, Kaz gets concerned if we only have one of something.

"Where is the Irenna bunny? The Irenna egg? The Irenna snowman?" he asks.

"Like twins?" I ask.

"Twins," he says. "Twins."

———

"I miss Irenna!" he screams every time he wakes up from his nap.

"No Irenna!" he screams when she's in my arms.

"No Kaz!" she screams when it's his turn.

———

At 4:30 A.M. I give up and we three relocate to the kitchen. The cabinet is full of mouse droppings and bright-orange yam flesh strewn everywhere. The septic tank off the bathroom is leaking. The ants parade around our floor as if they own the place. I shut the cabinet door and carry our misplaced mouse trap covered in ants outside, setting them out in the twelve-degree air to at least kill something for the day.

"What's next?" Irenna asks.

....

December 23, 2018
Letter | Two Years and Five Months Old

We are on a plane to Minnesota. Your dad sits across the aisle from us, unencumbered, while the two of you writhe on top of me and alternate screaming, "Mamma time! No Irenna!"

"No Kaz!"

He tries to pry one of you off me, but you will have none of it. It only makes the screaming worse.

We are the people on the plane whom everyone hates.

The flight attendant tries to push you, Irenna, down into your seat for takeoff. As she does so, your screams intensify.

The only way to keep you both from screaming is to relent. I give you, Kaz, the run of my hair so that my neck is cocked toward you. I snuggle you with my hair while you tug at every strand. At the same time, Irenna, you are tucked under my chin on the opposite side, with your thumb in your mouth and your fingers curled around my nose. We are breathing the same air—the same stale plane air—back and forth.

I am angry, again, at your dad, even though it's not exactly his fault. I'm mad at him because I cannot be angry at you. I go pee with you attached to me, Irenna. Then I watch the family in front of me eat over-ripe bananas from a special banana case as they look disparagingly at me for giving you the sugar-laden Spirit Airlines juice cocktail.

December 26, 2018
Letter | Two Years and Five Months Old

"The cheetah mother is always stressed," the narrator says.

I snort at the TV. Peter closes his eyes.

The four cheetah pups cavort on top of their mamma like she is a trampoline, burying their faces and butts into her chin and her armpits. The only difference I can tell between them and my twins is that they are covered in fur.

Here it is, I think to myself, *the irrefutable evidence that this is what females do.*

Twelve years ago during an Ethiopian sunrise on Lake Langano, I lay next to a man I was considering marrying. He told me that the females of any species were designed to take care of the young. The baboons were loud that day and had woken us up. Henry was in the coffee business but loved biology. He lazily stroked my arm and talked about how amazing nature was because of the perfect and true roles for male and female animals. With every word he uttered about the baboons, hippos, zebras, and lions, I took one step further from a future with him and his tweed blazers.

And now I watch and think, *How do I refute this? How am I as a woman refuting this daily? How do I pair this role in myself with my demand for equity elsewhere? Is everyone else this angry and not admitting it?* The cheetah mother is stressed, but is she pissed?

December 31, 2018
Letter | Two Years and Six Months Old

Michelle Obama is my ski companion right now. Or at least she is in my ear, reading *Becoming* to me during my daily cross-country ski tours in the White Mountains.

"I was a box checker," she says, "marching to the resolute beat of effort/result."

Is there any other beat?

As a child, any time I came home with a quiz in hand to proudly share with my parents the ninety-seven scrawled across the top in red pen, my older sister was there to tell me she remembered that same quiz and her score of ninety-eight.

"Was I good enough?" Michelle Obama asks.

I asked.

I ask.

Good enough could make me fit in. But of course it never did. Curly hair, glasses, and a Polish name impossible to pronounce set the stage for never fitting in early on—enough to make it never feel right when I almost did later.

The other day I pulled my eighth-grade school picture out of the photo box. What was I looking at over my shoulder when everyone else was looking squarely at the camera? My future over there?

Effort/result. I used to think that what I was doing was different. Now I know I am doing the same, forever doing the same, just trying to do it in an unconventional setting.

Michelle and I ski the miles together, and I wonder why we all push ourselves this much. I huff and puff up a hill and try to go a little farther, a little faster, a little more than last time.

January 2, 2019
Letter | Two Years and Six Months Old

I am not a big New Year's person. Or maybe I am, but I also know myself enough to not get overly hyped about what I want in a new year nor overly hard on myself about what has not come to pass.

But today, this New Year, with the two of you freshly two and a half, I feel. You read that right. *Feel.* Period. I feel everything. Today I sat down with giant sheets of paper covered with marker and crayon and stuffed a selection into folders with your names on them. I cried. Not because they were good drawings. But because they showed me how much you've changed. How much you are. How much you are mine.

Raw. Maybe that is the best word for my experience of motherhood.

I don't know what to do with all of this emotion other than to write. Other than to try to capture it, you, us—together in this giant vessel of love and questioning and learning.

"What is the point?" I asked Peter as we drove home last week from the airport in the increasing blackness that comes when you leave the city for the mountains.

If we can't visit happily with my sister, then why visit?

What is the point of family when it's hard?

What is the right plan with them?

Will more time together make it easier?

How are we raising you?

I am not the version of myself I like the most when I am with my sister. I am stiffer, tenser, more caustic, more like her than me. And it's made worse by my fear that this might be the real me if this is the real her. As if it's our DNA or the inescapable imprint of our upbringing.

January 16, 2019
Letter | Two Years and Six Months Old

I'm like a toddler. Irenna screams when she's having a tantrum—when she's awash with complex emotions. Even when she's not necessarily mad, she lashes out at me. And I do it to Peter.

My heart is breaking. So is my will. So is my mind. We have not gotten consistent sleep since November because of teething and colds and a lingering cough Kaz cannot shake, all making it so that now you almost wake up just for the sake of waking—and, each time, you need me. I feel like we have infants again.

My body responds to the fire alarm of screaming by automatically swinging my legs over the bed and walking. I fix the problem, lie back down, get up, fix the problem, lie back down. Except it's harder now. Or maybe I'm just more tired.

Last night I sat in a chair by your bed and listened to you scream for forty minutes. Do you know that in France one night you cried for seventy-four minutes? And then you slept. But then you were a year old and could only cry. Now you wail with words that break my heart.

"I want to snuggle."

"Please snuggle me."

"I want to hold your hand."

"Please, Mamma. Please."

"Help me."

"Sleep with me."

"Please hold my hand."

"Please sleep with me."

I am crying as I write this at 8:40 in the morning, having gotten less than three hours of sleep. I know we are building a way for us all to have more sleep, but I am breaking.

———

Today at nap time your dad texts me from the living room after you've been crying in my ear in your bedroom for fifteen minutes while we try to settle you down. *Are you with Kaz?* he asks.

I want to reply something mean, something like, *Yes, just like I was all the time when they were babies, just like I am way more than you.* Even though the night before he was with you from 4:45 to six A.M. But that was not midnight.

I am angry, I think. *So deeply, deeply angry.* But it is not anger, really, is it?

We work on our feelings together every day. "I can see that you're mad, Irenna. You're mad Mamma won't let you have more almonds. It's okay to be mad," I say.

But what about *my* feelings? Why am I mad at Peter over these forty-minute chunks of time I must spend with Kaz, trying to calm him down while he carries on? Is it because I don't have a name for this feeling? I don't have a guide? Maybe I feel put out. Uncomfortable. On edge. Too needed. Heart-strained. Is that an emotion? I feel heart-strained. As if I'm being stretched and stretched against all the edges.

What I should do is walk outside and tell Peter that. I should not be mad but say this to him instead. But mad is all I know. Mad is what I grew up with. Mad was the only other emotion available next to happy. If you're not happy, you're mad.

But that is not serving me, and it is definitely not serving our marriage. Our family needs more than happy and mad.

January 24, 2019
Letter | Two Years and Six Months Old

Difficult and different. It's what I've always created and thought I thrived on.

—w—

Rainy Pass, North Cascades, 1996.

I was a climber by then, and that meant climbing at any cost, at any time, all the time. If I could not find partners I'd head into the mountains by myself. I knew what I was doing, I rationalized, and most of the objectives had a relatively little actual climbing. The Northeast Ridge of Black Peak was one of the first on my list.

The four or so miles of hiking and then the lower-angle scrambling went quickly, and I sat on the high ridge surrounded by the craggy Cascades and pulled out my rock shoes for the three pitches of technical rock I'd climb ropeless above. I tied the laces, clipped my pack's waist belt and sternum strap, and went up. The climbing was a simple series of steps and reaches and pulls, with some exposure here and there. My body felt strong and lean, and I had everything I needed just as me—including Advil, athletic tape, a lightweight alpine harness, and a 120-foot small-diameter rope in case I needed to rappel. I took out my pocket climbing register at the summit and wrote "Northeast Ridge, solo" next to my name, and then underlined it.

Soloing made me feel strong and independent. Those might seem like obvious words to associate with doing something hard by yourself, but they were key feelings for me at the time.

I was nineteen, with a history of setting up independent literature studies in high school and already looking to create a personal study-abroad program in college. Taking a year off between my sophomore and junior university years to climb full-time synced up with my knack for placing myself outside various peer groups—rightly or wrongly. I didn't want to wait to find my group of climbing friends—and back then, I didn't know I was supposed to be looking for that group. It had never occurred to me that it even existed.

For each climb, I'd feel my energy switch on the moment I started packing up my red-and-purple Granite Gear backpack that was covered with hand-sewn patches. I can still picture most of them: green and white from Inuvik, Northwest Territories, to celebrate a forty-five day canoe trip; decals from Vancouver Island and Tijuana, Mexico, bookending a 1,700-plus-mile bike trek I did with my mom; orange and black oars for the Princeton Rowing team to go with the calluses I still had two months post–Eastern Sprints. Each brocaded insignia a justification for another adventure, another boost to my self-esteem.

Firestone Library, Princeton, 1994.

I wore the fact that I'd been admitted off the wait-list like a badge of honor while also using it as a crutch to help me fit in.

These were not my people. After all, I was not supposed to be here. I chose college like I'd chosen many things in my life—picking what was hard and what, when conquered, would be an achievement. When everyone told me that my first choice for undergraduate study, the University of Chicago, would be the hardest academic challenge I could undertake, that the neighborhood was rough, and that I'd have absolutely zero social life, I was inspired instead of afraid. "You can't want that," people seemed to say, so that is what I wanted.

Princeton saved me from my own self-sabotage in that way—giving me a literal ivy-covered second option.

Difficult and different. Jesus, Burhardt, using that as your guide was not a way to set yourself up for marital and familial success.

January 30, 2019
From the Notepad | Two Years and Seven Months Old

Last week, I said no to auditioning for a reality show called *Man vs. Bear* with a storyline exactly as the title suggests. Today, I am heading to DC to shoot a pilot for another reality show called *Middle of Nowhere*—which is about what it feels like in a near-whiteout on Route 25 at six A.M. today when your dad calls to announce that pre-school is delayed.

"Can you call your client and push back your start time?" I ask him.

"I'd rather not," he says. "I'd like to not have to."

Have to what? Be less professional? A dad? A real person? Midway through my wondering and his silence, we lose service.

The new normal at home seems to be that I cover these disruptions, rescheduling my meetings no matter the consequences. This is not mine to solve today. I'm already forty-five minutes away and have days to go before I'm home. I turn up the music and enjoy my time out of service.

—⁓—

Last week, I took a grant meeting on the phone in the minivan after my annual pelvic exam ran late. I did not share that detail, or any detail, with the potential funder.

We compartmentalize a lot. But I'm not sure it's doing any good.

"I wish someone had told me that to continue obstetrics within family medicine I'd need a stay-at-home spouse," says a college friend, Katie. She had done an additional fellowship year in high-risk obstetrics after a family-medicine residency, hoping to provide full-spectrum care to her rural community. But hospital politics left her without a team to share being on-call for those late-night deliveries. With an infant and a toddler at home, and a husband helping run his family's business, plus working full-time in family medicine, she was stretched too thin.

"Something's gotta give," she tells me.

Her "give" is now doing family practice without obstetrics, still a big job, but more manageable. The fellowship year had not been a total loss. "We got to live in Seattle for a year!" she says. "And I loved delivering all of those babies. But for me it was just too much. Some mom docs manage it all, with solo call; I just don't know how."

Something's gotta give. I bristle at the statement because it's true. In my head I justify the choice of not going to Patagonia this year based on the type of climbing I want to pursue, but the calculus also involves what I *can* have if I don't go.

At the airport en route to DC, I scan Instagram and see Kate, my now-former climbing partner, announced as the winner of this year's American Alpine Club's Underhill Award for "the highest level of climbing skill, courage, and perseverance, with outstanding success." I scroll past it, envious, confused, hurt by our collective inability to bridge the gap of my new motherhood.

Kaz's nights are filled with coughing and crying instead of sleep. For everyone. We're being constantly thrust forward into another day that takes forever, and filing away the nights and the weeks and the months behind us. But they are our life.

This is just temporary, I tell myself.

"We'll just get through this big push," Peter says.

You are two and a half. Just when are we supposed to feel like this is the life we're creating? Or maybe a better question is, *When will we realize it already is?*

―—―

How hard should I be fighting for equity? How much do you just let go? If one of us, Peter or me, could just cry uncle, it would be easier.

"Do you just want me to sell insurance?" my friend Kevin asked his wife, Claire, when their kids were young and he was guiding and traveling.

"Yes," she told me, recounting her answer to his question. "I wanted to tell him, 'Yes. So very much.'"

When Kevin and Claire met, they both worked for the National Outdoor Leadership School. From there Kevin shot off into climbing and guiding, and Claire into teaching. When they decided to have kids, she stayed at home to be the family's ballast. That was their plan. Peter and I never even talked about a plan in which this was an option for either of us.

What is a reasonable amount of time to be with your kids? To want to be with them? I demand Peter have an answer while telling him that since our work does not follow the traditional five-day workweek schedule, we can create our own reality.

But the other reality is that it's far from endless—or sometimes any—fun to be with our kids right now. It's real work. It's constant refereeing. It's hard to *want* to choose that over a climbing day putting up a first ascent. One leaves you sore and invigorated. The other leaves you worn-out and sneezed on, but loved.

Somewhere in me I have a formula for figuring out what is enough time. It's a ticking clock when I've been away for too long, when just an hour with the twins before bed will not suffice, when I know they need three times that and I shift my schedule and push more into less space so I can allocate more time with them.

What is Peter's formula?

And I don't know the cost of this long-term. I'm afraid of the toll on our marriage, on my sense of purpose, on my ability to make an impact, on the happiness of our children. How much more well-adjusted would I have been if my parents had been happy together?

February 25, 2019
Audio Journal | Two Years and Seven Months Old

I swing at another concavity between ice runnels. *Snap* goes the pick of my tool into the ice. I think of Irenna. *Don't think of your kids, Majka. Not now. Get yourself to the next foothold, the next microledge in the midst of the vertical ice. Swing, fracture, break the ice up, yell, "Ice!," swing, set, kick, and move up. Think about that.* I don't know what I used to think about when I ice climbed. I don't remember. I do know it doesn't seem helpful to think of my babies.

I'm midway through my first climbing trip since having the twins before I realize my problem. I'm temporarily living without kids in a rental apartment in Quebec and have what feels like endless time. Each morning I sharpen my ice screws and picks, I pack, and I wonder about how this choice might impact my kids.

"It's so good for them to see you doing something you love," says Gilbert. She is childless, for now. I don't have the energy to explain why I think that's overly simplistic. Because it's not just what I love; it's also what takes me away from them. And it's what could kill me.

Does climbing have to be worth dying for—big, gnarly, laudable objectives—to justify doing it over being with my kids? I don't even want to write these words. That is not my type of climbing. I do it differently. I am safe. But what if?

One thousand feet of climbing up, La Loutre's final ice pillar had a crack clean through it. I had no idea it was there until my right tool sat perched in its bottom half, the *whoomp* my pick made when it hit the ice telling me something far bigger than anything I wanted to deal with had come detached. I froze. I looked at the ice. A horizontal gap the size of my fist ran across the pillar—the crack where it had separated from the wall. The broken ice might explode when I took out my tool, and it certainly would if I hit it again. I pivoted, contorted, and strained around my tool and crampon placements, placing a screw in solid ice high and left to protect myself.

How far above a clean fracture is ice actually bonded without the bottom falling out? Can I reach that far?

—⁓—

Today is Gilbert's and my second day climbing; we're upriver from La Loutre on her more famous cousin, the Pomme d'Or. I stomp my feet and squat at the belay to stay warm as Gilbert picks her way up scalloped ice above that looks like parasols. I think of the blood in my hands warming up, to will it to do so. I think of all the things my kids say now that I want to remember before they're gone. Before "babbas" became "blueberries," as they did all of a sudden two months ago. I miss babbas.

"I want a come with me," says Irenna.

"I am going to share with myself," says Kaz.

Irenna sucks her thumb and shares her pinkie with me; Kaz kisses me by first taking hold of my head like a possessive lover so he can square his lips directly against mine.

—⁓—

The wind picks up by two P.M. even though the forecast said it would wait until five P.M. The wind has its own plan. Snow falls sideways and up—on top of down. I think a jet plane is flying around, then realize it's the wind on the Rivière Malbaie, a sliver of gray and bare ice four hundred meters below us. Soon Gilbert; her husband, Jason, who's shooting photos; and I rappel down fast and easily and thankfully. We set off microavalanches as we plunge into armpit-deep snow below the climb, two inches of slab releasing from the snowpack below. I choose to not worry about it. Somewhere in my brain I think how stupid it would be to die descending from the Pomme d'Or. Why would this be worth it? I bury the thought as soon as I have it.

———

Our last day of climbing dawns with zero degrees as a high and seventy-mile-per-hour gusts predicted. This is the storm that will generate a new record of 172 miles per hour on Mount Washington, and sustained winds of 130 miles per hour for thirty minutes back at home.

I'm done in Quebec, a nagging pain in my ankle is growing, and I want to get home. We scrap climbing for the day, and within an hour I'm driving back to you.

When I walk in the door you cover me within minutes, each carving out your piece of my real estate—a parcel of lap and a shoulder each. Irenna, you have my neck; Kaz, you have my hair.

Irenna: "Mamma, I was sad and I missed you."

Kaz: "Mamma, I want to take care of you. And I want to take care of your hair."

Oh, how I love you each and how I love you both.

March 10, 2019
From the Notepad | Two Years and Eight Months Old

Kaz: "Stop singing that song!"

Irenna: "I want to sing."

Kaz: "This is *my* house!"

Irenna: "No, this is *my* house."

Kaz: "This is our house."

Irenna: "This is *our* house!"

March 23, 2019
Letter | Two Years and Eight Months Old

We sent Ptarmigan the poodle to a farm in Vermont. It's not a euphemism.

"Poodle? Poodle? Oodle?" Irenna walks around and asks, playing a game of hide-and-seek that will forever go unrequited.

"He's on his way to Vermont," I say, "to be with chickens."

"Bock, bock, bock," says Irenna.

"Cluck, cluck, cluck," says Kaz.

"Woof, woof, woof," I add, because it's easier than sharing that the poodle cracked. It was just too much for him. He was snarling and snapping at me and Peter, and, we were afraid, he'd soon do the same to the kids.

His new family is bringing Ptarmigan from the vet's office to our house today, to say goodbye and to pick up his bed, food bowls, and leashes—and just like that, he will be gone. He has not been home in eight days, since that first morning when he growled and snapped at me and then ran away. I chased after him all the way into town, my ankle grating what I now know is bone-on-bone because it turned out to be broken. It's been broken for six weeks—I'm the lucky owner of an os trigonum, a bone that fewer than ten percent of humans have, and that I have now sheared off my ankle such that it's floating around in my heel, blanketing my ankle with stabbing pain with every step. Usually it's elite ballerinas who get this injury, but I somehow did it climbing, poodle-wrangling, and skiing. After six weeks of climbing through the pain when I thought it was just a sprain, I'm now facing surgery.

When Val drives up, I hobble to the door in a walking boot that is about to be replaced by crutches. Ptarmigan barks at me from the car, and I tell Val I will stay back and try not to stress him.

"I get it, buddy. It is too much," I say to him.

You two are mooing and neighing in the house by the time my tears are at bay and I've limped back to our to our carpet farmyard.

April 17, 2019
Letter | Two Years and Eight Months Old

I'm three weeks post–ankle surgery, and Peter has temporarily left me, again. (That is not fair, I know, but it's what I call it sometimes in my head. Really he is just gone.) We do it to each other, but I am fairly certain he does it more and more often. And that I let him. This time around he's in Tucson with the military.

"Mamma and Papa and me and Kaz," Irenna says. "This is my family."

When Papa is gone, they cry for him. "I want my family," Irenna sniffs.

Kaz wants stories, both pretend and real. Like the story of the bear who trades a banana to a moose for a cookie, and then the one "where Mamma was scared to go to bed."

"When Mamma was little, she was afraid to go to bed," I start.

"And her mamma helps her," Kaz says.

"Her papa helped," I correct him.

I pause, but what if this makes him miss his papa more? I continue: "Her mamma and her papa helped."

When do you tell your kids that, as far as you remember, you never had a mamma and papa put you to bed together? When do you just decide to lie for ease?

"Mamma's mamma and papa came in together and told her she was safe."

If you face forward in the car when you tell a story and don't change your overall velocity, most often your two-and-a-half-year-olds won't know when you're crying and driving.

I grasp for help. I text Peter: *I signed us up for an eight-week date-night plan with Gottman Institute—looked interesting and cool.*

One minute later I follow up:

I should have prefaced that with: Would you be okay with me signing us up for this? I'd like to do it. It's like therapy without the appointments.

Peter doesn't say yes. Instead he responds with: *Let's talk about it when I'm back.*

I want to dig further into our marriage when it's hard versus backing away and looking at it like a Monet painting. From a distance you can't quite see all the dead spots and fissures between the dots, and instead you pretend the overall view is "fine." Peter wants to stand in the back of the gallery.

The next night I have dinner with Garlick. We talk about our nuclear families blowing apart when we were kids. I tell her how my sister had a hard time, so I did not.

"I was the one who was fine, and so I was fine," I say.

"Doesn't that make you sad?" Garlick asks.

I contemplate an answer.

"Or the little girl in you sad?" she clarifies.

The restaurant's starched linen napkin sucks at wiping up tears. I try to find that little girl. But I don't know where she is. "I think I must have been fine—really," I say. "Or I was fine enough not to know how to be otherwise."

Here are two facts I know. My mom was violently raped by a stranger and then got divorced from my father. Maybe the events are not as related as I assume. This is both not my story to tell and the story I must finally understand as also being mine. Or give myself permission to make my own.

Today, eleven days before my kids turn two years and ten months, I slowly type my mom's name and "rape" into Google. I want to have the details show up on my computer screen. I want to read them and not have to ask her for them because I don't want to hurt my mom by dragging her back to this time.

"I get why marriages fall apart when kids are two and three and five," I say to other people—and have been saying for the past two years—looking for any safe harbor in which to express my desperation. Only now am I doing the arithmetic of my own life. It is not *marriages* that fall apart; it was my *parents'* marriage that fell apart. Which has left me without a template for how to keep my new family together.

—⁓—

What's the best way to begin a conversation with your mother about when she was raped? Should you start by calling your father and asking for details—so you in turn know what to ask her—gingerly navigating what will surely be an emotional minefield? Can I tell this story, even to myself, without first understanding it?

I didn't mean to end up with another husband. I was the one who was freshly divorced and told everyone that marriage was a bunch of lies unless you renewed your commitment every three to five years. My marriage with Eddie dissolved for a reason. Even dozens. But now I have another husband I married because he was the best man I'd ever met, and now we're entrenched in this life of family that can be as beautiful as it is fraught. Inside our union, I can clearly see plain vanilla resentment and anger and poor behavior building—mine, and some of Peter's, but a lot of mine.

Eighteen years ago my friend Libby told me that her first husband had turned out to be gay. She didn't know at the time that I was trying to understand why I had married my first husband and if I should keep him, because I didn't tell her this. But I resented her for it. Gay? Brilliant. Easy. Done. Now, eight years into my second marriage, I realize that I'd been unfair to Libby, who I thought had had it easy. Eddie's drifting into porn and pot, and him turning me down for sex again and again, were all my first marriage's equivalent of Libby's husband being gay. We'd both been burdened with what we saw as intractable situations. Now I have a marriage with fault lines but no cracks. Now, with Peter, I have the work in front of me and the acute realization on a daily basis that I might not be up for it.

"I'll take care of you, Mamma," Irenna says when I cry.

"I'll take care of you too," Kaz adds.

Did I say that to my mom and my dad? As they jousted in court, getting friends to testify to each other's shitty parenting in hopes of full custody? I've always told myself that my mom woke up screaming in the middle of the night from the rape, but what if sometimes it was the pain of her marriage failing and what that was doing to her family?

If I had another life, I tell people, I'd have more babies. I'd have more of them and be content with what that choice brought. Yet I don't know if that is really true. "I don't know if I can have kids," I used to say. "I am a resenter." I'm not sure now if I should be proud of myself for my self-awareness or terrified at my accuracy.

I want to be a man in this equation. I want to be the person who gets to go away for five days and then again twenty-six hours later for seventeen more. I want to have the partner at home who transitions through five different childcare providers during that time and puts toddlers to bed while they scream, "I'm sad, Mamma. I'm sad so sad don't you love me?"

Fuck it. I don't want to be that partner; I want that wife. And I hate that I am that wife, that this is where we've collectively gotten to, that this is the role I've stepped into. To wake up at three A.M. even when the kids are not screaming and lie there wondering if it's because I'm drinking too much wine or because I've become too much of a mother. And not being able to stop doing either. And also not being able to stop climbing, even though I'm pretty sure climbing makes things worse. Another lens to refract on each other. Another shared love turned into an equivocator.

I can't find the date my mom was raped. I find another truth instead.

April 21, 2019
From the Notepad | Two Years and Eight Months Old

Kaz is not asleep yet again. It's been five nights of a continuous battle getting him down, keeping him down.

Tonight we're already an hour past bedtime and he is whimpering. I miss the days when he was in a crib and would cry and I could leave him and know he could not get out. But tonight, with Kaz in his toddler bed, that is not an option. I clomp down the hall, my tread heavy thanks to ankle surgery and crutches.

I start with the same question I always start with: "Are you okay?"

"I love you," he says.

"I love you *too*," I tell him, emphasizing the *too* because he gets upset if he can't hear that part of the script that he's decided is the only way through a conversation.

"*Noooo, Mamma*. Irenna!"

"Baby, Irenna is sleeping."

"Irenna didn't say, 'I love you,' back!"

April 23, 2019
From the Notepad | Two Years and Eight Months Old

We spent $250 on the Gottman Method and watched twenty-eight minutes of the first eighty-minute session. Red and yellow playing cards with tips for creating more marital passion are now scattered throughout the house because you two have more time to play with them than we do. I set an alarm for every Thursday night to do more Gottman sessions.

April 24, 2019
Letter | Two Years and Eight Months Old

I have a pound of flesh to give . . . but to whom?

We're making such a big ask of people on Mount Namuli—to preserve their mountain forest when we can't seem to preserve anything we have here in the US.

There are days I wonder if I should change course and fight right here at home.

Against the people who get plastic bags at our local grocery store.

Against one plastic milk carton at a time.

Against airports not having composting available.

Against a political administration that doesn't believe in climate change almost as vigorously as it is accelerating that change.

Today I book tickets for California for round two of the fellowship. Then I brace myself. When I travel I feel sickened, seeing all the waste and conspicuous consumption around me. But travel I do—to speak about a faraway place and the people who are working to protect it. About their fight to feed their families and not have their land and futures wiped away in a mudslide. How does the carbon footprint of my travels compare to that of a few plastic bags?

Would it be better for me to give my pound of flesh here at home?

Better for my family, for my kids?

Better for us all?

May 17, 2019
From the Notepad | Two Years and Ten Months Old

"Lee is dead," my high school friend Paul tells me. "I had to call."

I'm outside our town library in my van. I stall with my hand on the ignition.

"She was a mom," I say.

"Three kids, Maj. She jumped off a cliff."

I have a mental process to justify the deaths of fellow climbers. But what is the process for grieving childhood friends who had to make it all stop?

May 20, 2019
From the Notepad | Two Years and Ten Months Old

"When we were babies, did we have milk?" Irenna asks me.

"Yes, you had a lot of milk from Mamma," I tell her.

Kaz pipes up: "Did we have enough?"

"You had more than enough."

"Thank you, Mamma," they say in tandem.

May 30, 2019
Audio Journal | Two Years and Eleven Months Old

Five days ago, when Peter was guiding, a two-foot-diameter wheel of rock rained down from above, narrowly missing him. A rockfall that could have just as easily killed or maimed him, changing his life—our lives—forever.

Peter's exposure to risk and injury and death feels so much more real with every near miss. Getting to this place feels so inevitable.

"The exposure is enormous," I tell him. "Hard stop. This is dangerous. You could have been killed." It's not news to either of us.

———

Ten years ago in Namibia, I watched Peter surf a recliner-sized granite rock down a boulder field and stick the landing. Had that rock flipped on him, it would have broken his leg at a minimum, if not ended his life. We were a day-and-a-half hike up the Brandberg Mountain putting up a first ascent on shady, golden granite. The night after we climbed the route bottom to top, we celebrated with our teammates Kate and Chris, and with the final crumbs of chocolate left after seven days at our remote camp.

Neither Peter nor I could sleep that night, and instead of trying to, we made love on noisy air mattresses. We tried to hide what we were doing by having a conversation in case anyone was listening. I have never felt more connected to anyone as I did on those nights camped under the Southern Cross. I've never shared so much of myself, tried so hard, and risked so much, with one person. And now it's even more.

Tonight, we process his accident. He's on the couch and I'm stretching on the floor.

"Can I come hug you?" I ask.

"Please," he says.

The next day, when Peter doesn't move the clothes into the dryer as quickly as I want him to, it suddenly seems as consequential to me as the rockfall. I feel like a giant raw and exposed wound—he can impact me always, in every way.

June 5, 2019
From the Notepad | Two Years and Eleven Months Old

Texting:

Me: "The oatmeal was amazing this morning. It's so hot when you make breakfast."

Peter: "I love how you took the kids to school today."

Me: "It was no problem, lover-man."

Peter: "Lover-man?"

Me: "It was that or baby lamb."

Peter: "Did you reschedule the tire appointment?"

Peter: "Did you reschedule the tire appointment, dear wife of mine?"

Me: "Dear husband, I can't wait to take care of that for us."

Our new therapist Natalie told us to flirt like we mean it. We're shaking off the cobwebs first.

Gottman's still in the drawer. This is better.

June 26, 2019
Letter | Two Years and Eleven Months Old

Your birthday is coming. It's only our third time celebrating you two, and already we're planning two cakes for your big day.

"Why not?" my mom says. "They're individuals."

Irenna wants "banilla," her version of vanilla. Kaz, strawberry shortcake.

After talking about it so much, Irenna changes and says she wants "banilla longcake."

"Mamma," Kaz says, "I love you."

A statement pulled out of the air. Sometimes I can trace the root. Other times, on the way to paint or make it to the potty, he tosses it over his shoulder for me to catch.

"Mamma, can you stay with me forever?"

I sidestep this, even though the reality of my leaving for fifteen days is just three days away.

"I will love you forever," I say, and it seems weak even to me. I consider getting into it with him, but it's eight P.M. and getting my kids to sleep on time so I can sleep seems more important at this moment than being honest with Kaz. Which, even as I write this, makes me cringe.

Irenna crawls into my bed within ninety-five seconds of her wake light turning on. Hoisting herself up today, she checks in and checks up on me.

"Mamma, how was your date? How is your ankle?"

She still curls her pinkie finger around my nose, sharing her thumb-sucking with me, her curled fingers again a tunnel between only us.

June 30, 2019
Letter | Three Years Old

"Bring them with you," she says to me.

I'm wandering JFK again on my way to Mozambique and have run into this woman who has twenty-six-year-old twins. She tells me it's what she did.

But how good is this woman's memory, really?

I nod my head as if *of course* I agree that I should take my kids with me. But what am I supposed to do with them? Am I lacking the parenting ability that magically transforms two three-year-olds having double tantrums into a calm working environment? Who would take care of them while I work? Or is the expectation behind this that I'm not supposed to work—but then why would I be going? And if I am working and they come and I bring a nanny, who pays the thousands of dollars in extra travel and childcare expenses to make this great experience happen?

When Peter, en route to South Korea to work with the military, chatted with someone in the airport and divulged that he's a father, was he told repeatedly that he should bring the kids with him? Somehow I doubt it.

—⁓—

The reality of life on the move with kids is clear to me: if I bring them with me, neither motherhood nor my work will get done properly.

I wander the airport, taking care not to strain my ankle, which I still can't climb or hike on even three months post-surgery—even though I was told that based on typical recovery time I'd be back in action after three weeks. I wish I had a tighter connection so I would not think about how much I want to turn around and fly home instead of eighty-five hundred miles away. It's been just a few hours, yet I already feel like I have lost time with my children that I will never get back.

—⁓—

Your kids will appreciate that you do this, yet another friend texts me. *It's so good for them to see you out in the world.*

Is this what we tell ourselves in the interest of staying sane? What if I could stay home for six years and *then* do this work? That would be what I consider impressive, and almost impossible. So I barter again with the system. I will do *this* now so I can do *that* later—when my kids probably won't need or want me. But I cannot explain that broken calculus to myself very well, let alone to my well-meaning friends.

"Your future self will think it's cool that Mamma does this," I imagine saying to them. "Future. Can you say *future*?"

When I think of my parents, I don't think about appreciating them for their accolades or travels or the complexity of the problems they solved at work. But my sister and I benefited hugely from their success, with food and clothing and comfortable houses and vacations and ski passes. I was proud of my hard-driving parents, but I didn't know any other reality. Can I say for sure I would have been less proud if they'd done less?

July 5, 2019
Letter | Three Years Old

My computer clock is on home time, and I watch the minutes tick until you all wake up. In front of me is Mount Murrabué—guarding Namuli just out of sight. Motos sputter past, punctuated by the gentle whir of bicycles trailing behind.

My stomach has gone south again—it's the malaria meds. One trip a year feels like too little to become ingrained here in the work in Gurúè and on Mount Namuli. And yet it seems like too much for my family.

We spin through the city and countryside to finally get to the winding road into the mountains. The tar breaks apart, exposing dangerous potholes. We swerve, then just moments before tipping, we straighten.

This feels more like home to me.

How will you help these people, really? I ask myself this every day. It's been five years of working here—hearing people tell me they want their kids to be healthy, not just the forest to be healthy; years of saying, *But I can't help with that*. What if we could say yes? I thought conservation was the sector for this work. But it feels too narrow and inhumane. What if Legado can create another way?

July 26, 2019
From the Notepad | Three Years Old

You're three years and almost one month old. All goals I had for staying on top of my letters to you have gone by the wayside, just like my uninformed, pre-motherhood fiery assessment of people who sleep-train their kids.

Irenna, you still suck your thumb and come to me saying you have not snuggled enough. When things are outside you tell me they can "wind away." Today, you disappeared down the hall to try to squirrel away water in a jewelry box, and when I caught you at the bathroom sink, you yelled, "I am meditating!"

August 8, 2019
Letter | Three Years and One Month Old

Today, when I was talking to your dad on the phone, I called you two "little shits." It might be my new parenting low point.

He's in New Hampshire training future mountain guides. We're in Colorado because, ankle be damned, I wanted to have an adventure like I had before I had you. I cringe even to write that down—having never wanted to say aloud that there is a difference between the before and after, having instead wanted to see my life and our marriage on a continuum. But there is nothing if there is not a line between them.

This "adventure" is about family and work meetings. But we are only three days in, and I have canceled plans on friends as well as all my meetings because I realized that what you need more than me coming into and out of a new place is me being around this new place with you.

Or I need to be a different kind of mom—one who can handle your meltdowns with grace and aplomb. I have started handling them with threats, hobbling after you—limping first and then with a cane—and no longer wondering why the surgical ankle repair that was supposed to take just weeks to heal has now landed me back in a removable-cast walking boot four months later.

I held your baby cousin today. Anna is eight weeks old, and started nursing my bicep so strongly I have a hickey to show for it. Feeling her lips and tongue engage and pulsate against my skin brought me back to my two years of nursing you. I want that time back. I want to travel to it when I need to see and understand it. Holding Anna made me ache with wanting another baby—made me yearn for another chance to have that connection. I want to stop time, or at least repeat it, to embroider the memories in steel thread on my mind and heart.

My oldest childhood friend, Liz, had another baby four years after her twins because she wanted to know what it was like. "Just one," she told me. "Imagine, just one." She told me that having that baby was the best decision of her life.

"I want another," I told Peter last week. "I miss my babies as babies," I cried.

"Are you crazy?" he asked.

Then, the next time I said I wanted more, he said, "You have your babies. They are down the hall sleeping. Go wake them up and play with them."

How can I want more if I cannot always handle what I have? Every single thing I am straining against—the reality of my twin-pregnancy-induced abdominal-wall separation, which makes it so I still cannot climb overhanging routes let alone do sit-ups; managing the tantrums; the discrepancy in parenting workload between Peter and me—would be exacerbated by having another child. This has to be the very definition of illogical thinking.

And yet, I still want it.

Last week, Irenna was screaming at me, "I am *not* listening to you."

Kaz came over and held my head in his hands. "I will listen to you, Mamma. I will take care of you. I will be with you all summer."

I inhabited that peacemaker role my whole childhood—leaving me with zero idea of how to handle my anger as an adult.

Kaz and Irenna trade roles. One behaves while the other melts down—declaring their compliance in contrast to the other's defiance. "I'll take care of you, Mamma," they say.

"It's not your job to take care of me," I tell them. "That is Mamma's job."

Oh, what am I sharing with them that I don't even want them to have in the first place?

I was their age when my mom and my dad . . . what? I don't even know the details. I cannot imagine sitting my kids down today and telling them there would be no more Dad and Mom together.

August 14, 2019
From the Notepad | Three Years and One Month Old

Words from My Mother

On working from home:

"I just don't think anyone who works from home is really working. I know that sounds tough, but in my heart of hearts I think, *Oh come on, get out of bed and go to work.*"

On weaning her four-month-old horse, Huckleberry:

"If we put him with another mare, he'd try to nurse and risk getting kicked. This way, if he tries to nurse, he's sucking on a gelding's penis. It's win-win."

On my fifteen-year-old niece, who is spending the summer with her:

"Well, I'm not going to just hang out with her if she doesn't want to spend time with me."

Her world is the safest, primarily consisting of the horses, the ranch, her workouts.

If I could throw a tantrum and yell, my script might be, "Mom, why can't you hang out and just be?"

And then I think, *Irenna and Kaz's script might say the same thing.*

August 17, 2019
Letter | Three Years and One Month Old

Kate got married in Jackson today. I took us on this crazy western trip for an adventure, but now I know it was to be with my community. With you, with them. As an us.

"You came," Kate said when she spotted me.

"I had to," I said.

We spent the night dancing and learning that the new boot I'm wearing to immobilize my ankle makes for a great pivot point. I grabbed my friend Jasmin and her one-year-old twins and dove in and asked her about what was real, what was hard, what mattered.

I hungrily wanted hours more of this: conversation with a working pro-athlete, climbing-mamma doppelgänger. I saw Julie Kennedy and cried with her—not about losing Hayden, her son, but about what marriage takes. You two slept on the campervan floor; all night long, I kept peeking down from my bed to make sure you were real.

September 1, 2019
Audio Journal | Three Years and Two Months Old

They say a primary understanding in psychotherapy is that if you didn't process something when you were a certain age growing up, you will go through it as soon as your kids reach that age.

Well, guess what?

It turns out I didn't process a ton of shit when I was three years old, when my parents were getting divorced. How could I have? Right now, I am not handling it. I feel both so angry and so scared of the work it will take to free myself from that anger. And no matter what I do, I feel like the key for me to be the mom I want to be with my two three-year-olds, and in a good partnership with Peter as we co-parent, is all smashed together with what happened forty years ago.

All I want in interactions with Peter is to point out the things he is doing wrong, yet I also want him to be nice and loving to me. And I know that when my sister does that to me, or did that to me as a kid, all I wanted was to run away from her.

But then how do I speak up for myself and get credit for everything I am doing, without doing it the way she does it, and without alienating Peter?

This ongoing kernel of frustration—of not being seen and feeling so taken advantage of—is eating me alive.

September 19, 2019
Letter | Three Years and Two Months Old

"What happened when you got divorced, Dad? How did it feel?"

I am on a journey to learn answers to questions I have never been able to ask.

"Your mother worked until seven thirty or eight. She was at meetings or who knows . . ."

I don't ask him what he means by "who knows." *I won't take the bait,* I think at first. Then: *I won't see it as bait,* I think second.

"I was home every day at 5:10," he tells me.

I don't trust his answers, but I'm not sure why. What if I could just learn to listen?

―――⁓―――

"You were afraid of the wolf," my dad says. "I remember that."

I don't remember any wolves but probably don't remember ninety-nine percent of my life back then.

I tell him I have to check on the kids, in part because it's true and in part because I am not yet ready for this conversation. I am not sure I want to hear his sadness or if I can process this information without feeling protective of my mom. But why? Do I inherently trust Mom because she had an affair? My stepfather and she met and fell in love while she was still married to my dad, and everyone has always known that in my family. Do I feel like this truth being out there means my mom is more believable in her accounting of my parents' marriage? That is not fair, and I know I will have to find a way around my bias. I don't know how to listen to my dad though. I am too used to defending my mom to him, defending him to her, and straddling the middle of a family long after it ripped apart.

Who would know the unadulterated truth? I search for an impartial source in my head and wake up at three A.M. thinking of Becky—our nanny from when I was one until I was five. I haven't talked to her in five years, maybe more.

I write out a list of questions to ask and leave them on my desk. Then I add to them daily. Three days into my list-making, my sister texts to say Becky died. She went fast, days after being diagnosed with a rare cancer.

I'm sobbing as I read the obituary, write her family, and damn the fucking universe for its perverse sense of timing.

September 30, 2019
Letter | Three Years and Three Months Old

For me, you being three years old is harder than you being two years old. I think two of you at three years old might be my maximum.

I want to write all that is great about you, but at 9:21 A.M., I am finally digging into work after getting you out the door with your dad to daycare. And after having been yelled at by tantruming toddlers for the greater part of the morning, I just want to say how hard it is.

—

Here is what I don't understand: if I ask my mom or dad about me when I was three years old, they don't remember. How can they not remember this age?

I've started to see another old therapist, Angie, to try to better understand and manage my emotions. So much of my time right now is spent helping you through major feelings—everything from wanting another peach to not wanting to get a splinter out. But I'm without the tools I need to help you because my major feelings are at capacity. And I know this is only just the beginning of this new ride.

I don't want to write any of this down right now. Because the reality of it, stark on the page and meeting me eye to eye, is sure to make me feel like I am not handling much well. Except that is not true. I am handling work very well. This must be why people work. That and the fact that they need to make money to support themselves and their families.

———

I know I want things to be better between Peter and me, but I can't seem to get them there.

"Can you please be gentle to me today?" I ask him. Then he turns away.

How can you be gentle with each other or really be *anything* with each other when you have two three-year-olds almost constantly yelling at you, asking for you, and demanding things of you?

I've been saving up this time to write as if it's a treat, and now that I'm here, nothing but anger and frustration is coming out of me.

What else?

———

Kaz and Irenna, you can bike now. You climb on your Strider Balance Bikes, run your feet quickly along whatever surface we put you on, lift your feet up, and fly. Irenna, you're terrifying on your bike going downhill, tensing your hip flexors and hinging to lift your legs so that slowing yourself isn't an option. Coming to an eventual slowdown is the only way you'll stop. You career into the woods ten percent of the time but are otherwise mastering the ride.

I'm still recovering from my ankle surgery, seven months since hurting it, and while I know I could sprint after you in an emergency, I watch you ride and fly over logs and rocks and see everything I cannot control appearing in front of me in your wake.

You come into my bed every morning. Today, you told me that I should not be sad when you leave because grown-ups come back.

Kaz, you have new language every day. New phrases, new tenses, new Spanish words. You run your way into a room and announce what you want or you cuddle with my hair instead. You're exploring your emotional options, always. "How was your sleep, Mamma?" you ask me. You cannot go to sleep without your dad and me checking in and following up endlessly. I fear you're learning how to control the world and we're not pushing back on you enough, but the truth is that I am all out of pushbacks when 8:30 P.M. comes around.

———

I feel like I already don't remember what just was. I can't remember what I did when you needed us in the night and I was still nursing you. And that was not that long ago. I think we were in a better place with sleep than we are now.

What should I remember from now? Irenna, you snuggle my armpit wanting *skin skin,* and know exactly how to get it by unzipping or unbuttoning or yanking down anything that is in your way.

October 15, 2019
From the Notepad | Three Years and Three Months Old

"I didn't like or trust my siblings," my mom says. "I didn't have a place with them. And if you like them, Majka, then you must think I am the one who created the problem."

She goes quiet for a beat, then continues, "I don't want to talk about this and have you thinking I'm the reason for every bad thing in your life."

"Oh, Mom," I say.

"And," she adds, "I don't want you to think I am the reason for everything wrong with them."

I'm not sure if I should point out that she's casting fear in every possible direction.

How am I supposed to navigate my own sibling relationship and foster a marriage when this is my template?

I want a different template.

"I'm not the only person with trust issues in my marriage," she tells me. "And if you get to seventy-three and don't have trust issues, then congratulations."

Later, on the phone with Mom and the twins and Peter before hanging up: "I love you all so so much. Peter, that means you too. I love you too."

My mother takes my breath away.

October 27, 2019
From the Notepad | Three Years and Three Months Old

"Mamma, my bum hurts! I need cream!"

I chase after you with a finger full of Aquaphor ointment. When I catch you and smear it, you nuzzle my hair.

"Mamma, did you know I like to smell things that touch my bum? Like my fingers?"

"Let's wash your fingers, Kaz."

"I did it twice, Mamma."

"Washed your fingers?"

"Touching my bum."

"Let's give your bum some space, okay?"

"Okay, Mamma. Sorry I touched my bum."

October 31, 2019
From the Notepad | Three Years and Four Months Old

Mom on Going to the Convent

"I liked to do the unusual," my mother explains at lunch on her visit. "I was sandwiched in my family, nothing special, but I could be unusual by being super Catholic." I can see my mom growing determined just by saying it, even when she says it now over sixty years later.

"There was a new pope when I was in high school; it was a big deal. I read all about him and was inspired by the scriptures again. I had not been a good girl—I stole the money we were supposed to give to the church and bought cigarettes. But when the new pope was elected something shifted, and I chose to pursue God."

I can't imagine my mother doing this. Except for that seed of persistence, nothing is familiar to me about this version of her. Sometime after the convent, she tells me, she took all of her money and spent the summer in Europe, where she had a fling with an Italian whose name she cannot remember.

"We could barely understand each other," she says.

I don't point out that the same thing happened with Dad. The only difference was that they got married and he was Polish. Though, to be fair, by then she was fluent in Polish and had tried to live in Poland, and all of that was inspired by crazy, head-over-heels love.

She'd spent her first year of college at the convent. "One night I was pressing my habit—we had to make them ourselves. I was pressing out the pleats and smelled the wet wool and knew I had to leave. I told Mother Superior, and within hours I was out of there. Back then they separated you immediately if you decided not to pursue becoming a nun, as if you might be contagious to the others. I never remember her trying to change my mind."

I try to reconcile, again, this vision of her giving her life to God. It's not just about the vow of celibacy, though I bet if I had met her at twenty,

I would have wondered about that. It's about the full-fledged adoption of an ethos. It's so hard to picture this woman who spent her life pushing and creating a new way. Who was this woman who was willing to follow?

When I was growing up, we had a sign in our kitchen that read: LEAD, FOLLOW, OR GET OUT OF THE WAY. Maybe, after the convent, following was no longer an option for my mom.

"I suppose, if you were into psychoanalyzing, you could say I was trying to find a place in my family by going to the convent. S. was the oldest, M. was the boy, and I was the pious," she tells me. She didn't mention what J. and F., the brothers who came after her, were.

"I feel shame," she says, unprovoked. "Shame I had to leave. Still, today."

I know in this moment I have gone far enough with my questions. Her eyes are shifting, and soon I will get answers from her fear and not from a place of trust.

—⁓—

Oh, how I want to be the champion for my mom back then—to cheer along her decisions, to help her fit in—but then again, without obstacles in her way, maybe she would not have become such a fighter and achieved so much. Maybe that would have blunted the edges she needed in order to carve out her path so sharply.

Who am I to know what she needed?

I want to know so much more.

November 1, 2019
From the Notepad | Three Years and Four Months Old

Mom on Discipline

"Kaz, get over it! Irenna, tell Kaz he's being a baby and to get over it."

At the restaurant, my mom's coffee is dangerously close to tumbling off the table and spilling on Irenna. My mother takes a full pat of butter and works it onto one pancake, but it is her statement—the tone caustic, clipped, and familiar—that derails me. *Get over it*, I suddenly realize, was the mantra of my childhood. Said again and again. Until it never needed to be said again because apparently I did just that.

The reality is that I'm a good mom, but my mom doesn't have the rubric to know that. She doesn't see that I'm purposefully giving my kids love, time, and space to have a tantrum. She doesn't see me as a leader—connecting, redirecting, and managing my children's energy. Everything I'm doing feels silly and inefficient to her—which likely means I need to do them even more.

My proudest moment of her visit was not saying anything to push back the whole time. I learned quickly that day twelve of seventeen sans Peter but with two three-year-olds (one of whom is birthing molars) is actually not the time to have Mom visit. *Do not talk to her about why you want to parent this way*, I coach myself. *Just do it.*

"I actually have no idea what it was like when you were little," she then says. And in the next breath: "You need to ignore them more. Don't give in so much."

I want to go back in time and see how she ignored me when I was three years old. I want to see if she and Dad ever noticed that I didn't express any emotion because the one place I was supposed to be safe was anything but stable.

Mom on Being Raped

"When I was being raped I was afraid I was going to die. To be under someone else's control so thoroughly made it clear to me my life could end. Maybe later I used that as an excuse. I was raped, I almost died, I deserved a divorce.

"In my mind, the day after I was raped, I went to see my therapist and he told me I had tried hard enough. I can still feel what those words felt like—like they washed over me.

"How could I have done this to such a good man? How could I have had an affair? Your dad was the good man.

"Your dad and I, we fell romantically in love: language, espionage, and that—excuse me—*fake* Polish accent of his."

My heart follows her story, relayed in snippets, and feels hopeful that she's trying to be honest. Then I'm let down when she protects herself by saying something powerful and damaging. And then she goes and says something real: "It was so hard. I remember it being so hard. But not for you girls—we worked to make it easier on you girls."

Later, I ask my mom how it's possible that everything could have happened that quickly—to be raped in late August, get separated by November, and finalize a divorce by April.

"Maybe . . . maybe it was a year and a half," she tries to recall.

According to my stepdad's memory, she was raped when she was already separated from my father. But she and my dad concur it happened when they were married. I don't point out the discrepancy.

"I had sent him away to Kansas City when he got a job offer there," she says, referring to my eventual stepdad, PapaD, and him leaving Minneapolis to work in Missouri. "But then I called him the day I was raped. And he was great, and so was your dad."

I don't push her to line everything up from *A* to *Z*. It will never line up from *A* to *Z*.

November 17, 2019
Letter | Three Years and Four Months Old

I'm supposed to teach you about feelings. But I am learning every day that I can barely deal with my own feelings. When I am mad, I, too, want to be mad—just like you insist you have a right to be. I want to scream and shout. Definitely at your dad. Not as much at other people. I want it, but I don't do it. Just the wanting is terrifying.

Kaz and Irenna, you're learning how to cope in life from someone who never really learned coping herself. I grew up with a sister who was hot and cold with me: I was both her best friend and her punching bag. I wonder if I was the safe person for her—the only person she could be like that to in her life. She was never the safe person in mine.

I wish that someone had grabbed me close when I was little and asked me how I was feeling. I wish they had taught me how to process my feelings when they happened. Instead, I learned how to stuff them down and be rewarded for that.

If parenting gives us an opportunity to be the person we needed when we were young, then I have no way through this but through it.

November 19, 2019
From the Notepad | Three Years and Four Months Old

"Thanks for giving time," Irenna says.
 And just like that, I come undone.

November 22, 2019
Letter | Three Years and Four Months Old

Dear Irenna and Kaz,
 I'm tapped out. My whole body hurts.
 Last night, you, Kaz, called me down the hall for the eighth time to look for your fairy stick, a felt-and-pipe-cleaner toy we'd made earlier that day. After bringing you an ice pack (what might forever be seen as

the oddest item to give to sooth a kid, but that seems to work for you), giving you another sip of water, threatening to shut the door, having your sister fall asleep and then knowing I could no longer shut the door because your screams would wake her—after all of that, I shook you. I clenched your shoulders and squeezed and shook you as I pushed you down into your bed.

"I can't do this," I said, releasing you.

You're not a baby. I need to write that down for myself. You're big enough now that I could not have shaken your brain or done damage to you in a physical way. But there are so many other ways. I don't want to share this with you, really, or anyone. But next to that shame, I feel deeply lonesome.

I wish I knew what my mom had done. She was recovering from being raped, was in the middle of a divorce, and had a three-year-old and a five-year-old of her own—how could she not have done the same thing? Or did I just never push her, having long since learned not to?

I have help. You two are in a great preschool, we have a part-time nanny, and still, I curled my fingertips into the soft, fleshy parts of your triceps.

"Mamma, that is aggressive," you rightfully told me.

"I know," I said. "I am so, so tired. I cannot do this now."

What is the line between showing our kids we're human as parents and shielding them from becoming our protectors?

———

I'm on day twenty-five of solo parenting while your dad is out west working. Today your father texted Aliah, our nanny, asking her to help you get me flowers. When I saw you after nap time, finishing my workday at 3:30, I read the cards you'd made me and you covered me with kisses. I tried not to cry. I feel like I'm not supposed to cry right now. But I failed.

"Mamma, I will wipe your tears," Irenna said. And you gently blotted my cheeks and only slightly gouged my eyes.

"Oh, Mamma," Kaz said, "I love you."

"You're a good mamma," Irenna said. "Why are you crying?"

All I wanted to do in that moment was cry the way I needed to, but it seemed to be undermining the very faith you had in me as your leader. I want you to know I can be vulnerable, but I am scared to death of burdening you with taking care of me.

———

There are stories of my mother's childhood about how she was afraid to upset *her* mother. How my grandma would cry and cry all day and then wash her face, do her hair, and get dressed before Grandpa came home. It would crush my mom to know I think of Grandma this way, and so for most of my life I have only focused on the other stories, about my grandma being the only kid in her family of eleven siblings to go to college, let alone graduate school, how she put Grandpa through college, how she led her five kids to serve their community and made sure they always had beautiful clothes she sewed herself. But it's the other side I need to see now. The side that links to my mom and her emotional devastation—I can't help but know that her mom helped to make her so.

"Mamma is tapped out," I said to you today.

"What is *tap out*?" Irenna asked.

"Oh honey, it's when you feel like you have nothing left," I said.

December 3, 2019
From the Notepad | Three Years and Five Months Old

I knew all the words of Tina Turner's cynical "What's Love Got to Do with It" by the time I was eight years old. Mom, my sister, and I would belt the song in unison every time we were in the car.

You and I sing Katy Perry's self-empowerment anthem "Roar" together. It's better. It's on the road to better, for sure.

ABOVE: Me and my mom celebrating after one of her marathons in Minneapolis, circa 1983. She ran all during my sister's and my early childhood, and then became a triathlete, long-distance cyclist, and equestrian. *Photo Majka Burhardt Collection.* BELOW: Dad and I out on the Colorado slopes when I was roughly four years old. He brought his Polish skiing roots to Minnesota; I grew up chasing him downhill, and he can still out-ski (and out-bike) me at age eighty. *Photo Majka Burhardt Collection.*

LEFT: The first ascent of Vertical Baboon (5.10+), a classic jam crack in Tigray, Ethiopia. This was the first climb my three teammates and I established on Ethiopian sandstone during our expedition in 2007. At the time, very little rock climbing had been done in the region. *Photo by Gabe Rogel.*

RIGHT: On an expedition, climbing partners become more like life partners. This is me in 2009 feeding Kate Rutherford high on Namibia's Grand Spitzkoppe formation while she belays my then boyfriend, now husband, Peter Doucette, as we climb the existing twelve-pitch route Herero Arch (5.12b). *Photo by Gabe Rogel.*

LEFT: Peter, Kate, and I atop a first ascent in the Marienfluss Valley in Namibia in 2009. This trip to the northern Marienfluss was plan A, but temperatures were hitting more than 110 degrees Fahrenheit each day. So we quickly opted for plan B, a shaded first ascent on the Brandberg Mountain, Namibia's highest peak (8,442 feet). *Photo by Gabe Rogel.*

ABOVE: Me starting off the crux pitch of Southern Crossing (V 5.11+) on Brandberg Mountain in 2009. Peter and I cleaned the new, twelve-pitch route over the course of a week, while Kate (here, belaying) recovered from being sick. We linked this climb up the mountain's Orabeskopf face in a final one-day push, to complete its first ascent. *Photo by Peter Doucette.* BELOW: Love is applying sunscreen to your partner's face while their hands are gloved up at a belay. Or it was for Peter and me on the Palisade Traverse in California's Sierra Nevada, a technical concatenation of multiple Fourteeners along the spine of the range that we climbed over three days in late summer 2011. *Photo by Gabe Rogel.*

ABOVE: Ato Sha'le Bokal and I in Sidamo, Ethiopia, in 2011 when I had the honor of giving him a copy of my second book, *Coffee Story: Ethiopia*, which features stories of him and his family and how coffee interweaves with their rituals surrounding love, marriage, and reunion. *Photo by Andi McLeish.* BELOW: Sarah Garlick and I pack for a climbing attempt on Mozambique's Mount Namuli in 2011. This was my first expedition to Namuli. During our eleven days on the peak, Sarah and I obtained permission from Namuli's community members to climb, verified scientific interest in the mountain with the herpetologist Werner Conradie, and made it up a handful of virgin pitches on the mountain's granite to confirm that climbing here was possible—all of which helped launch Legado. *Photo by Paul Yoo.*

ABOVE: Climbing Mount Namuli's sweeping slabs required alternately balancing on micro granite edges and divots and body-lassoing giant grass hummocks. Here, I'm climbing one of the crux pitches of Majka and Kate's Science Project (V 5.10+), a new climb Kate and I established on the southwest face of the mountain during our thirty-day expedition in 2014. We picked the line to give scientists access to a hanging forest midway up the mountain as well as to the pockets of vegetation barnacled to the upper granite ribbons. During the expedition, we also supported science and conservation teams working in the forest, rivers, and villages below. *Photo by Rob Frost.* BELOW: New Year's Day, 2015—Peter, Anne-Gilbert Chase, and I celebrated it by climbing the Supercanaleta route on Patagonia's Cerro Fitz Roy. The range had just had a serious snow event, and we climbed what is more often done as a rock ridge under full alpine conditions that also included a bivy, or night out in the middle of the route, just below the summit. Here, I'm heading out across Fitz Roy's southwest ridge. *Photo by Peter Doucette.*

LEFT: The last photo taken of Peter and me in 2016 before we became parents. My mom snapped this shot as we headed out the door to the hospital, where I would be in labor for a total of forty-one hours before I got to hold the twins in my arms instead of my belly. *Photo Majka Burhardt Collection.*

RIGHT: Day one of parenting—Irenna with me, and Kaz with Peter. Our friend Anne Skidmore took this photo of us in the hospital courtyard when she came to visit. This was also the day we bought a new house, because sometimes you do it all at once—even if each piece is the biggest thing you have ever done. *Photo by Anne Skidmore.*

LEFT: My nursing reality every two hours with three-week-old twins. I printed this picture out and framed it; it sits next to me in my office, and I look at it every day. It's one of my favorite photos from the early days because it shows everything: face still swollen from pregnancy and Pitocin, yet also etched with a smile of mamma pride and possibility. *Photo by Anne Skidmore.*

LEFT: Climbing and wrangling twins, aka trying to learn how to put the "this" of my life all together when the twins were only four months old on our disastrous, truncated family trip to the Red River Gorge, Kentucky, in 2016. *Photo by Bernd Zeugswetter.*

RIGHT: Peter giving his first climbing-geography lesson to the twins, when they were just seven months old. Peter took the photo he's holding of Cerro Torre and the surrounding Patagonian peaks from across the valley during the final pitches of our climb together on Fitz Roy in 2015. *Photo by Majka Burhardt.*

RIGHT: Peter and Irenna at nine months, practicing walking on the dock at his parents' house on Forest Lake, New Hampshire, where Peter himself played as a child. *Photo by Majka Burhardt.*
BELOW: Proof of a climbing date in 2017 when the twins were eleven months old. Peter and I are at the top of Whitehorse Ledge, New Hampshire, after we blasted up one of the formation's 900-foot slab routes. Only fifteen minutes from our home, the cliff provides a quick fix for busy climber-parents. To make things even more efficient, on Whitehorse, Peter and I will often "simul-climb," moving together while tied into the same rope, placing protection between us (though not stopping to belay) to arrest a potential fall. *Photo Majka Burhardt Collection.*

ABOVE: Grandparents galore with the almost-one-year-old twins. From left to right, my father with Irenna, my stepmother, and Peter's father and mother with Kaz. Having Kaz and Irenna has brought Peter and me closer to our parents, and our parents all closer together. Peter's mom and dad live one hour from our home, so we see them frequently. Most of the time when my dad and stepmom come from Minnesota or my mom and stepdad come from Montana, we'll also gather as a pack. *Photo by Majka Burhardt.* LEFT: Kaz and my father, his Dziedek (Polish for "Grandpa"), in 2017. *Photo by Majka Burhardt.*

ABOVE: Women in Love is a climb on Cathedral Ledge I somewhat arbitrarily decided would be a benchmark signifying that I was "back" as a climber after having the twins. I picked the route's second-pitch 5.11d finger crack as my fall 2017 project when the kids were fourteen months old; I climbed it after a handful of tries and cried at the top, after hyperventilating my way through the crux sequence. *Photo by Rob Frost.* BELOW: On my first trip away from Irenna and Kaz, when they were fourteen months old, I came home after five days in California to them playing in our yard in the waning September sun. They saw me and immediately stripped down to nurse naked, to be as close to me as possible. *Photo by Peter Doucette.*

ABOVE: Taking a break to pump milk for the twins, sixteen months into mamma life, on Cathedral Ledge with Peter and the photographer Bernd Zeugswetter. I told Bernd he should take a photo of my unfiltered reality as a climber-mom to young children versus just shooting the usual glory images of rock climbing. *Photo by Bernd Zeugswetter.* BELOW: Before kids, Peter's and my gear room was a locus of organization and preparation for our vertical objectives. The kids quickly co-opted the room, however, and so we outfitted it with swings and jumpers and padded obstacles to also make it into a playroom for the various phases of their development. *Photo by Bernd Zeugswetter.*

ABOVE: In 2018, when the twins were just over two years old, I returned to Mozambique for the first time since becoming pregnant and joined my team for a legacy workshop with Mount Namuli's Lomwe communities. Here, I'm celebrating the program's success with my team members Filimonio Felizardo (far left) and Galio Zecas (center), as well Filimonio's mother and community leader Basilina João (left) and community leader Rosita Faustino (right). *Photo by Curtiss Conrad.* BELOW: I sometimes think that the best thing about having twins was that someone besides me always got to hold a baby. From day one, Kaz and Irenna were passed around to willing and loving arms—some of the most willing and loving were always my mother's. This shot was taken when the twins were two and a half, in early 2019 when my mom visited during a polar vortex. *Photo Majka Burhardt Collection.*

My friend Anne-Gilbert (belaying) and I continued ice climbing together after I had the twins, when she'd visit during the New Hampshire winters. Then, in 2019 when the kids were two and a half, we met up in Quebec on my first climbing trip away from them. There, we climbed dual routes on Mont de l'Équerre, including the 1,200-foot La Pomme d'or (V WI5+), pictured here, eking it out between two massive winter snowstorms. *Photo by Jason Thompson.*

ABOVE: I never knew when I moved to New Hampshire's Mount Washington Valley in 2008 that living here, with immediate access to so much climbing, would play such a critical role in my ability to simultaneously be a climber and a parent. This shot is of me in 2019 on Cathedral Ledge's Black Crack during a four-hour climbing romp while the twins were toddlers. In this picture, I unknowingly have a broken ankle, having fractured off a bone in the back of my heel after twisting my ankle in hard-crusted snow en route to climb one month prior. *Photo by Brent Doscher.* BELOW: Celebrating Mount Namuli—and its people and their lives and futures—by dancing with Queen Adelina Jackissone during a festival at the Mucunha-sede school in Mozambique. This trip was in 2019, when the kids had just turned three. *Photo by Stephanie Mladinich.*

ABOVE: The family's inaugural van-camping trip up in Crawford Notch, New Hampshire, in 2019. Before the twins, Peter and I often traveled around the United States in our van to climb; as parents, we've wanted to keep that tradition going. Not pictured: the marshmallows the twins smeared all over the inside of the vehicle. *Photo by Peter Doucette.* BELOW: When I was eight, my mother converted a closet into a darkroom, and started taking and developing photos as a hobby, beyond her professional career in business. When she was fifty, she started woodworking, and has now made over 50 percent of the furniture in our house. Here, she shares her love of creating with the twins in 2019, helping them shape clay figurines. *Photo Majka Burhardt Collection.*

ABOVE: One month before COVID-19 gripped the world, my friend Anne-Gilbert (belaying, not pictured) and I went to climb a coveted ice line, Valhalla (WI6), in New Hampshire's north country, nabbing the first female ascent of this ephemeral smear. As an ice climber, catching something in rare conditions just when climbing is possible makes the experience all the more electric. *Photo by Peter Doucette.* BELOW: A picture of the twins at age six, out climbing on Mount Oscar in Crawford Notch, New Hampshire, just as *More* goes to print in 2022. These days, we all climb together as a family—sometimes. We also bike, swim, hike, do puzzles, read, and learn about our emotions—and do it all again and again.

December 31, 2019
From the Notepad | Three Years and Six Months Old

"Papa is my husband," I tell Kaz and Irenna.

"Am I your husband too?" Kaz asks.

"You are my son."

"Mamma, I love being your son . . . But who is your moon? And who are your stars?"

January 11, 2020
Letter | Three Years and Six Months Old

It's easier to parent without him.

Truer and more dangerous words were never spoken, I think to myself.

Or better put, I have more joy when I parent without him because I'm the only one letting myself down.

January 14, 2020
Letter | Three Years and Six Months Old

Kaz is watching *Frozen*. Olaf is running through the dark woods saying, "This happens every time."

I'm trying CBD oil these days to see if it helps get rid of my neck pain so I can sleep. I wash it down with red wine. I do this every time . . . too many times recently.

"If you can slow yourself down, then you can catch up," our therapist Natalie says right after she tells me I have anxiety.

I'm seeing her by myself now in addition to seeing her with Peter. First we had to make sure it was okay with all of us.

"Just so you know," I told Peter when I asked about it during a session together, "you have stuff to work out too."

Then I closed my eyes.

Natalie sat there on Zoom waiting for me, for us.

"Take two," I said. "This is what I need."

I'm merging and unmerging our life as a young family with my life in my family of origin. White-knuckling it to keep it right and organized so as not to lose my shit.

Cheers to you, little snowman.

January 20, 2020
From the Notepad | Three Years and Six Months Old

"I always thought if I could just have the time to explain things well, people would agree with me," my mom says.

I'm cooking dinner. My mom is on the phone announcing that she is now not holding herself back from any level of feedback or input on a county planning board.

"I am unleashed," she says.

January 25, 2020
Letter | Three Years and Six Months Old

When I was in high school, my dad used to try Polish calculus to help me with my Minnesota math problems. It never went well for either of us.

What if Peter and I have the math all wrong? I can't understand how at the end of his ledger he comes up with time to spare and I am always in the red.

I ask him to empty the kids' backpacks from school, and the next morning I find a pair of wet, tuna fish–smelling mittens in Kaz's pack.

I tell him it's on him to plan the childcare when we go away on a three-day climbing trip to the Adirondacks together.

But then I end up doing it instead.

Garlick tells me of a recently divorced dad who now truly feels connected—inextricably—to his kids. Being thrust into the primary parenting role half the time did this for him, *to* him.

What are we all doing wrong? *Mental load, invisible labor, the second shift*—I know all the buzzwords. I see them in articles and in thinkpieces and hear them from other women. Yet I still just wrote myself a reminder email to tell the preschool we're staying for next year instead of asking my husband to do it and then wondering if he followed through.

"Who did this all for you?" Natalie asks.

"No one," I say automatically. But is that right? Everyone? Myself? My dad's commitment to us suddenly looks different seen through the lens of Garlick's divorced-dad tale. Did split custody make him do more for us, and in doing so, love us more too?

How do you break the cycles?

I want something in return.

I tell Peter, "I did the thing."

"What do you want in return?" he asks.

"I don't know yet, but I'll tell you," I say, adding *figuring out what I want* to my mental load.

January 27, 2020
Letter | Three Years and Six Months Old

Dear Peter,

Maybe the thing I have been fighting against is the thing I should have been writing toward all the time—you.

I am trying so hard. My default is anger, but even that is stuffed inside of me instead of well expressed. I am fighting for us. It might just look like I am fighting. I hope you know it's toward you.

February 12, 2020
Letter | Three Years and Seven Months Old

"How much rope do I have left?!" I yell down to Peter. He is somewhere below me belaying, at a distance I hope is not quite two hundred feet—the length of my rope.

"Forty feet," comes his answer.

I look up and guesstimate the height of the final ice headwall of the aptly named route Midlife Crisis. We're five hours from home in the Adirondacks in New York, just us, while the kids are at home for three days held by school, Aliah, and Grandma and Grandpa.

I count the screws on my harness: two. I climb up into steepness and do what I have been doing all winter. Stretching longer and taller between pick placements, snapping my crampons into the ice, and no longer thinking about my now-healed ankle—just climbing like it's what I was made to do.

March 14, 2020
Letter | Three Years and Eight Months Old

I should treat Peter like I treat Aliah, our nanny.

So far that's the best solution I came up with in the middle of the night. I like her. I am nice to her. I have good days with her.

Last night, Kaz and I were thirty minutes deep into abject screaming that worsened whenever I left the room.

"What do you think is a solution, Kaz?"

"I don't know!" he said.

"Don't touch me, don't touch my bed," he yelled. "Cuddle me. Don't touch me. I need so much *thing* from you!" he wailed.

Buddy, I feel you.

I feel like I am trying to shift something monumental—that involves a shift in how gender roles have played out for generations—yet I worry I have a greater chance of tanking my marriage through the process than saving it.

I need to meditate. I need to clear my own personal shit. And I need to find a way through the wilderness.

—⁓—

Back when I was sixteen at my friend Stuart B.'s house, I saw Mrs. B. on her hands and knees, crawling the perimeter of the living-room area rug. What for? I don't know—and I surely didn't know then. I watched with a queasiness that bordered on disgust. *Get up!* I wanted to scream. *I can see your stockings! Why are you wearing stockings? Why do you insist on me calling you "Mrs." when you should be a "Ms."?* What a pathetic housewife. I want to delete that sentence. But I think I need to keep it.

Last night, I was on my hands and knees digging dried coconut oil out of a crack in the floor and the bordering carpet edge. Two hours earlier, I was on all fours wiping up apple cake and yogurt. Mrs. B., I want to ask now: Did you have a job? Did you come home from working and growing your career and clean the floor without thinking about it? Or did you do it with frustration? And Mr. B., you asshole, why weren't you the one down there?

Of course, for all I know Mr. B. had cleaned the floor the night before and the two of them had an egalitarian approach to all domestic labor. But it was 1992, so I doubt it.

I'm convinced that if I can just articulate this problem and find an egalitarian solution, I can fix it. But what I cannot articulate is the commitment to getting this work done—the ethos, the timing, the focus. Yesterday's family day consisted of my cleaning up the house while taking care of the kids during my shift. Peter's shift ended with lentil soup not even scraped out of the bowls on the counter, let alone into the sink. Do I say something? What is the cost?

I am becoming like my sister. Eyes flashing contempt and dissatisfaction at every turn. I know what it's like to be in that aura. I know how much contempt it eventually creates in the other person. But I don't know how to stop it.

March 20, 2020
From the Notepad | Three Years and Eight Months Old

"Mamma, I'm going to grow up just as you," Irenna says to me.

"Great," I say back. "Let's work on growing up together."

—⌁—

March 27, 2020
Letter | Three Years and Eight Months Old

These days we play the Closed Game. *Mamma, is the pool closed? Is the museum? Is the bagel shop? Is school still closed?* Yes, yes, yes, and yes. It is all closed.

We are thirteen days into COVID-19. Will this forever change our lives?

Things are changing so quickly it's hard to even keep up. Three weeks ago, your dad and I were exploring new ice lines together and making up new yodels to find each other as we bushwhacked down through the woods from the cliff. Last week, I was livid because Peter wanted to go climbing and I felt it was too selfish with the world shutting down. Now, with recreation areas closed off in our state, we're wondering if legally we even can.

If I tell you now to conserve your food, will you grow up forever worried about having enough? If you overhear the word *unemployment* for the tenth time in a day, will you know what it means? What are you absorbing behind the tantrums and the relentless *Frozen* character drawings?

I want to write you something large and compelling about this time, but all I can do is scroll the internet, survive until it's time to drink wine, and burst into tears over snippets of news—especially about what it's like to be immunocompromised during Covid. I think of my best friend and her MS, or about an elderly woman dying alone with no one to hold her hand or tell her goodbye.

Will I see my parents again? I feel so radically far from them. Montana and Minnesota. It's not helpful to think like this, but it's in the back of my mind. How long until someone I know dies of this? But perhaps that is overly morbid. Perhaps that is a fear reaction born from bearing the news of climbing deaths, having gotten less than seven months into my life as a serious climber before loss touched me. It's the same ticking time bomb.

March 28, 2020
Letter | Three Years and Nine Months Old

I'm horrible at figuring out what I want. But I am trying.

I want to do the right thing for our community and our world right now. I want to not climb or ski until the lockdown order is lifted. I want to take this moment as a pause, to be with our family. I want endless support as the only one working in that family—you can't guide when travel and face-to-face contact are no longer allowed. I want Peter, with all his newfound free time, to step into the additional burden of household management and kids so that I can work more.

And I want him to do it the way I want it done.

I can see in a gauzy vision that what's best is for both Peter and me to feel balanced. But what is clear and right in front of me is that I want to control him. But this is not entirely accurate. Perhaps it's more about me and my own discomfort at not being able to control his choices. It's a fear that reaches back to my failed first marriage.

Eddie used to lie to me about where he was. He'd come home late, and I'd assume his guiding day went long only to learn the next day from a friend that they'd been out climbing together after work. Did I create that? Eddie and I certainly did in some way.

—◦—

This was our crux before Covid. What if, while we wait for our community to explode with this pandemic, we can finally fix this and all of the other broken dynamics that seem to keep trapping us?

Does it count if I can say I don't know what I want, but I do know what I don't want *you* to do?

I don't think so.

Look at yourself, Majka.

Look at what he is doing.

Try.

April 4, 2020
Letter | Three Years and Nine Months Old

I binge the news when you're not around. I can't have it on when you are—there are only so many times a not-even-four-year-old should hear the word *dead*, and one minute of any news today adds five to an amount that should be zero in the first place.

Today, while I drive alone to do our two weeks' worth of grocery shopping, I listen to a NPR story about teaching kids to process death and loss. "The first thing kids need to know is what death actually is," the expert says. "No matter how a person dies, every person that dies stops breathing."

This person runs a center in Utah where they run exercises with kids who've lost their parents to guns, suicide, and now Covid. "Do it with me," they say to the kids. "Breathe. Again. Stop."

"What these kids need is a system in place to name the loss, identify the loss, and talk about it," the expert explains. "Only once they can talk about it do we consider them ready to heal."

I'm crying, of course, and now I'm wishing I'd grown up in Utah, even though I doubt Utah in 1979 had the same system, or that it would have also applied to divorce—though maybe we need one that does.

When my parents split up, I was the "okay kid." Then I was supposed to be okay, apparently forever.

No one suggested I talk about it aloud, process it, get mad, feel lonely, or feel scared. I watched my world implode while I sucked my thumb and was rewarded for being the kid who was all right.

Who would not want to be the kid who's all right and gets cookies for it?

My sister couldn't be the "okay kid." I don't know why exactly; I just know she couldn't. Maybe it's because she didn't suck her thumb or stop her questions or hide her sadness; maybe it's because she was older and saw it all, heard the fights, understood the harsh words overheard from behind our bedroom door. And she didn't know any better than to take her pain out on me by yelling at me, controlling me, throwing things at me, and keeping me in her shadow. That was not coping; that was controlling. I'm starting to understand the difference.

Right when I was almost finished building my house in Estes Park at age twenty-two, I got a job at a Williams Sonoma in a mall eighty minutes from my house. I still have a cutting board that works only for a roast, a matching set of eight steak knives, and a combo cake display/ punch bowl. Why the fuck did I think these things were what I needed to spend my twelve-dollars-an-hour pay on?

I was too smart to think, *If I create it, it will be perfect*—wasn't I? But then I'd never seen a complete version of singular, loving bliss because mine always came in two flavors: at Mom's house and at Dad's house. I thought the solution was to go all in on one life and auger Eddie and me in together with custard bowls.

But then it wasn't. Because Eddie and I had ways to not know each other and ways to make our marriage worse. No amount of steak knives could help that.

I thought I'd done the work back then. Three years of therapy with Eddie, then four more without him. But now it's fifteen years later, and I'm doing all I can to save my and Peter's marriage—and realizing I have so much work to do to even start.

"We help kids mourn," the woman on the radio says.

Will the center in Utah take me? Will they teach me how to mourn forty years after my parents' divorce and fifteen years after my own?

"Tell a story of when your mamma and papa didn't let you eat chocolate chips at night," Irenna asks as I trade stories for a pee before bedtime. Here we are again. Do I keep making them up? Do I tell the truth? Do I keep it simple? I can't tell stories anymore about the hypothetical childhood I never had.

"How about a story of when my mamma and PapaD and I walked across the frozen lake?"

"But who is PapaD?" she asks.

April 13, 2020
Letter | Three Years and Nine Months Old

I am so tired.

But who isn't? Who isn't overwhelmed by the tsunami of Covid and our president's tirades and the hurt of the world?

"I need a break," I say to Peter.

"Mamma, I need you," Kaz says. "Mamma, I need you now. Mamma, are you done yet?"

I am having dreams that Peter is having an affair. I also dream that I have to go to work in Ethiopia, but the world has not been cleared of Covid and I have to risk catching it to support the family. Then my logistics in Ethiopia fall through, and I am there on my own. I wake up and reach for Peter's hand and squeeze it. He tugs me close even in his half-sleep.

I want this to feel easier. I want to not have to think about what I want and make sure I plan for it and say it. I want to not be the presumed point person for everything—by default, all the time.

But Natalie says it's simple.

Mom abandoned me and my sister.

I was mad, wanted connection, and looked to my sister for it. She in turn treated me like shit and tried to control me. She didn't know any better.

I now seek to control when I am hurting and want to connect, because I never learned otherwise. When my defenses are down, I am drawn out, or I am at my most raw, this is my behavior.

Which means I control the variables in my life by constantly cramming it full, by being a working mom of twins who is also trying to be an athlete, maintain a sane house, and have a good marriage.

It makes sense. But it hurts. "Your mother abandoned you . . ." When Natalie said it, I raised my shoulders and held my breath. *My mother did no such thing. Why not say my mom and dad both abandoned me?*

I made myself breathe.

Feel it, Majka. Feel it in a safe space. It doesn't mean it's the only part of the story. It doesn't mean you don't love her. It doesn't mean she doesn't love you. Find yourself. Find me.

....

April 14, 2020
Letter | Three Years and Nine Months Old

"Roody is a reindeer who is strong and confident and a girl . . ."

Check. I turn up the podcast and drive to the river the long way, the kids in their seats in the back of the van.

"But, Santa, why can't I pull your sleigh?"

"Because you're a girl and girls can't pull sleighs."

Uncheck.

"Why did that stop?" Kaz asks.

"Mamma, I like that story," Irenna says.

"Oh, that story stopped working," I lie to them.

"No it didn't," Kaz says. "You just turned it down."

For the past three-and-a-half years, I have changed names and genders in books and removed from our house books framing women as weak and homebound and men as unconnected to their kids. To be honest, I'm quickest to snatch away the ones with women portrayed in aprons and skirts waiting for their men. I gently (and not so gently) suggest other genders for creatures my stepdad, dad, aunt—anyone— spots. "See that squirrel? What do you think he is doing?" is a common framing. Never do we ask what she is doing.

Perhaps I would not focus so much on this if I did not have two children of opposite genders. I went to buy celebratory undies when we potty-trained and spent some of my best intellectual capacity for the day standing in front of princesses and unicorns for girls and trucks and superheroes for boys, searching the back racks for plain undies, longing for something basic that didn't have an inherently gendered message. It's not that I didn't want Irenna to have unicorns or Kaz to have superheroes; I just didn't want her to only have unicorns and him to only have superheroes. I left the store empty-handed and found a site online for colored undies, no messaging.

Struggling with gender portrayal is not something new to me. As soon as I could spell *woman* I turned around and spelled it *womyn*. But that got hard to maintain in school, and I eventually chose a perfect score on my spelling test over my lexical rebellion.

May 5, 2020
Letter | Three Years and Ten Months Old

Eight years ago, your dad and I sat on a lumpy couch in a therapist's office to talk about the kids we did not have. I'd insisted on the appointment. I wasn't sure I wanted kids, I told your dad, but I wanted to have the option—with him. I also told him that I was afraid I might become a resenter if we had kids.

"You'd resent our kids?" he asked.

"Never," I replied. "But even though we would have done this because we wanted to—because *I* wanted to—I am afraid I might resent you and the world for the additional load I'd take on for having and loving them."

And now here you two are. I was accurate in forecasting my resentment, but the force of my love for you two helped keep it at bay. And then came COVID-19.

In the past week alone, between playing "mixed-up puzzles"—our new game in which I dump three puzzles into a box and stir up the pieces in a desperate attempt to refresh what we have—and writing Legado's donors about our COVID-19 response, I have read articles in five different news sources about women taking on even more of the child-rearing and household work as their male partners' jobs take precedence in the pandemic era. But here in our family, the opposite is unfolding.

Six weeks into being our family's sole earner, I feel proud and terrified. And beside those emotions, the ever-familiar resentment is mixing with something unexpected: a sense I need more, and may even be entitled to more.

Last Tuesday, amid a harrowing workday that was supposed to end at five P.M., I asked your dad for more time in the office.

He sighed. "Haven't you already been working all day?"

I stormed back to work. How dare he be anything but effusively supportive of my work? After all, it was the only solvent thing our family could count on.

And then the thought came: *My newfound status in our family entitles me to anything I want.*

It's not news to say being a mom is complex, and all indexes point to it being even more so in a pandemic. What I suddenly and desperately wanted to know was if women are the only ones working, does the housework-child-rearing-dish-washing model flip?

Resentment is, by definition, the bitter indignation at having been treated unfairly. My pre-kid premonition wasn't far off. The therapist from eight years ago? When I told him we were there because of my fear of resentment, he deduced I felt that way because I didn't feel I was getting enough credit from Peter. Perhaps, he suggested, what I needed to do first was support Peter. When Peter got home from work, I should understand that he needed downtime; bring him a drink; and ask him if he wanted to talk or watch the news. The fact that Peter doesn't drink was beside the point. We never saw that therapist again.

The therapist we have landed on has helped me understand that what might help me fight the resentment is cultivating a sense of fairness.

Covid, in some ways, has helped our family reach a point of fairness. But instead of celebrating this marker, I want to go beyond it and get a chance to drink and watch the news before I drop in to family, dammit. Is that how entitlement starts? I also want to be a good and present mom for you, and hear you and your dad thundering around the house playing hide-and-seek and its chase-the-hider-when-found variation. If this becomes our norm, is this what I want? Peter starting our garden from seed and doing morning plant checks with you both in our sunny loft as I log into Zoom?

Sociologists worldwide caution that a gender-role reimagining is underway. They say this, largely, as a warning that women's roles will go backward. To keep these roles from regressing, we have to include the voices that push things forward. Maybe it's time to ask ourselves and our loved ones to imagine themselves in our positions—an imagining that might not be as hard after we've seen each other's realities as starkly as we do now, all quarantined at home together. And then sit down together and not get up until we have created a new model based on this understanding.

I began adding my voice at home last night. Though my anger and resentment were pushing me to tell Peter I deserved more, I chose empathy, using my most effective twin-conflict-deescalation tool: questions.

"How would you feel if Irenna painted your lovey?"

"How would you feel if Kaz composted your soccer ball?"

I turned to Peter with all the weight of the past two months in my heart, took a deep breath, and asked, "Where do we go from here?"

"The only place we can go," he said. "Forward."

....

May 13, 2020
From the Notepad | Three Years and Ten Months Old

"Mamma, how much older until I die?" Kaz asks.

I reach for his foot behind me in the car. "So many years," I say.

"Until I die I have a lot of growing to do. Right, Mamma?"

"Right, Kaz," I say. "Let's focus on the living."

"I have another mamma, you know. She's so old—she's fourteen, and her name is Coleslaw."

May 16, 2020
Letter | Three Years and Ten Months Old

Here is what I love . . .

That you use my body as your own—launching onto me willy-nilly and contorting with no regard for where you stop and where I begin.

Irenna, you tell stories now. Long stories. Stories that last through dinner.

Kaz, you used to sleep under Irenna's bed and still won't go to sleep unless she's tucked in her bed next to you.

These days we can't get far into any subject without a question. "Stewball," our current favorite goodnight song borrowed from my childhood days at camp, is particularly good fodder.

"What's a 'poor boy in trouble'? How does Stewball drink wine if he's a horse?"

Irenna, just so you know, I'm on to you. You suck your thumb any chance you get, but it doesn't make you docile; it makes you razor sharp. *Pop!* goes your thumb as you de-suction it to explain any answer to any question we have. *Pop!* as you put it right back.

Kaz, you are tough and rough and brawny and shy, but you won't tell anyone that yourself. Instead you ask Irenna to tell people for you.

"Kaz," Irenna told you today, "it doesn't matter if you're shy because you can't touch anyone anyway because of the coronavirus."

I didn't used to be scared of Covid. Now I am.

May 25, 2020
Letter | Three Years and Ten Months Old

Kaz: "Irenna, people die, and flowers die. But loveys don't die."

Irenna: "That makes me sad."

Kaz: "But don't worry, you still have a lot of years left to live."

You have this conversation in the living room, oblivious to my overhearing it. I am in the next room, in bed at four P.M. Yesterday at midnight, I had my appendix cut out of me to save my life. But I am pretending that has nothing to do with your conversation.

I was supposed to be putting up a new climbing route on a thirteen-hundred-foot granite face on Mount Ribáuè in Mozambique right now. Would my appendix have failed there on this exact day? While I was searching for lichen that could show the impact of climate change and for bats that only lived on that mountain?

"I'm fine," I told the nurse at the hospital triage station. "Or I have Covid."

"How about we admit you?" she asked.

"Either way, all I need is a test," I said.

I stood up to fetch my purse and my insurance card but stayed crumpled and hunched as I shuffled instead of walked. She looked concerned.

"This happens all the time," I said. "I have two almost-four-year-olds."

I didn't tell her about the last time I came to the hospital with stomach pain and was told I had the most impacted bowel the ER doctor had ever seen. Your dad loved telling me I was full of shit after that one for weeks. The only reason I came here this time was because I was afraid of being the one who killed your grandparents if it was Covid and I didn't know it.

"But can you take care of them right now?" the nurse asked.

I thought about lying down. An IV. It seemed luxurious.

Five hours later, I was down an appendix and in a hospital surrounded by PPE-ensconced staff. I was filled with fear and hope, and grateful for the help. I came home to you this morning, and I will not leave my bed for days. But I am sure this has nothing to do with your being worried about dying.

June 8, 2020
Letter | Three Years and Eleven Months Old

"He died," you, Irenna, tell our nanny, Aliah, first thing in the morning.

"A policeman put a knee on his neck. George Floyd. That was not kind."

"Police are normally kind though," I say, realizing this might only be true because I'm a white mother telling it to my white children.

"We're going to the protest because people need to be kind," you continue. "It's not kind when some dogs don't get to have ice cream. All dogs should be able to have ice cream."

Peter is back working more and more now, and we're podded up with Aliah to make it all possible. She is as deft at wrangling you out biking and hiking as she is at being by your side as you process the world through your three-year-olds' eyes.

"Oh Irenna-bear," Aliah says, "I know they do. Should we make posters together?"

"What's a post-er?"

"Come on and I'll show you."

Yesterday, I—a forty-three-year-old, privileged white woman—tried to explain racism to you. You and your brother automatically associated it to Ptarmigan the poodle and Ello the retriever. Somehow ice cream got involved. But you're not wrong.

We've talked a lot about colors of skin before, but this is different. This is not a small trespass. This is a life taken and a reckoning I have no idea how to lead you through. I only know we have to start.

We wrote George Floyd's and Breonna Taylor's names in chalk on the sidewalk outside of your Great-Grandma Keller's nursing home. First we spoke to her on the phone, seeing her through the window.

"Why are we writing these names on the ground? Are they your friends, Mamma?"

"These are people who were killed by the police because they were Black," I say.

"Can you tell the story, Mamma?"

June 28, 2020
Letter | Four Years Old

Will you remember your fourth birthday as the year of the contactless birthday party? You donned your birthday capes and crowns and sat on our tailgate as your friends drove by and waved.

"Isn't it so nice Ms. Brooke came?" Coupled with: "Give Ms. Brooke space."

Again, and again, and again.

But it's not only this. I hope you also remember going climbing on Square Ledge—up on a rope for your first time.

"This is what Papa does," Irenna said.

"This is what Mamma does," Kaz said.

⁓

I tuck you in bed tonight with extra songs, kisses for Irenna, and hair sniffs for Kaz.

"Happy birthday, my babies," I say.

"I'm so happy to have you in my life," Kaz says.

I smile and start to walk out.

"I'm just four years old. I have so much life still."

"Goodnight, Kaz and Irenna," I say.

"How much old are we and how are we going to have to die?"

"Oh, Kaz."

"How much old was George Floyd?"

August 21, 2020
From the Notepad | Four Years and One Month Old

"I hate to give my spouse ammunition," my mom says.

I debate explaining to her that I'm trying to find a more gentle and generous side of myself. Before I can, she continues, "You never want to give them something they can use against you."

I don't keep ammunition for Peter. I count instead. Everything. I'm keeping score of everything, even when I pretend I'm not.

To stop doing so would mean relinquishing control.

I counted through my parents' divorce. Who got what? Who got us? What did we get?

I counted through my divorce.

I counted to survive.

To have power.

To keep track.

But now I'm not sure what I've been counting all this time.

What did I measure? Does it ever really add up?

September 23, 2020
From the Notepad | Four Years and Two Months Old

"I support you if you want to bank sperm in case I die and you want to have more kids with someone else," I tell Peter.

"It's like you haven't met me," he says in response.

I can think of thirteen other, more appropriate responses.

"If you don't want more kids, then why can't you get a vasectomy?" I have been asking him to get one for the past two years, and I'm out of entry points into the conversation.

"I don't want to have any unnecessary surgeries," he says.

Who gets to decide what is necessary? When I jump, my stomach jiggles with skin that will never go away. I can still fit Irenna's whole fist in the space between my abs.

October 8, 2020
From the Notepad | Four Years and Three Months Old

Swimming, biking, hucking stones in the river, climbing—that is the current order of your outdoor passions. I would not have it any other way.

Two weeks ago, we all were in Acadia National Park together and your dad and I took you up the Beehive, a one-and-a-half-mile round-trip that brave hikers do using ladder rungs and rails to keep them safe, and that we did with harnesses, helmets, and ropes as your first big climb. At the top, after we celebrated with Sour Patch Kids, I told you that you could take your harnesses off for the trail we'd take down the back side.

"I'm going to leave mine on," you said, Kaz. "That's what climbers do."

My outdoor priorities run in the inverse order of yours. After months of not climbing when Covid started, I am climbing every week again. Today I was at Rumney, one of the best sport-climbing areas in our country, just ninety minutes from our house. And no matter what I did, I could not make myself stay attached to the rounded edge of the black and gray corner of gneiss on the climb Black Mamba. I tried stacking my fingers differently, used my heel, said to hell with my heel and tried to toss my body upward—all to no avail and all resulting with me hanging on the rope again.

I am trying harder than I have since getting my appendix out four months ago, and the safety provided by expansion bolts drilled into the rock lets me do it. My climbing partners Art and Terry are below me, and soon I'll swap ends of the rope with them while we all stand six feet apart.

I drop you off at school and drive over the Kancamagus Highway each day I climb here. In the mornings, I have meetings with my team in Africa via WhatsApp both before and after I cross over the pass; in the early afternoons, I drive back and talk to my mom, my sister, and my dad, ticking through the three dimensions of nuclear family until the White Mountains blot out my cell service and I get to just be.

October 17, 2020
Letter | Four Years and Three Months Old

My mom was raped when I was a little girl, I write to my hiking friend Kate—my other Kate—who told me on Mount Pemigewasset today that she volunteers at a sexual-violence hotline. I read the words and consider how I have never written them purposefully for someone else to read. Who is the subject in this sentence? Who needs to be?

How much does this violent event, done to my mom, shape me and my sister? Is it too far a stretch to think that I took control of sex and explored what it could be like with whomever I wanted in my life as a teenager and again in my late twenties so I would not be powerless against her rape as part of my narrative? Did my mom ever talk to me about how to understand her rape inside my own sexual and relationship decisions? Why did I skew in my direction, and why did my sister skew in hers—toward a single long-term boyfriend before marrying a childhood love? Saying these things are all tied to Mom's rape feels overreactive. But how could they not be?

Does she think of being raped as one of the crucial events in her life? I don't know. Does she connect or conflate it with her divorce and her affair and more? I'd imagine that if a rape were part of my history, then I would not want to give it that standing. As if giving it more power gives it more power.

I don't remember my mom ever talking to me about sex except for birth control. She never talked to me about men trying to have power over me. But did she, and I just cannot remember it? And if she didn't, why not? I remember by the end of high school knowing she was raped. But for me, then, I think it was about fighting for her for women's rights, not asking myself how that might inform the sexual politics I was creating for myself at that time.

Can I talk to her about this?

November 12, 2020
Letter | Four Years and Five Months Old

"Your sister was the most important person in your developmental life," Mom says to me today on the phone.

She doesn't have to add that it wasn't supposed to be like that. I don't tell her I understand why it happened that way, and that I'm starting to realize how angry I am that she and my father did that to me. They left my sister and me to be the consistent relationship, without giving us any support for how to do it well.

By the time you become a parent, will there still be people who tell you that you're bound to mess up your kids somehow, so it's best to start a therapy fund now?

If there are, you should tell them to suck it.

I want a different version of parenting, where my job is to give you the best tools I can to help you chart your course.

I'm trapped in the dual tension of being mad at my parents for what they did to me and understanding how damn difficult it was for them.

Compassion and anger layered and layered again, but in a way that feels more confusing than right.

I try to sit in the anger to understand it, but I don't know how. My favorite compliment to receive as a kid was to be told I spoke like a grown-up.

Slow down, I want to tell that little girl. *You don't have to be the nucleus for everyone and make them happy. Feel the anger. Feel the sad.*

November 19, 2020
From the Notepad | Four Years and Five Months Old

Juliet, my babysitter from when I was ten until I was eighteen: "I was brought in to help parent you. You needed more parenting."

Kaz: "Mamma, when are you going to be as big as Papa?"

Mom, after I finally tell her I'm going to tell my sister to stop being mean to me for the first time in my life: "I have to go now. It's not that this isn't important; it's that I need to move on."

November 21, 2020
Audio Journal | Four Years and Five Months Old

I wonder if one day you're going to have a four-year-old (or maybe two four-year-olds at the same time) and be emotionally wiped out from trying to understand what is happening in your life and what the heck your mom was going through when you were four.

This seems to be what I spend all my time thinking about now. The irony is that all this perseverating makes me a heck of a lot more emotional and less functional as a mom in the moment. And a lot busier.

For example, if I weren't deep-diving into therapy right now, and needing the space to process my emotions, then I could have more time with you. And we'd be creating even more good memories together.

But let's be very clear that right now, when you are almost four-and-a-half, I am having a hard time.

I don't know what the right amount of time to spend with you is. I don't know what is enough. There's probably no such thing as too much where you're concerned. But there's a lot of too much where I'm concerned. I'm learning that I grew up with a mom and dad who were not very hands-on parents. I'm not stuck on my dad now because he is not as important in my path to my own motherhood; I'm stuck on my mom. And I want to use stronger words to convey the damage their hands-off version of parenting might have caused.

But I'm afraid that if I speak them—even into the ether of a voice memo, in a minivan driving on the 113, from Maine to New Hampshire—that the words will somehow come back to bite me, and her, in the ass.

I want a linear explanation for this. I want to be able to draw a line that clearly demonstrates how Mom's rape resulted in her leaning on work more and leaning on parenting a lot less. Because parenting for her brought up a ton of emotions, and parenting meant dealing with my dad. So she did what made the most sense and what she needed to do to support us: she worked. Work gave her affirmation, promotions, logic puzzles, and challenges to be met. And home and parenting became the more difficult things to do.

But I don't know if she ever saw it like that. I don't know if it was ever simple like that. I don't know if in the 1980s there really was any other choice for a woman trying to have the kind of career that she had. And because she *did* have a career at such a level, I was able to go to good schools, model myself after her as a strong woman, be a leader, fight for equity, and speak up.

I want to see the linearity-and-causation diagram because I know it's all constantly overlapping. And maybe I'm making my story her story.

What I need to know is if staying married, being in a good marriage with your dad, will do more for you than anything else I could ever do. If we stay married, maybe in your later life you won't be so fixated on the amount of time you got to spend with your parents—because you will have seen me all of the time, and never known that the other option was just half of the time.

I've never thought about it that way before. For me, for you, or for her.

———

I feel doubly sad these days—sad for me and sad for my mother. Maybe this isn't a story to you. Maybe it's a story to my mom.

Maybe it's a story to all of you.

All I want to do is call you up, Mom, and ask you all these questions. But I know it's going to break your heart. What I don't know is if I need to know the answers badly enough to do that to you.

November 21, 2020 (Later)
Audio Journal | Four Years and Five Months Old

Dear Mom,

I don't know if I'm brave enough to send you this. I do know I'm not brave enough to do it on the phone. However, with us being thousands of miles away from each other, with no real knowledge of when I'm going to see you next, maybe a letter is just what we need.

Did you know that every morning, Irenna crawls into bed with me? "Snuggles!" she says, patting the bed before crawling up, before inserting herself under the covers. She sucks her thumb and tucks her nose into my armpit. For real, my armpit. That's the place in my body she asks for by name.

What was it like for you to cuddle us when I was four?

I remember we couldn't touch you very much. I have juxtaposed memories of being in bed with you and of standing in your doorway as you had nightmares. Watching you, I didn't know what to do.

By the time I was eight or ten, I'd already made up the story. Or I had internalized the idea that you didn't want us to touch your neck.

Was that true? Or is that something I've invented myself?

I know that man held a noose around your neck.

How tightly?

Did he cinch it?

Did you have red marks on your neck?

Did you forget about it? Or did you think about it when you wore choker necklaces later in life?

I love cuddling those little kids. I can't imagine what it must have felt like to you.

But here's one thing: I think maybe I make a bigger deal out of your rape than you do. It seems to be the thing I need to understand and talk about with you, but I'm wary of bringing up something that you've long since processed or don't want to dwell on. Maybe it *is* at the center of everything, or maybe it *was* at the center. If so, everything would make more sense. Because my logic goes something like this:

Things weren't good for you and Dad. Things were good for you at work. Then a man jumped out of the woods, put a noose around your neck, held you to the ground, held the knife to your throat, and violently raped you. You escaped, but not before . . . god, what do I say? Not before he violated you.

Jesus.

You went to the hospital. You got a rape kit, and then you went to work. Who does that?

I don't know if that means that you are the bravest, or the most stoic, person I've ever known, Mom. But then again, I might have been alive in 1979, but I wasn't the one going through it.

I wasn't the one making my way in that career. So damn determined not to be looked over. Not to be looked at as a woman who didn't have skills.

And then, in my mind, that event sets the tone for everything that happened over the next four years. For you and Dad to get divorced, for you to go back to D., for us to have childcare who became as important as our parents. Oh, shit. This is so complicated. I don't think you can single out any of it.

December 3, 2020
Audio Journal | Four Years and Five Months Old

Dear Irenna and Kaz,

I realized today that what I'm trying to do is guide you through your wobblers and encourage your big emotional powers and knowledge, while at the same time trying to figure out my own emotional know-how.

I want to be down there on the floor too, kicking and screaming, trying to figure out how to have a good marriage and how to be a good mom, because I now understand that I never saw those two things together. I wish I'd understood the world I was raised in when I was two and three and four. When the tracks for who I was going to be and how I was going to respond were being laid in my brain and my heart. But I didn't.

What I know are the facts. Or my interpretation of the facts. Mom and Dad's tough marriage. Mom's affair, Mom's rape. Mom and Dad's divorce, their heinous custody fight, my emotionally bullying sister. I wish I had parents who felt safe about remembering how it was and whom I could trust to talk to me about those rough years.

That space was the darkest part of my family's life, and it's the part that I'm trying really hard to be in with you. But there's no beacon to show me how to do it.

So all I have is us, trying to learn our way together.

December 4, 2020
Audio Journal | Four Years and Five Months Old

Dear Peter,

Last night I climbed on top of you for the second night in a row. I nuzzled your neck and you said no.

Don't you know that our deal is to never say no?

He said no to me. The other one. The husband before you. The other mountain guide. The other six-foot-and-change-tall man. He said no again and again.

I should be able to handle your being tired, but the fear I have about your rejection is so much bigger. When you tell me you're too tired, or when you tell me after we make love that you don't have the energy you wish you had, my grown-up brain tells me to accept this and be loving. My reptilian brain tells me to bolt.

The other side of me wonders if I'm coming on too strong or asking the wrong way. Would it help if I changed the exact chemistry of my words—if I could just say them a little lighter, a little more playfully, a little less playfully, a little faster, a little lower? Would that unlock your desire?

I am fifty percent sure this has nothing to do with you and me and this moment. And I am fifty percent terrified that it has *everything* to do with us. If I don't speak up now, and if we do not right ourselves, will this be the moment when we stop connecting?

When we watch a show or a half a movie (my current maximum before I have to crawl into bed), I've started to turn the sound off during any fighting or violence. Without the noise it's just a scene, and I get to choose how I absorb or react to it.

What if we could turn off our volume when it gets hard? Not to mute our partner, but to instead create the silence that lets us hear what's happening and find our way through it with intention?

December 5, 2020
Audio Journal | Four Years and Five Months Old

Dear Aon Bon,

Is it right to call you Aon Bon, the made-up nickname that always seemed to signify a closeness of relationship we did not have?

Dear Sister,

I wish I could wave a wand for you and make it easier. Not for you now; you at age five. You the bigger, older, more cognizant counterpart to my three-year-old self.

What if we missed our callings? I text you.

What if we were supposed to be traveling guitar players and singing sisters, and instead our life imploded and we had to become high-functioning humans as little girls?

———

What if I am a mom who can sit with you through any emotion and tell you it's okay?

What if I am a mom who is not exasperated?

What if I am the mom I am trying to be instead of modeling the one I know?

December 11, 2020
Letter | Four Years and Five Months Old

"When I am a mamma, I am going to have thirty-one babies."

"Really?"

"Yes. And I am going to milk them two at a time, just like you."

"That sounds so good, Irenna-bear. I will help you."

"But, Mamma? When I have babies, they are going to come out of my vagina." Irenna makes a flushing motion with her hands from her stomach as if moving the babies down the birth chamber into the vaginal canal—a noncompliant cervix apparently not being an issue.

I will not cry about not having a vaginal birth with my four-and-a-half-year-old daughter. I will not feel C-section shame in this moment.

"I hope they do come out of your vagina, Irenna. I wanted that for you and Kaz so much, and I am so, so glad we could all be safe and be in this world together. That is what Dr. Lauren made possible when she cut you out of my tummy."

"Did you get cut out of Grandma Pooch's tummy too?" Kaz asks.

I close my eyes for a moment, and by the time I open them Irenna is straddle-snuggling me, pushing the straps of my cotton negligee aside to make unobstructed contact with her cheek. "Mamma, when can we go to Montana again? I want to hug Grandma Pooch," she says.

You two can tell when I cry now. It's almost as if you feel the air changing in my lungs, the breath catching in my throat. This time, Irenna, you look up and hover your wet thumb by my cheek, holding my chin with your fingers. "Sometimes parents get sad about their parents," you say, nodding.

I nod back and let myself do just that while you pop your thumb back in and return to your place in my armpit.

I don't know if it's doing us any good for me to tell you the truth about how much I miss my parents right now. I make promises I have no idea if I can keep. We will go to Montana soon. We will be able to hug them again. You will know them, and this will not be a year you will never get back in the waning years we all have together.

December 13, 2020
From the Notepad | Four Years and Five Months Old

The *thud* comes first.

I wait.

"Yeeeeeeooooooolllllleeeeeee!"

I go.

"What's going on, team?" I say before I've even rounded the corner from the bedroom to the living room.

"Irenna . . . pushed . . . me . . . *down!*" Kaz says, hiccupping through tears.

"Kaz punched me . . . in the stomach!" Irenna wails.

Is it important which came first?

I sit down on the floor and open my arms, and Irenna and Kaz each come to me automatically. I still have this power.

"You bugs," I say. "We have to keep working on being kind."

"I'm sorry!" Irenna yells, her fists balled up.

"I'm sorry!" Kaz adds, his eyes narrowed.

If I teach them how to do this better, will they knit themselves closer to each other than my sister and I did?

"Who can say *empathy?*"

"Path-y," Irenna says, with her thumb in her mouth.

"Em-pathy, Irenna," Kaz corrects her.

"Good job to both of you," I say, "*and* let's just answer for ourselves, ok?"

I take a big breath and our group hug expands and contracts as I do it.

"What if Mamma did something to Papa, like stepped on him? How do you think he would feel if I said, 'I'm sorry'?" I ask, making my imaginary apology in as gruff a voice as I can.

Kaz and Irenna both give me a scared look and stay quiet.

"Would it be better if I said, 'I'm so sorry, honey. Are you okay?'" This time I'm all softness.

Irenna raises her hand. "The second one, Mamma."

"Okay, then. We can do that, right? Mamma and Papa are here for each of you, and for you to learn how to be together."

December 15, 2020
From the Notepad | Four Years and Five Months Old

Today I met the woman who might help us all. She's not a nanny; she's a PhD biologist who specializes in chimps—and if I play my cards right, she's going to come and work with my team at Legado as we grow. Even better, she is a biologist who knows it takes more to protect biodiversity than traditional conservation work has been doing.

Kenya is next. We have a new partnership there to test our plan to support local people *and* their forests, rivers, and streams. To support their priorities for their kids, their health, their culture—and their biodiversity. All year, I have been working so hard on building this expansion that I'm now holding Zoom meetings in my dreams. All year, I have thought of the people on Namuli showing me that conservation was not enough—that their livelihoods and lives matter just as much as the flora and fauna. Our board, our funders, and so many others are behind us. We even have a partner in Kenya who wants to test this with us. Thriving Futures: that's what we call the model and program we're running—in which we support thriving people to live in thriving places. Your mamma builds thriving futures, and I've learned to build them because I saw I could be doing it better. But I'm most excited about Sonya, the chimp lady, because I might have finally grown Legado big enough that I can now step back and do less.

December 18, 2020
Letter | Four Years and Five Months Old

I don't want to write to you two right now. I don't want to tell you about
the block of ice more than forty times your combined weight that my
arm exploded into the world and on top of me today.

It was supposed to be a simple day. My friend Laurie and I were getting in early-season pitches at Frankenstein Cliff in Crawford Notch, but
so were others. The ice was busy. "It's all good," I said. "Let's journey up
the Penguin even though it's not quite in." It was a route I'd done more
than a dozen times before, but when I took the lead on the third pitch, I
found the fresh ice to be unclimbed, unorganized, poppy, and fracturable.

I went up, placed a screw high in the first mini-headwall, and looked
up. It was four moves, tops, to a break in the terrain. *I've done this more
than a dozen times,* I coached mysef.

I took a breath and felt my hesitation. I looked down at Laurie.
"Watch me on this; it's not usually so pushy," I yelled.

And then the next swing was an explosion.

―――

I wrote your dad a text from the hospital: *A chunk the size of a refrigerator.*
And with those words, my breathing stopped. Those are the words they
used to describe the ice that killed Rod Willard in Vail, Colorado. A similar
chunk, eighteen years ago, ended his life. But what does this one do to mine?

I drove myself to the hospital, by the way. It's important to tell you
that. I went just in case, because as a mom it felt like the right thing
to do—to be extra sure I was okay. Plus it hurt, a bit, to walk. They
X-rayed my hip, gave me a shot in the ass, and said I was good to go.

I can already feel myself rationalizing it. When the ice cut loose, I
held my stance. The ice tool I held with my left hand stayed put, my
legs balanced between two columns, stuck in place by the monopoints
on my crampons.

I have two options right now, and I hate to admit how well I know them.

Option one is to understand that I did something wrong, getting on the Penguin before it had fully formed.

Option two is to do all of option one and then shrug my shoulders, literally or proverbially, and keep doing the thing that makes no sense. The thing that could have ended without my being here to write you today.

To the outside world, ice climbing makes little sense. Even to the *inside* world, the world of climbers. Among those who have dedicated their lives to climbing, many of them opt out of the frozen vertical. It's too cold, too slow, too reliant on equipment, and simply too dangerous—as a medium, rock is much more permanent. Still, I have been back inside it since you were less than six months old. And yes, I will tell you now that I think I can control the risk. Or I thought I could.

"Where are you going to file this one?" your dad asked me after hugging me more tightly and longer than usual when he came home.

I told him what I'm telling you now—that I don't know. And with each hour that passes, I inch closer to climbing again.

December 25, 2020
Letter | Four Years and Five Months Old

"This is for you," your dad said, sliding me a card covered in aster through the boxes and stockings piled on our living-room floor. I looked at it and knew, so I tucked it in my robe for later.

It's later, past ten P.M., past my bedtime. And even longer past by the time I read Peter's card for the third time.

> *Merry Christmas, Majka.*
> *I love you. 2020 has brought more challenges and opportunities for us as professionals and parents than I could have imagined only a few short years ago.*

I'm proud of you and I'm proud of us for the hard work we do even as we're pulled in so many directions. I admire the way you engage with the difficult decisions and opportunities with equal enthusiasm. I know you care deeply about family, loved ones, and friends, and I admire the balance you strike.

I wish that in 2021 we can continue to strengthen as a couple, to laugh more together, to be easy with one another, to become even better at this team sport of marriage and parenting.

I want to be the best role models for Kaz and Irenna that we can be. To continue to build our family culture of curiosity, love, gratitude, and respect. I want to be there for each other in the ways that matter.

In love and support,

Peter

He heard me. He's been hearing me.

December 29, 2020
From the Notepad | Four Years and Six Months Old

Covid babies and Covid puppies. We have neither. I'd have both. But not in this life and this marriage. What would Peter have in another marriage? A wife who says yes more?

I spent three hours on a Zoom call with my team this week. Leigh, who runs communications for Legado, was set back from her screen, rocking with her newborn, alternating nursing him and snuggling him to sleep the whole time. I alternated between pinning her Zoom window to the top of my screen and hiding it.

"I want a baby," I tell Peter. Again.

"I know," he says. I wait for his punch line—the "You have babies; they are right over there" one. But this time he shifts on the couch to make space for me and asks if I need a hug.

December 31, 2020
Letter (from Irenna) | Four Years and Six Months Old

Dear Wild Kratts,
    Not all animals are he. You always say he.
    It's more kinder to not say he unless you know.
    You know a lot.
    Please be more kind.
        Irenna
        A she

January 2, 2021
Letter | Four Years and Six Months Old

It's been two weeks since I took the fridge-sized ice block to my hip.

"Guess what?" I say to your dad while climbing today. "I only envisioned the ice collapsing three times on me on this lead—progress, right?"

I am not sure if I should be proud or horrified.

I look down from my perch at a belay 120 feet off the ground. I count eight screws, perfectly spaced as if an alarm went off in my head each time I found myself exactly twelve feet above my last protection point. I watch Peter climb rapidly up to my stance, as if he would have led the pitch without any screws.

He seems impatient. My goodwill turns to frustration. "I know you are better at this than me," I say, "but can you at least say, 'Good job'?"

"I said it five times when you were climbing," he says.

Really? I think. "Whatever," I say. "One time, you can tell me at the belay."

—⁓—

I finish the climb and wonder why I feel I should be like him. Peter never seems to think he needs to be like me. I used to think we were the same, and maybe we were. We were paired perfectly at the start, challenging each other and mirroring each other's progress. On rock. But as much as I want to pretend we were on par with each other as ice climbers, it has never been true and now it never will be. I kick and swing at the ice and think about two back surgeries, carrying twins, a C-section, and an appendectomy. And that's just what's happened to my core. He's had one knee surgery and seems to be stronger than ever. How could we be the same?

When we're back on the ground, Peter starts racking up for another climb while I pack my backpack to leave. We're supposed to be a team, but neither of us is discussing why we're going in opposite directions.

"Time to get back to the babies," I say.

Peter sighs.

I know all he wants is big days—days when he can lose himself in the climbing. All I want are days when I can climb and be your mom in a way I know you need. Your dad doesn't question how much he needs to be a dad; he just *is* a dad. He equivocates over a week or a month—coming home early some days, being out for fourteen hours on others. For me, it resets every day. For you two, it does as well. Have we taught each other this? Would I have it any other way?

When I get home, you clamber on top of me demanding we get farm animals. Almost an hour later, you, Irenna, have finally passed out on top of me after one of your largest emotional expenditures of shrieking and sobbing to date. I created this by telling you that no, we would not be getting a bunny or a pig. I could have missed this if I'd kept climbing. I think of that alternate timeline as somewhat good for me and likely bad for you.

January 5, 2021
From the Notepad | Four Years and Six Months Old

"Tonight, it's movie night," I announce to you both as your dad cuts you veggies and pours enough milk to get you through an hour on your own.

"Have a good time at therapy," Kaz calls after us when we head upstairs.

January 5, 2021
Letter | Four Years and Six Months Old

Today I got to talk to the Queen of Namuli. Or did by proxy. My co-workers Filipa, Stephanie, Elizabeth, and now Sonya and I are working to build Legado 2.0, and I needed the queen to know it even if Covid is keeping me homebound.

Nine months ago we put together funding to hire and train more healthcare workers to help the Namuli community face Covid. It was just the beginning.

The priorities community members have shared with us again and again form the map for our work. Land rights, livelihoods, health, more.

This whole approach is what we're launching in Kenya.

"I wish I could be there to tell the queen this, to tell everyone this," I say to my team.

"Why can't you?" asks Filipa, our senior program manager. She is about to go to Mozambique, and can deliver a letter for me. "You can do it through me."

Dear Rainha, I write. *I wanted to be the person to tell you that we're now working in Kenya too. You and your community inspired this. You inspired us to do more and to do better. You know all that work we've done on legacy together? Your legacy, your family's, your community's, mine? That's the work we're building it all on.*

January 10, 2021
From the Notepad | Four Years and Six Months Old

"When you're president, you can decree no jam can have chunks," Peter told Irenna at 6:12 this morning after she rejected the toast he'd prepared for the second time.

"Papa, I'm not going to be president," Irenna said.

"Why not?" I asked.

"Because I'm going to be a mamma."

Breathe in, breathe out, I tell myself.

"Irenna, do you wanna know something amazing?" I say. "You can be a mamma and president."

"Mamma! My babies want me to be their mamma."

"Oh," I say. "I see."

January 12, 2021
From the Notepad | Four Years and Six Months Old

Your mom and I have appointments to get the vaccine on Friday, PapaD texts me.

The sobs start like a whoosh of trapped air, released from a tunnel I didn't know was inside me.

"Why are you crying, Mamma?" Irenna asks. "Are you crying because you are happy?"

"I am crying because I am relieved," I say.

Because now I am breathing and didn't know I hadn't been for all this time.

January 20, 2021
Letter | Four Years and Six Months Old

For exactly forty-eight minutes this morning, you, Irenna, cried about your *Frozen* Elsa dress. The dress I had gotten you with the help of your allowance, against my better judgment and typical distaste for overly marketed flouncy, girly baloney. Today was supposed to be easy. Peter is climbing, and I am being generous. I never planned for the Elsa-dress factor.

Did you know that when you two were little, I accomplished entire days once I got you into your car seats? I'd strap you in and run inside, play music for you on my phone, and go to the bathroom, eat, do the dishes, send an email, and wipe avocado off the underside of the counter before we left to whatever destination. Eight to ten minutes of bliss. Moments of breath. I still feel them. The second I activate the last of the six clicks to fasten you two inside your car seats, my body relaxes.

Today I owned it. "Wow, folks. Mamma is feeling anxious."

Irenna, you clutch your Elsa dress (which we have compromised can come *in* the van to school but not *to* school) and say, "Oh, Mamma, you should calm down."

Kaz: "Maybe you should go to the calming corner."

Irenna: "You could have a drink of water."

"You could take two deep breaths."

"Or draw."

"Or take a rest."

All the way to school you two offer me ways to calm down. I wait for a pause. "You know," I say, "when Mamma feels one way or another, it's Mamma's feeling, not yours."

Irenna: "We know that!"

"You are safe and I love you," I say.

Kaz: "Mamma, of course you love us."

Irenna: "Kaz, I love you." Then you giggle.

Kaz: "And I love you, Irenna, and you, Mamma." You giggle back.

"All right, silly bears—one more thing," I say. "Irenna, what would have helped *you* calm down this morning?"

The car is quiet, and I let it be

Then you pop your thumb out with a *schlock*. "Mamma, I am not sure anything would have helped. I was too sad. And when I am too sad, I can't do that."

"I know, honey. Mamma feels the same way—can we work on it together? So when we're too sad or too mad—"

"Or too anxious?" you interrupt.

"Exactly. If we're any of those, we can still learn how to calm down."

Kaz: "Okay, Mamma, sure. Maybe next time you can throw a snowball, real hard, at a tree. Or even the sky."

January 23, 2021
Letter | Four Years and Six Months Old

Crash, click, thud, squeak—ice makes all of these noises when you climb it. Today it's more of a whispering *thwack*, my wrist snapping my tool just enough to get my pick in the ice but not enough to break the great frozen panel that I'm attached to. I'm at the bottom of Dropline in Crawford Notch, tacking my way up a veneer of ice to a tubular column above. I'm only six weeks into this winter's ice season, but already my body is fluent in the medium.

I spy a dribble to my right where the route Last Exit comes in sometimes. I wonder if I can link the patches together. I shake my head to clear this greedy thought. There are not enough opportunities for protection to make this a safe option. And so I can't—and won't.

Maybe I had kids to keep myself from being insatiable as an ice climber, after all.

January 26, 2021

Letter | Four Years and Six Months Old

My skis scrape against the icy runnels of the cross-country track high off Rocky Branch Trailhead in the White Mountains. My ankle wavers, I dodge a rock, a noise explodes in my head.

The noise comes off my left shoulder. A man, not in skis, walking in big, heavy strides toward me.

I wave.

I freeze.

A man in the woods.

I have told no one where I am. I rarely do.

My mom came to visit me in Boulder, Colorado, fifteen years ago, and we went on a hike on one of the most popular trails in the Boulder foothills. Halfway up Mount Sanitas, I nodded in greeting to a solo man coming down.

"Aren't you ever afraid, Majka?" she asked.

I couldn't imagine anything happening to me in the light of day on one of the most well-trodden trails in Boulder. But I didn't say that to her. We never imagine the worst.

I see a snow machine up ahead. The man is a groomer, cutting trees for work. I start skiing again.

I used to think I was escaping to the woods because I loved them. What if all this time I was conquering the fear of them for both of us?

Is my mom afraid now? At seventy-six she goes on solo horse-back rides in the Absaroka Range. I think of her going back to running just days after she was raped, but from then on always with a friend. Soon she was back running marathons, then triathlons, and then crisscrossing North America on a bike all before I'd graduated high school. Maybe she's done this all because she loves the athlete's strain on her body and her psyche, but also because she refuses to stand down.

My mom had a choice to go to work that day. But she also didn't. She was already on a path toward success; her ambition set her apart. The more self-aware, more difficult choice would have been to step away from that path. You get knocked down—literally—then you get up.

You add more.

February 9, 2021
From the Notepad | Four Years and Seven Months Old

"Can you imagine? Can you, Mamma? If you had no kids?"

"What would happen, Kaz?"

"You'd be sad," Kaz says. "You need kids and a wife."

"You need Grandma Pooch too," Irenna adds.

Later:

"You know mammas come in all shapes and sizes and . . . types, right?" I say.

"Yes, Mamma, we know."

"Do you know my type?"

"You."

February 9, 2021
Letter | Four Years and Seven Months Old

Somehow you each have different ways of opening doors. Kaz, you crash through the door and swing it into the adjoining wall; Irenna, you nudge it open, a subtle click announcing your presence before your eyes appear in the sliver you've made. Today it's your turn to see if you can get Mamma out of her office.

"Mamma, what are you doing?" you ask.

"Working," I say.

"For Legado and the mountains?" you ask.

My to-do list is scrawled on both my giant whiteboard and on a sheet of paper beside me. But I just opened a blank document to write to you. I try not to lie to you.

"I was actually working on a book for you," I say. "For you and Kaz, and sorta for Papa."

"Read it to me, Mamma," you say as you stick your thumb in your mouth and levitate onto my lap.

"Irenna, we don't spend time in front of the computer together," I say.

"But I want you to read me the book," you say.

"Oh Irenna-bear," I say, "this is not a book for you now. It's a book for you later."

Shlock goes the sound of your thumb releasing from your mouth. You use my thighs as a turntable and pivot to face me next.

"But, Mamma," you say, cupping your hands on either side of my head and looking me in the eye. "I want you now."

"I want you, now, too," I say. I close my computer on the blank screen. This is time I don't want to miss.

February 19, 2021
From the Notepad | Four Years and Seven Months Old

Irenna to Kaz: "Are you really going to marry Ollie?"

Kaz: "Really."

Irenna: "But you said you were going to marry me."

Kaz: "I can marry you *and* Ollie."

Irenna: "If you marry Ollie, I am going to marry Arianna."

Kaz: "But if you marry Arianna, who will take care of the poop?"

You both giggle and run screaming down the hall to doctor your loveys. I trot after you. "What if everyone takes care of the poop?" I say.

February 20, 2021
From the Notepad | Four Years and Seven Months Old

"I'm thankful for Papa and Mamma's dinner," Kaz says.

"Papa made dinner, honey," I say. "Mamma did what is called *invisible labor.*"

Everyone looks at me.

"Mama paid bills, found your face mask at the bottom of your backpack and replaced it with a new one for tomorrow, and texted your doctor about the rash on your underarm," I add.

"I'm grateful for Mamma being invisible," Irenna says.

Your dad and I then laugh together about that all night.

February 23, 2021
Letter | Four Years and Seven Months Old

"Birth control," I say when Natalie asks what we want to talk about.

It takes three volleys back and forth about a vasectomy before Peter says, "It's just not what I can see, now or maybe ever."

All that comes next is silence. I open my mouth to speak but no words come out. And then my breath locks midway through an exhale. My chest collapses as I close my eyes. I start to rock.

"What's going on?" Peter asks. "Are you okay?"

His voice is far away, then eclipsed by one in my head asking questions: *How fast could I get to the hospital? How long would they keep me there if it's just a panic attack? Could I pretend it was something bigger? Medicate me, anesthetize me, take me to the numbness.* That is one way. I can see it. Collapsing on the floor. Crying uncle and stepping away from it all.

Except I can't. Because I want the way that takes me through. I breathe and make it all slow down, and in between each breath I can hear you two downstairs discussing who gets to eat the last carrot.

"I'm here," I say to Natalie and Peter.

"Good job," Natalie says.

Peter takes my hand.

February 25, 2021
Letter | Four Years and Seven Months Old

My inbox pings. "Addiction and mental illness in my family of origin" is the subject of my mom's email.

It turns out we're all processing this together—my sister, Mom, and me—at the same time, thousands of miles apart, from Montana to Minnesota to New Hampshire. "I will tell you what I know . . . ," my mom writes.

Before reading further, I offer thanks to the universe that over the past months I've stepped away from my nightly glass of wine. I'd told myself I was "getting through Covid," but really I was just becoming dependent on alcohol.

Why do I think I will escape that ill-fated list? What if the women in our family were pissed off before they went crazy? What if they went crazy because they were pissed off? What if the men went crazy because they were avoiding it all? What if it all it comes down to is who does how much of the fucking chores?

If we solved that, would it take the pressure off everything else and make a better life possible?

———

Courtney, a fellow mom, and I speak over rolled-down minivan windows as we pass each other at contactless school drop-off. Her four-year-old daughter was out of school for three days and she also has an almost two-year-old at home, but for once Courtney was the parent with the immovable in-person work. And so it was her husband who mainly handled the sick time. When I ask her how it went, she shakes her head.

"He was in such a bad mood when I came home each day. Last night I asked him if he was mad at me," Courtney says.

"What did he say?"

"That he's angry," she says. "He said it twice."

Neither Courtney nor I say anything for a moment.

I don't know her well enough yet to know if I should be candid. *Good,* I want to say. *Now he knows what it's like.*

But does that make things better? Or more terrifying?

February 27, 2021
Letter | Four Years and Seven Months Old

"Did you know when you were little that Grandma was sick?" I ask my mom today on the phone. Even though my mother was the one who sent the email about addiction and specifically mentioned Grandma's name, I am wary of asking directly about Grandma's alcoholism and depression.

"What I remember is that we all had to be perfect—and equal," my mom says. "Sometimes I think of her before she was a mom—she was the president of her high school class, graduated with honors from college and grad school, and then put her husband through college."

"And her first job was making toast," I add, thinking of my grandma's solo train ride from Minnesota to Montana's Glacier National Park, where one summer during college she worked making breakfast for guests at the Lake McDonald Lodge.

"But she stopped all of it once my dad could make enough money. And then had five kids."

We're both quiet for a while.

"Do you ever think she wondered what had happened to her life?" I ask, to break the silence.

"I don't know, honey. I know she wasn't happy."

I think of my grandma making holiday clothes for five kids, mandating they get all As in school, and sometimes drinking vodka from a coffee cup. "Maybe she had no language for it. It's not like there was a cultural rubric in the fifties to want more as a woman," I say.

"It's not like there was one for me in the seventies either," my mom agrees.

"You had to become it," I say out loud to her. Then one more time in my head.

Last night, I sat in a camping chair in a dirt parking lot twelve feet from Garlick and Janet. We drank beer and went nowhere. Between the three of us, we've spent over sixty years putting up first ascents in over a dozen countries, in all types of alpine environments. But this year, throughout Covid, we have been circling our black, gray, and red minivans in the dirt parking lot of the Cranmore ski area come sleet, rain, or black flies. The conditions change, but we're always having the same conversation—how to have careers doing meaningful work in the world while simultaneously being good parents, partners, and climbers.

Our parents attempted a similar version of this quest in the 1970s and 1980s—and all of our parents' marriages failed. Seemingly undeterred, we are all adding more factors to the equation: trying to embody a new standard of parenting wherein you actually meet your kids' emotional needs and acknowledge their vulnerabilities, show up for your partner, and have a productive and proactive career, all while not giving up your passion for adventuring and climbing.

"We need a model for this," Garlick said.

"What if we become that model?" I asked.

March 4, 2021
Letter | Four Years and Eight Months Old

Someone told me after you were born to trim your fingernails and toenails with my teeth. For weeks, I found myself constantly trying to make time to bite the ends off forty nails before I decided that person had never had twins. Today, Kaz, you and I trade hair cuddles for nail trims.

"Mamma, who's going to pick us up at school today?"

"We're not sure—who do you want to pick you up?"

You take a deep, loud whiff of my hair. "You."

"Why do you want me to pick you up?"

"Because I just want to see my mamma."

"How do you feel when Nick picks you up?" I ask, mentioning our new babysitter.

"Like I just want to see my mamma."

———

"Mamma, I need more Mamma time," Irenna says in the car to school.

Did I ever ask my mom for the same?

Maybe it doesn't matter. Maybe what matters is that I answer you.

"Mamma's going to try," I say.

March 10, 2021
From the Notepad | Four Years and Eight Months Old

Peter does not get up at five A.M. That is my thing. But today he slides onto the couch next to me at 5:12 A.M.

"Whatcha doing?" he asks.

"Working," I say.

"Is that what we're calling 'working on your book' these days?" he asks.

I look up and try not to act surprised.

"Don't think I don't know what you've been doing this whole time," he says.

"Not all the time," I say.

"Some of the time?" he asks.

"Some of the time," I agree.

"Do you think there is an irony in taking on more to write a book called *More*?"

"Very funny," I say. But I know it's true.

"Are you almost done with it?" he asks.

"Almost," I say.

"How will you know?" he asks.

"I just will," I say.

"Have you considered writing a book called *Less*?"

March 15, 2021
Letter | Four Years and Eight Months Old

"Vince is guiding Huntington, and Justin and the boys are leaving for the Neacola Mountains," Peter announces from the passenger seat.

We're driving home, taking the outside of a right-hand bend under what's left of the season's ice climbs in Crawford Notch. Today we stayed away from them and went rock climbing instead.

"Do you really want to go to Alaska?" I ask. "Really? Or do you just want to pretend that you do?"

"I'd absolutely love to climb in Alaska right now."

I arc left, and then straighten the wheel.

"What type of climbing?" I ask.

"Not what Justin is going for—two notches down."

I think, but don't say, that this adjustment might still be 159 notches above what most in the world would consider okay for a parent. And that the same might be said for so many of Peter and my climbing choices.

I think of the last time Peter was in Alaska and I went to Montana. That was before there were easy mobile-linked devices that let us text from our tents deep in the backcountry. That was when all we had was a sat phone for emergencies, when the crappy coincidence of a middle-of-the-night phantom call followed by days of silence until a real call came through from Peter with news of his success sent me into an anxiety tailspin.

"I don't want to climb like that," I say to him and me. "Maybe I will one day again. Right now I just feel such a responsibility to be with our kids. I can do that ice and rock climbing. I am not sure I can do that alpine climbing on giant objects in faraway places."

I keep taking us safely down the road at fifty-five-miles-per-hour exactly, as if not wanting to break the spell we have cast that makes this conversation possible.

"I want to be healthy, be able to use my body for anything I want. That is enough for me right now."

"That's good to know," Peter says.

"But I'm not saying never . . ." I trail off.

I spin through the notch, to Kaz and Irenna, pulled to them like magnets. I have spoken my truth and am settling into it, breathing through it.

March 20, 2021
Letter | Four Years and Eight Months Old

Just thinking that a week from now I'll be hugging you and cuddling those twins! my mom texts. *Please tell them no squirming away!*

The last time my mom visited was fifteen months ago, before Covid, before vaccines, before I had nowhere else to be but here with you and your dad, and nothing for us to do but figure things out.

I call her instead of texting back.

"Mom," I say, "do you think I can have cuddles too?"

"Of course," she says. "But no squirming from you either."

March 25, 2021
Letter | Four Years and Eight Months Old

Tonight at dinner I tell Ailis—whom I'm courting to be one of Legado's newest board members—that my November trip to Kenya is happening.

"That's not what you told me," Peter says. He stops eating and is looking at me.

"Can we talk about this later?" I ask.

———

"You didn't tell me you were going," he tells me later.

"We have been talking about it for a year," I say.

We both pause.

"How do you feel about it?" I ask.

"I'm scared."

"It's Africa, not a climbing trip to Alaska," I say.

I watch him pick up his phone.

"I'm sorry," I say. "I know that feeling. Tell me why you're scared."

"You said yourself you would have died last year if you'd been there with your appendix . . . You don't have a community there . . . You've never been to Nairobi . . . Is this really the time?"

We work through each piece, piece by piece.

April 1, 2021
Letter | Four Years and Nine Months Old

Dear Kaz and Irenna,

I have been wanting to write to you all day but am not sure why. Something about today mattered, to me, to us. And then I looked at the date and realized why.

When I was four-and-a-half years old, my dad took me and my sister to an ice-cream parlor to sweeten his bitter news with chocolate malts.

"Today, your mom and I got divorced," he said.

It was April 1, and I had spent the day throwing water balloons at my friends and making fart noises whenever my sister sat down. You spent today doing your version of the same.

"April Fools'?" I asked.

If memory serves me right, I not only got to have my own malt that day, but also half of my dad's.

———

This book, these letters, these past five years of growing you in my body and on the outside, I now know have been a promise to you. I will give you a different life, beyond these first four-and-a-half years.

I used to tell people I wasn't sure I wanted to have kids. I now know that was a lie hiding a big truth: I was terrified to be a mom. It took me this long as a mom to discover this: I was scared that my intensity, my drive, my desire to do so much so fast would make me into a mom I wanted to be like in part—but not entirely. And *that* mom, *my* mom, surely did her best—but in the end, as her kid, my life came unhinged as a consequence.

Each day I feel the reverberations of my childhood—the gaps left in my upbringing and how these echo in the face of my family's challenges.

But my mom also taught me how to rise. And how to keep rising, no matter what.

I hope I can teach you how to do the same. I hope you can know that when it's lonely and confusing and hurts more than you ever imagined it would, you can stand up and keep going.

It took the two of you coming into my world to understand that I can do more *with* you—and that it will be hard and wonderful and fraught and beautiful if I do it this way. And, in the end, that there is no other way for me to do it.

But this *more* is not carte blanche; I cannot do everything. However, what I see now is that I can keep trying like hell for more—as long as I keep you two, and your dad, at the center.

I almost didn't have you because I couldn't find any other couple or parent I wanted to emulate. Now I know I have to become that parent myself. And I am not scared of it anymore.

It's time for me to do that outside of these words—with you, and for you.

Afterword
October 31, 2022

Dear Peter and Mom,

Stashed away in our attic in New Hampshire are boxes upon boxes of my journals. They date back to the age Kaz and Irenna are now, though the twins' handwriting is already more legible than mine ever has been. I don't ever remember *not* writing; it's always been my way of being truly me, of finding me.

When I found out I was pregnant, the first thing I did was reach for a way to write. I filled up my phone with audio files and notes when I was on the go, and poured my words into a never-ending Google doc when I had my computer. I was not writing a book then; I was writing me. And then on one day at the end of December 2020, I sat down with it all and asked what this could be. *This* is the this.

No experience in my life has been more illuminating than becoming a mom. I am still becoming a mom because I know now that it's not a singular moment of transition; it is instead a lifelong evolution of understanding and unearthing.

The process is also inextricably tied to you both. I am not a mother without each of you. I am not myself without each of you. More than any other people, you have each shaped the person—the woman, daughter, partner, leader, and athlete—that I am.

I also understand that my experience of your early years is just that: mine. Yours will be different. You might have different versions of each small piece or even of the whole. You may remember some of these moments of our lives in vivid color, and others may be foreign to you. Ultimately, you might want to burn it all to the ground.

Before you do, I want you to know why I have worked so hard to put our story out into the world.

This book is first for Kaz and Irenna. It is a time capsule of me for them—to use if they need a window into their past. In my dreams, I imagine them opening it as they wrestle with where they have come from, as they chart their courses into the great unknown of the future.

This book is for you, Peter and Mom. I am sure there have been more than a few moments when you've wondered if we would make it through. Moments of darkness when I was unrecognizable. I want you to see that I was fighting to find myself the whole time—to do better for myself and for all of us.

Finally, this book is for the other women in the world—those who feel alone or confused, or terrified of their own *more*. I believe so strongly that if I can give even just one woman a hand to rise when she feels like she can no longer stand up and fight for her future—not even one more time—then writing this book will have been worth it.

For each of them. For each of us. This is *More*.

Acknowledgments

Peter, I see you. I have seen you this whole time, but not enough. I know that now. I know that because you bravely picked up this book and read it and still loved me. And still love me to this day.

I wrote *More* in a fury, albeit one spread out over five and a half years, in snippets of precious time each moment I could grab a pen, speak into my phone, or tap on my keyboard or phone. Were I to write this book now, as a retrospective, our life might look more balanced, more beautiful, and less raw. But that is not this book—it was instead written in real time, because that is how I live and think and operate. And because that is the reality of being a parent to two young twins, and being pulled constantly in so many directions by their love and their demands.

What *More* is, is intense, just like me. When I was seven I had a crush on a classmate, Colin Davids, and he eschewed my affection and told me I was too intense for him. At the time, I didn't know what being "too intense" meant, but I decided then and there that I would henceforth think Colin Davids was a tool and become even more intense and own that intensity next to my curly hair, glasses, and weird Polish name. Peter, you married the thirty-five-year-old version of that girl—you know you did.

The first thing you said to me when you finished the book was that it hurt. That it hurt to read how lonely I was when you were right there beside me, trying your hardest every day. I heard that, and I hear that still. You were always right there. You are right here. You show up; you have given your life over to this family, to these babies, and to me.

But it was also so much more conscious than that. You have made this your life; you choose it every day.

All of the questions, doubt, anger, and hurt on these pages tell the story of me trying to carry a hot ball of fiery unknown through these months and years—and not let it burn us. I know I am not easy to be married to; I know this book made it harder. And I know that *More* being in the world in print is a testament to our ability to walk through this together. It is also a testament to you as a husband whose kindness shows me again and again how to love.

We are different today than we were amid the mayhem—when the kids were one day, six months, two years, four years old . . . of course we are. This book made us revisit the love and the ache, but also the strength *of* you and me and the strength of the *us* we've created together.

So thank you, Peter, for being my partner on this journey. Thank you for the physical and emotional space you gave me to write this book. And thank you for understanding that writing *More* and putting it out there for others to read is part of how I grow.

———— ᴡᴡ ————

Mom. You made me strong. You made me brave. And you made me love and care and try. Perhaps most importantly, you taught me never to stop.

When I told you I was writing this book, you said, "Good, you should. I hope I'm in it."

"Oh, Mamma—" I started to respond, but then you interrupted me.

"Lots," you added.

This is the lots.

And I know it's a lot.

And I know it's missing a lot.

Today, as I write this, you are downstairs entering hour three of a Lego-athlon with Kaz and Irenna. There are plans for you three to also make plaster handprints during your visit to New Hampshire, and a stack of drawings of future woodwork projects you'll tackle together the next time we're at the ranch in Montana. You love, Mom. You love, and you give to these kids each and every time. And you have been doing it their whole lives. You have been doing it my whole life, too. I know that I've failed to convey the breadth of your love on these pages, so I'm saying it here. When I was writing, and experiencing, the events in *More*, life was often a matter of minute-to-minute survival. Your love and presence were not confusing to me—it was everything else that kept dragging me toward an internal reckoning.

I don't think we ever know what our mothers (or fathers) are really, wholly doing. I know now there was so much that I missed when I was growing up—so much I did not know, should not have known, and could not have known. I had to pass through these last six years to reach that understanding, and what helped me along the way was writing out what has been the most difficult. I hope after reading this, you can hear me when I say that <u>I am so damn proud to be your daughter.</u> Now that I know what it truly means to be a parent—the power and conviction and unwavering love for your children you need to get through each day—I can see how much you did and continue to do for me.

Thank you for believing in me and my writing at every step. Thank you for loving me and holding that love around me like a giant balloon I can crash around in while I find my way. Thank you for going first so I could follow your path and create my own.

—⁓—

For the rest of you who shaped me in my first expanded iteration of family—my dad, my stepmother, my stepfatfer, team Burkefley, and my sister—thank you for having my heart and my back in life and in learning. I could not write this book and take these leaps without knowing you have me and love me.

—⁓—

For Sarah and Roger, thank you for expanding my understanding of family and what love can look like and helping me always make that love bigger and stronger.

⸻

This book took shape as a book because of my friend Leigh Shumann, and I am forever awed by her willingness to wade through page upon page of transcripts and notes and to say she saw it in here. You believed in me and this book, Leigh, and I profoundly thank you for virtually sitting next to me every step of the way.

⸻

Sarah Garlick, you have been my ballast and my mirror as a friend, colleague, mom, writer, and fellow human trying like hell to understand it all. Thank you for telling me to keep going, always, and for reading this early on and telling me it was worth it.

Scott Gould, you gave me just the right pushes each time I called and asked for them. Thanks for being my friend and coach and telling me I could do it. Natalie Baszile, thank you for jumping in and reading my first excerpt and telling me to try to make it real. Matt Samet, you have been my authorial conscious for so long—thank for you being a mentor for me in my writing and for being part of this in the homestretch.

Elizabeth O'Neill, I am so damn glad the world put us together eleven years ago. You have been with me through all of this as a friend, a mentor, a sounding board, and a person who helps calibrate my moral and emotional compass as a woman, a mom, and a wife on a near-daily basis.

Sasha Tracy, you are my reflector, and while you are only in these pages once, your conversations and your readiness to go anywhere and everywhere in them have taught me how to keep moving forward with the complexity of caring and trying. Thank you.

Sally LaVenture and Cameron Elmendorf, thank you for the early reading, wisdom, and friendship. Kate Rutherford and Anne Gilbert Chase, thank you for traveling around the world with me to climb and for creating friendships that can come out on the other side of motherhood. Janet Wilkinson, thank you for building a friendship step by step, missteps too, to get us here. I am honored every day to have you in my corner and to be in yours.

Nancy and Wayne, thank you for lake time and the extended love that is always at the ready.

Susanne Conrad, thank you for being my teacher and friend.

To my team at Legado—Stephanie, Filipa, Sonya, Monicah, Tita, Ana, and Matt—thank you for the support and belief you gave me each time I shared news of the book getting closer to its arrival in the world. Thank you for being a team of beautiful people who get it—all of it.

To my agent, Esmond Harmsworth, for reading this book again and again and asking for more of *More* each time. To Jessica Case and the team at Pegasus for seeing that this story needed to be told and helping me tell it to the world.

To all of you who let me bring a piece of you into this book and who, when I asked if it was okay to use your name, not only said yes but showered me with love and encouragement.

And to the mountains of this world, which have given me a place to find myself, be myself, and grow even when I didn't know I was doing it.

And finally, to Irenna and Kaz. Thank you for becoming you so I could become me.

Thank you all for getting me to here, to the here as a mom, to the here with this book. There is more to come.